Count It All Joy

Norma-Jean Sims-Coachman

This book is a memoir and depicts actual events in the life of the author as truthfully as recollection permits.

Editorial Services: Remembering the Time
Book Layout and Cover Design by FormattedBooks

Count It All Joy/Norma-Jean Sims-Coachman—1st ed.
ISBN: 978-1-959670-69-8 (paperback)

Dedication

For my children Charles and Alisa, and their children and their children's children. May you find joy every day. May your life be filled with Love.

CONTENTS

CHAPTER 1

Jitterbug Obsession

O n the night of August 13, 1949, Mama and Daddy were out doing the Jitterbug. It was one of their favorite things and they could really move.

World War II had facilitated the spread of the Jitterbug from the dance clubs of Harlem, New York to Europe. That's where my parents met and discovered a love of dancing and each other. By the time they married they had danced many nights away trying to forget the horrors of the war.

When it came to Jitterbugging, Mama told me it was a term referring to someone suffering from alcoholic or drug nervousness. Cab Calloway described one dance club, "They look like a bunch of jitterbugs on the floor," and the phrase caught on and swept the nation. It was a dance of fast bouncing movements combined with swing or what some used to call the Lindsay Hop. After World War Two some traditional dance halls posted signs that read "NO JITTERBUGGING" because they felt the moves were so alarming!

Mama was obsessed with Jitterbugging and loved the fun moves and dancing with Daddy…it made her forget everything. They would go to little juke joints in New Jersey or New York and sometimes to the NCO Club (non-commissioned officers club). But wherever they went people would gather around and cheer them with rhythmic clapping, chanting, and words of encouragement. It made them want to show off even more. Especially her! So that August night Mama bounced and turned, twirled and flipped, spun and laughed the night away with determined joy. She stopped now and then for a sip of something cold and just long enough to catch her breath. She had a ball that hot, humid Jersey night. Nothing would stop her.

Mama had perfected a duplicate of a dress she'd seen in a store but could not afford. It had a fitted bodice, with a straight skirt that flared just below a sassy kick pleat. Capped sleeves and top stitching trimming the collar, bodice, and slanted pockets finished the dress to perfection. The style, the soft, polished cotton fabric, the fit…it was definitely an exquisite little summer dress.

She couldn't wait for nightfall; she was so anxious to wear that dress. I can imagine the deep green fabric reflecting in her lovely light green eyes like foliage over a pond. I wish she had kept that dress for me.

Pumps and seamed nylon stockings completed her stylish dancing clothes. Her light brown hair was cut in a chin length bob and carefully finger waved. The only makeup she wore was bright red Revlon lipstick, just enough to accentuate her full lips.

Mama was twenty six and Daddy was twenty four. He was suave and handsome with dark wavy hair and a neatly groomed mustache. Neither of them can remember what he wore that night, but they loved to talk about Mama and how beautiful they looked together.

That night's chosen dance hall was a little juke joint, hot and muggy under a blanket of humidity. The place was packed with people and became hotter, muggier, and smokier as the night wore on.

…it was another night to hear great music and dance her beloved jitterbug…the crowd gathered around them…

She didn't care one bit about any of that. Not the architectural design of the building, nor the furnishings, or even the location. What mattered was that it was another night to hear great music and dance her beloved jitterbug. She said the little place jumped and swayed with the music and she felt incredibly happy. The crowd gathered around them clapping in rhythm to the music. They passed no judgement on her and fully embraced her. She doubted they had seen anyone like her that could jitterbug so well. She was a European woman in the midst of the most soulful little place and loving every minute, every beat, and every handclap! She danced all night long, losing herself in the fun.

Her green eyes twinkled with sheer joy any time she recounted a night spent jitterbugging. Especially that night.

By her own account Daddy was a mediocre dance partner, not as light on his feet or quick to step as she was. She had grown up in a culture of polkas and waltzes and now here she was in love with a crazy dance.

The morning brought not only a new day, but also a new beginning. Their life took a detour in the breaking dawn as they drove to Camp Kilmer Army Base and checked into the base hospital. There were many unusual things about being at that particular hospital on that particular day.

At one time Camp Kilmer was a thriving military installation. It was organized as part of the Army Services Forces Transportation Corps and activated in 1942 as a staging area and a part of the New York Port of Embarkation. It was easily reached by the mainline of the Pennsylvania Railroad as well as the port. Troops would receive medical injections, send personal effects home, and get supplies needed before loading onto transport ships to overseas. It became the largest processing center for troops heading overseas and returning from World War II, handling over 2.5 million soldiers.

But, on August 14, 1949, there was no war going on. The 1,000 bed hospital was under orders to deactivate by autumn and all but a few people were gone. The personnel had been transferred to Fort Dix.

So here they were, Mama and Daddy in a nearly deserted hospital. The corridors were long, linoleum floors buffed to a glass shine and marked with stripes leading the way to various departments. Room after empty room sounded like hollow caves as she was wheeled past. It was like a ghost town hospital. Thank God the staff left behind was the best.

She asked for no gas, no putting her out. She feared that. They gassed people in concentration camps. But no, they didn't listen. They placed a mask over her face and she tried to fight them. When she came to herself, all she remembered was jitterbugging the night before.

"Tell us your name. Can you tell us your name?" She shuddered and recoiled. She felt the cool, wet washcloth on her forehead and heard the question again. "Can you tell us your name?" Opening her eyes, she said in her thick, Latvian accent, "Alice" (pronounced Ali-sa). "Alice Erika Ariya Tennis." Then, she faded out and forgot where she was. Then it came to her. "My name is Alice. Alice Jackson."

They placed a mask over her face and she tried to fight them.

The reason they were at the hospital would come as a shock. The night before she had been jitterbugging in the lovely green dress with the fitted bodice. There was no evidence she was pregnant and she certainly didn't act like a someone about to have a baby any day.

I had made my way into the world a little after eight p.m. and when the mental fog was lifted she asked, "Where's my baby?" When they brought me to her she counted ten little toes and ten little fingers and looked at my face surrounded by a full head of hair. Before passing me to my daddy she proclaimed that she would call me her "jitterbug baby!" They all laughed at my new nickname and it was a day of joy.

I was told I was the last baby born at Camp Kilmer during that go round for the hospital. They reactivated the camp again in 1950 so I am sure more babies came after me, but I doubt that any of them were called "jitterbug baby."

That, as they say, was "The first day of the rest of my life." Another army brat was born! Mama loved to tell me how shocked people were to see her with a baby, remarking, "You didn't show at all." "Weren't you just jitterbugging the other night?" She said her answer was "Yes! And this is my jitterbug baby."

At that time we lived in a little house in Colonia not far from Camp Kilmer. The camp closed in 2009. Grandma's home was modest with a small garden and chickens pecking in the yard. A big weeping willow tree provided shade. She grew green beans, tomatoes, and all sorts of other vegetables. Much of the produce she canned, including peaches from the local market. She taught Mama to cook delicious soul food.

Mama sewed stylish wedding gowns for all the aunts when they married: Aunt Elizabeth with James Wilson, Aunt Laura with Uncle John Jennings, Aunt Vivian with Richard Mickey, and Aunt Alberta with Donnie Faison Sr. I remember playing with Donnie Jr, taking naps together, and even being thrown into the bath with him. It was a warm, close family. In recent years I've loved my telephone conversations with Uncle Bobby Jennings.

Due to some sort of birth complications Mama had to go back to the hospital for a few days. Daddy

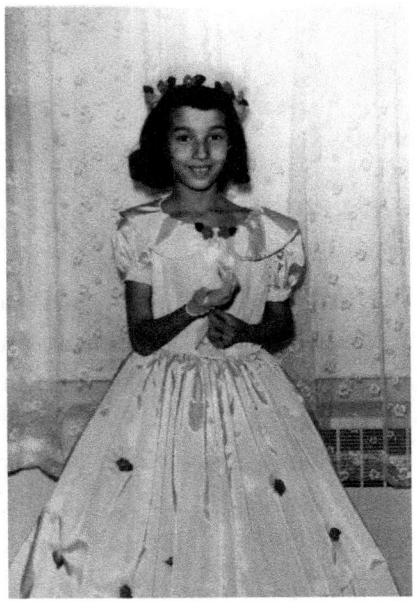

Norma-Jean, wearing a flower girl dress designed and sewn by her mother.

5

was at home doing his best to take care of me when our neighbor from across the street came and knocked on the door. Violet Greenlee never divulged how she found out he was home alone with me. He didn't stand a chance against her determination. She told him she was there to take me home with her and he could go back to the hospital to be with Mama or go back to work, the choice was his! With that she walked over to my bassinette, picked me up, cradled me in her arms and declared herself to be my Grandma.

As I write this Grandma has passed away, but she lived to 103. Her age was another testament to her determination. I can't imagine my formative years without Grandma in my life; she was such an integral part of our family.

When Mama was released from the hospital Grandma welcomed her with opened arms and treated her like she had always been a member of her family. My mama loved being included.

Anti-miscegenation laws criminalized sex and cohabitation between whites and non-whites between 1923 and 1948 in America and thirty out of forty eight states enforced the laws. Thankfully, New Jersey wasn't one of them. That didn't mean people didn't hold the belief that a white woman shouldn't be with a black man. Really, however they felt in the mid 40s wasn't going to change because it was now 1949. People who had issue with it were still outwardly prejudiced. It may not have been apparent in their actions but it could be felt in their demeanor and attitudes.

Oh yes, I suppose I left out some facts about my parents. Key facts that contributed to who I am today. Not because it isn't important, it is vitally important! It speaks to the core of the kind of people my parents tried to be.

When I was growing up my parents knew of course that they were an integrated couple, but it was never talked about. They didn't judge others by the color of their skin, but rather on their character. Color was incidental. That is how they raised me.

So let me say that, incidentally, my mama was a white woman. She was born in Riga, the capital of Latvia, a small Baltic country by Lithuania and Estonia. She was talented, intelligent, and well educated, and spoke five languages fluently. She was the daughter of a fashion designer. Riga was at one time a fashion capital of Europe. Her father was a merchant sea captain who died at sea when she was just a little girl. She had one brother who aspired to be a musician. After the first invasion of their homeland by a series of other European powers she never saw her mother or brother again.

Mama had incredible drive and courage and lived through unspeakable horror and nightmares. She would come right up to the edge of saying something to me about this time but would stop short. She never revealed very much about her experiences but I sensed it. She had been in a labor camp and escaped and yet, here she was in America, the land of the free and home of the brave. She belonged here because she was brave and she was now free. She was married to a black man, my daddy. As an adult I would learn that there was much more to the story. Some of it miraculous!

Top - Alice Jackson
Bottom - Olden Jackson,
high school graduation

My parents met by chance one day in Munich, Germany. There was a war going on and Daddy wasn't looking at her and thinking about her being white! He was thousands of miles from his hometown of Chicago, Illinois. There were no women of color for him to talk with. There were no choices to be made based on color. They met and began talking. A simple act, having a conversation with someone. They were from opposite corners of the world and just interested in hearing each other's stories.

His story was so simple compared to hers. Daddy was born in New Orleans, Louisiana. By the time he was four. my grandfather, Adolph Jackson, decided to move his family north for better employment opportunities. He and my grandmother Hattie moved to Chicago where he went to work for the railroad as a Pullman Porter and she stayed home to raise their three children. Al was the eldest, then Edna, and Daddy was the baby in the family.

After completing high school he tried his hand at a few jobs, but in the end Daddy enlisted in the Army. A few years later, he was standing in Europe gazing at a beautiful interpreter for the U.S. Embassy. Color wasn't even a factor in their meeting or their attraction to each another. It was very *Laws or no laws, people were prejudiced and people can be mean.* unlikely that a young woman born in Riga and a young man born in New Orleans would meet, jitterbug nights away, fall in love, and get married. But they did! Now, here they were in the United States. She was clearly white and he was clearly black, or colored as the time defined him, and as a result they had to face some ugly days together. Laws or no laws, people were prejudiced and people can be mean.

Military life would take us up and down the eastern seaboard from post to post. I was growing up in true army brat fashion. Before I was ten we lived in Fort Dix, Fort Devens, and Fort Monmouth. We were always close enough to visit Grandma, who always treated us with love. In fact, many times before I started school she would visit us, find an excuse to go to the store, but her destination would actually be home with me in tow. She would call my parents with an announcement of when she intended to bring me home. It was always fine, of course. That changed once I started school but it was a precious time.

My parents had many close friends when I was growing up, all of whom I called Auntie and Uncle as a sign of respect. I was not allowed to call adults by their first name and Mr. and Mrs. was too formal for close friends. Mama's best friend was Aunt Sigrid and her husband Uncle Pat was Daddy's best friend. He witnessed their wedding. I grew up playing with their son Claus who was like a brother. After his sister Monica was born, we still played for hours on end while our mothers chatted. They would switch back and forth between German and English to try to keep us nosy little ones out of their adult conversations. Claus and Monica were also biracial children. As very young children we didn't realize anything special about our ethnicity.

One thing about life on or near a military base is you are in an ethnic melting pot. I had aunties who were white, black, Filipino, Japanese, Korean, German, or Polish. I had uncles whose skin color ranged in hue from white with farmer tans to skin so dark it looked like smooth black velvet. All of my uncles had in common their service in the US military. All were welcomed in our home and all were treated with equal respect with no reference to their race or hue. My parents taught me by example and not their words.

CHAPTER 2

Something Changed

S omewhere along the line my parents had a drastic shift because their life no longer looked like or sounded like a love story. Not the beautiful story I had been told. It was so far from where we began and for me there seemed to be no end in sight from their daily misery.

When I look back I realize that although I was taught great values, my childhood was strange in many ways. I was fairly resilient to the dysfunction in our home and tried hard to rise above it. My mother was not interested in domesticity. She showed no interest in housekeeping or decorating, although she was the world's best seamstress. It must have been in her blood.

At the age of seven I took on the task of cleaning the house. I remember one year, after admiring the neighbor's shiny

Norma-Jean, first grade 1956.

floors, I asked for a bottle of Johnson's Liquid Floor Wax for my birthday. What a weird little girl I was! After school I did dishes, dusted, made beds, picked up clutter and tried my level best to make things look lovely. I was very domesticated. Mama's polar opposite.

I was a latch key kid before the circumstance had a name. Mama went to work and that was where her focus remained. She fell in love with her career. It wasn't what she was educated for but working for the US Government in any capacity made her happy. Her attitude was "the heck with the house or what it looks like." Our house didn't look pretty to me, but it was filled with lots of books and interesting things.

I suppose it sounds contradictory to say when Mama wasn't at work, she was cooking or sewing. Those two domestic tasks she did exceptionally well. Sewing seemed like therapy to her; she would lose herself in it. Often while she sewed, I sat on the floor near the sewing machine playing with fabric remnants and she would tell me stories of the past.

At times I would rub her leg feeling a ridge of bumpy lumps under her soft skin. When I was older I found out her skin was like that because of shrapnel.

Daddy could have cared less about decorating. I think he had no sense of interior home beauty, but he always wanted the dishes to be clean. Funny, he never wiped the stove, or counters, or swept, or mopped a floor. Instead, he spent countless hours reading when he was at home. He had a comfortable chair next to a floor lamp with an attached table where he kept his pipe and cherry tobacco pouch. He read a bit of everything, from travel books with accompanying slide shows, to war histories and wildly contrasting religious books. Someone had to clean and that someone was me!

Even as a child I recognized my parents' intelligence. I thought they had to be two of the smartest people on earth. They really didn't notice that our home didn't look like our friends' with clean, shiny floors, dust free furniture adorned with starched doilies, and pictures neatly placed. Mama and Daddy could have cared less about a nice looking home. The odd thing was, the inside of the closets and dresser drawers were in perfect order, a sign of Mama's organizational ability and Daddy's military training to keep uniforms and clothing in order. I used to wonder how I got such smart parents who saw things in such a different way than I did.

Aside from the lack of interest in housekeeping, Mama was prone to screaming fits of anger directed at Daddy; complete with throwing things and spitting in his face. Her way of talking was very expressive, using her hands and showing lots of emotion in a very European manner.

My parents loved each other very much, but certainly did not seem to be *in love* with each other. They did not get along. Daddy was what some would call a "womanizer", talking to or flirting with women of all colors, shapes, sizes, and walks of life. They were pretty, they were plain, it didn't seem to matter. He was suave and handsome, drawing the attention of women wherever he went. If they would listen to him, he'd talk to them, appropriate or not. I used to wonder why. I don't know, maybe just because he could. His behavior was similar to an addict seeking a fix. Sad, given the fact he was married.

One time my parents had a huge fight over a photograph he brought home. It was of a beautiful chocolate skinned lady in an evening dress with her shoulders exposed. I had no idea who she was; I hadn't seen her before. I'd seen a lot of ladies talk to him, but not her. My Mama looked at the picture, read the dedication, "To Olden, Amour, Amour, Amour" and went ballistic. She tore it up and threw it in his face. They fought so long on that day that I was afraid. Why did he have to bring such a stupid picture home? I'll never understand.

Normally, they fussed from the time they woke up in the morning until they left the house for work. Then it started all over again when they came home until they went to bed. This was their existence. In between the daily bickering they would have bigger blow ups like the one over the picture. I lived in the midst of their miserable existence and yet I still had a desire for joy. Their friends joked about them or just ignored their behavior. I was embarrassed.

My parents were like oil and vinegar. It's a nice combination when you shake it up, but otherwise it separates and it becomes clear that one is always separate from the other. The more I noticed their bickering and discord I became nervous. I chewed my fingernails, cried, and wished I could disappear. Most of all I would say to myself, *When I grow up and get married, it is never going to be like that and I will never talk to my husband like that!*

According to Mama and Daddy they loved each other and stayed together because of me. They both gave me a lot of love; I was their little girl. I believed that they were trying to ensure I was growing up knowing how loved I was. They tried their best. Whatever dysfunction was at home was familiar to me and my parents were never cruel. I was not the problem, nor was I the solution.

> *My parents were like oil and vinegar. It's a nice combination when you shake it up, but otherwise it separates...*

When I was not within the walls of my parents discord, I was a different child. I skipped everywhere, hummed constantly, and giggled easily. I was full of joy all by myself or with one parent or the other. And I was a masterful daydreamer.

⟨⟨◎⟩⟩ Beatnik Dreamin' ⟨⟨◎⟩⟩

My artistic side dreamed of many things. Right from the beginning I thought outside the box. My parents often told me that my aspirations weren't quite complete and they tried to get me back on the grid. "What else Norma-Jean? Have you thought of something else?"

One of my aspirations was to become a beatnik. I didn't know why they didn't agree with me that this would be wonderful! I had seen pictures of them. I had heard all about them. I saw how they dressed. I saw their unique, inclusive culture on television and in magazines and decided that these were my people. I walked around saying "Daddy O", snapping my fingers and bobbing my head to the rhythm of their music. I liked everything about them, their music, their stylish tight black pants and berets, their poetry recitations, and their general air of "coolness". I knew I wanted to be one. I wouldn't smoke the cigarettes, but I would stand and recite poetry, listen to music, and drink cocktails in Greenwich Village. I heard there were a lot of beatniks there. Yep, just as soon as I grew up.

Or maybe I would just keep dancing. I mean maybe if I did every arabesque, plie, grand jete, and pirouette a gazillion times, I too could dance in the *Nutcracker* in New York City and travel the world with a dance troupe. Everyone always commented on how long my legs were, perhaps I could become a Rockette. I had seen the Radio City Rockettes perform in New York City; they were wonderful.

Or if I practiced the piano enough hours every day, maybe one day I could grace the stage at Carnegie Hall. I had so many dreams; perhaps I could be a veterinarian and help sick animals, I loved animals. Or I could be a Christian missionary and travel to places where the people needed lots of help and needed to hear about Jesus. Or being a teacher would be safe; it would be something Mama and Daddy would like me to do.

I knew that I really wanted to have a family. Oh my goodness, we could be a beatnik family because most of all, out of everything, I wanted to be a mother. This would combine the best of both dreams; a Beatnik's mom, smart and free to be different. For months I talked daily about the way a person could balance being a mother and a father and a beatnik. I had it all figured out. It would be economical. No need for lots of different wardrobe pieces and just a small place to live. No car required. I sketched my Beatnik family in their oh so cool

"Daddy O" clothes. I had a black and white composition notebook filled with poems I was writing. I would stand in the living room, pop my fingers close my eyes… *yeah, yeah, yeah… and this is how this poem goes.*

For a while my parents humored my day dreaming. Mama made me a "beatnik" outfit with black pedal pushers, a top that looked like a French sweater, and a matching beret. Daddy bought me some sun shades. Oh yeah, I was it! I was in! They explained that I had to understand it was just an outfit! I had **not** become a beatnik. "Right, Norma-Jean?" "Right!" That's what they thought. My young inner-self was as beatnik as I would ever become. "Oh yeah, Daddy O." Jeanie, that was my nickname, was a beatnik through and through!

I sketched my beatnik family in their oh so cool "Daddy O" clothes.

Then the ruling came down. Yes, they liked the beatniks too. Yes, Daddy agreed that they were representative of deep thinkers. "For the most part," he laughed. "You stick to school and we will worry about this later. Study hard and do well, doors will open."

⤬◉⤬

But outside of daydreams the world can be a cruel place. It was a hard transition from home to school. When I went to school, although I was with children who, like me, were in a racial and ethnic melting pot, there was always somebody who had been taught different values at home. I was taunted and teased about various things.

Many times my young classmates with straight hair teased me and said I had a "Toni." I didn't even know what a "Toni" was, I now know it's a home permanent, and I went home in tears because it just sounded so negative. Whatever it was I didn't want one! Mama sat down with me and told me I had some of the most beautiful hair she had ever seen in her life. "Those girls are just jealous. You go back and tell them you don't need a 'Toni.'"

A few days later someone else would have something to say, "Why are you that color? Your skin isn't white and it isn't brown. Are you tanned?" I wondered, "Is tanned something bad?" I'd go home crying again and Mama would sit and tell me, "I have to sit in the sun to get a nice tan. God gave you such a perfect color. It's right in between your daddy and me. He knew exactly what would look perfect for you. God gave everyone what would look best on them too. He *always* knows exactly what he is doing. But some of us try to change it just a bit, because just like I wish I could have your curly hair, I wish I could have your pretty skin." Sometimes I would ask, "Mama, why don't the children like colored people?" *Colored* was the term back then, very few times did we hear the word "Black." She would say, "They are just jealous, look next time we go to the beach, everyone white is trying to get a sun tan so they can be brown!" "Oh Mama, you are so funny!" "It's true," she would say.

Why are you that color? Your skin isn't white and it isn't brown. Are you tanned?

The next time we went to the beach she said, "See, Norma-Jean, do you see how everyone is laying in rows in the sun just trying to get brown and yet people say mean things to you? You tell me, Sweetie, does that make sense to you? You be proud of how beautiful God made you." Mama was just building me up to deal with the cruel and insensitive kids. She wasn't trying to make me feel better than anyone else. She just didn't want me to feel inferior to anyone else. She gave me a regular dose of self-confidence when I came home with my head hanging low. That was petty stuff compared to what was ahead. I thought the world was safe and good. All that changed when Daddy was transferred to Fort Huachuca, Arizona.

CHAPTER 3

Unforgettable Roadtrip

The day I left Fort Mammoth, New Jersey was pretty sad. I thought I was headed to the land of thirst and rattlesnakes, mirages, and cactus, nothing more, nothing less. I thought it would be a vast desert scattered with ghost towns just like in the western movies. My ten year old imagination pictured cowboys with spurs on their boots and guns on their hips walking through saloon doors to challenge one another to a duel in the streets at high noon. I was really scared and hated the thought of leaving my best friend Rhonda. We had so much fun together. I thought I would never see her again. Most likely, she would hear that we were found dead in the desert. She'd hear we were skeletons with clothes on. I was such a sensitive child, I cried at the drop of a hat, not just sniffles but blubbery, snot dripping ugly crying. Our goodbye was extremely painful and tearful.

My parents took some of the pain away by promising to stop at Disneyland before going to Fort Huachuca. The idea brightened my day and made the journey seem more enticing.

They bought a brand new Chevy station wagon for the trip. We bid "adieu" to everyone and off we went. Daddy was behind the wheel,

Mama next to him, and me and my little cream colored Pomeranian dog Cookie had the back seat to ourselves. I had had her since she was a little fluffy handful.

All was fine the first part of the trip. As a child, I had no concept of how far we drove. It seemed far. I decided that everywhere we stopped to eat I would eat the same thing for lunch each day, the same thing for dinner, and the same thing for breakfast. That way my parents wouldn't fuss at me to eat my food since I was a very picky eater. I would have things I liked and promised myself to eat as much as I could to avoid getting in trouble and spoiling the fun of the trip. I had it figured out, I'd order a cheeseburger, fries, and a chocolate shake for lunch and the same thing for dinner. For breakfast I would have pancakes and hot cocoa.

The first day we sang songs like *This Old Man* and *One Hundred Bottles of Beer* as we traveled along. I did indeed eat my cheeseburger and we stopped at rest stops to stretch our legs and walk Cookie. When night fell we stopped at a roadside motel, put gas in the car and the next morning were on our way. Once again we sang songs and stopped at rest stops. I'm not sure where things went wrong. I only remember snippets of the rest of the trip. My memories are like excerpts from a bad nightmare. I try to forget but I just can't.

I remember stopping for gas and a big, burly looking man in overalls and a T-shirt coming over to my daddy and calling him "boy" asking him what he wanted. He replied, "I just want to buy some gasoline." "We don't sell gasoline to any niggers!" Daddy lunged at the guy and was going to fight him for calling him a nigger. Mama was screaming, "Olden no! No! Let's go!" The guy was really mean and ugly looking. He wanted Daddy to fight him. He was a much bigger man and would probably do some damage. Daddy walked away. When we started down the road he was cussing and pounding the steering wheel. He was saying he should have just kicked the guy's ass! Well, that wouldn't have worked. Clearly, he made the right decision. Soon he asked, "Alice, how far is it to the next town?" She had the map in her lap, trying to read it and figure it out. They were watching for road signs and at the same time watching the gas needle drop lower and lower.

It wasn't until hunger for another meal and the need for more gas that things once again became troubling. We stopped at a hamburger stand and just before we got out of the car Daddy cracked the windows to let fresh air circulate in the car for Cookie. We walked into the restaurant and everyone in the place turned to look at us. We took a booth and sat down. People weren't just looking at us, they were staring at us! Staring like we had just stepped off a spacecraft. After a few tense minutes, a waitress came over to the table and said, "We don't serve coloreds." Mama looked at Daddy, he looked back at her. Neither one of them looked at me. I just sat there frozen. Finally, I felt my hand being pulled as I was tugged toward the door. I looked back over my shoulder to see all the people still staring and some laughing out loud.

After a few tense minutes a waitress came over to the table and said, "We don't serve coloreds."

At the next town, Daddy pulled up to the gas pump and it was almost a repeat situation except this guy wasn't big and burly and he wasn't ugly. He just called Daddy "boy" and told him he wasn't going to sell him any gasoline. Daddy went ballistic. He grabbed the pump and started pumping the gas himself. The guy started to scuffle with him and pretty soon a couple of other guys surrounded them. I was screaming and crying and Mama got out of the car. She pleaded, "Stop, please stop!" Finally all the confusion stopped and the other men turned and looked at my mama. One of them said, "This nigger got himself a white woman. Boy, don't you know there's laws against a nigger having a white woman?" I huddled in the car, curled tight in a fetal position, crying so hard I could barely see. When I heard this I thought "What are they talking about?" Daddy said, "Look, I'm a soldier in the U.S. Army. I have fought for this country. I don't want any trouble."

After the scuffle Daddy got back in the car, tears of rage streaming down his face. Mom reached over to touch him and he jerked away. I buried my face in Cookie's soft fur and tried to shut out the world. Cookie was my friend.

Late in the day we pulled into another town. I don't know how long we had been driving because I had fallen asleep, exhausted from crying. I guess my parents had worked out a strategy for getting something to eat without another incident. When they spotted a hamburger place Daddy parked down the street as Mama walked to the restaurant and ordered the food to go. I felt confused and wounded, it just didn't make sense to me that we couldn't all go in together and sit down to eat. Within minutes Mama came back with our food. I was so hungry I gobbled mine up without being coaxed to eat more. I don't think I even remembered to thank God for the food but I was thankful no one had hurt Mama or Daddy. In the back of my mind I wondered when we might get another meal like this one. Looking back, I think I had a slight eating disorder, never wanting to eat and always having to be coaxed, but my parents handled it well.

I prayed that my parents wouldn't fight like they had earlier. They had never gotten along very well, but they had never, ever said a racial word to one another ever! After the incident at the gas station, Mama had tried to jump out of the moving car during the angry bickering with Daddy. Dad slammed the brakes on, throwing me off the backseat and sending Cookie flying. That was just the craziest thing I had ever seen! I was stunned. My heart broke for my daddy who I knew was hurt and humiliated too.

They decided that when it was time to stop for the night it would be best for Mama to get the room and not to mention Daddy or me. Things were never like this before. I couldn't wait to get safely to a

Scars heal over but there's still so much more to tell.

military base. That much I knew even as a child, the behavior I witnessed would not be tolerated on a military base. As far as my parents, I just hoped they would put this behind them and we would get back to normal, whatever "normal" was for us.

I wish I could say the remainder of our journey west was sweet, wonderful, and uneventful, but that wouldn't be true. It was traumatic and scarred my heart forever. That journey was like ink splatters on parchment paper; see them as beauty or see them as ugly. I think I will choose beauty. Scars heal over but there's still so much more to tell.

By the time we reached Anaheim, California I was in dire need of the make believe world of Disneyland. Mama bought me a pair of moccasins at an Indian trading post somewhere out in the middle of the desert. She also bought me a very pretty cowgirl hat with a matching shirt and pair of lavender cowgirl pants. To top it all off, I got a fancy beaded belt. I saved the outfit to wear to Disneyland. I had convinced Mama to cut my hair before we left, so I was feeling fancy! I was convinced that anyone who looked my way that day was admiring my snazzy new outfit and cute haircut. That good, beautiful day is etched in my mind.

Where else on earth can you ride up and down the Amazon, spin around in tea cups at the Mad Hatter's party, take a dive under the sea in a submarine, hug fairy tale characters who were walking the streets, and then go to Tomorrow Land all in one day? It's only possible at Disneyland. I was in love with the place and we all were having the time of our lives. My parents held hands, smiled, and posed for pictures. My favorite rides were the Teacups and It's a Small World. It was the perfect ending to our journey through hell.

After a couple of days of fun in the California sun we retrieved Cookie from the Disneyland kennel and headed back toward Arizona. I felt that nervous tumbling in the pit of my stomach when Daddy insisted on checking the burlap water bag he purchased to hang on the front of the car. "In case we break down in the desert," he said. I enjoyed watching the pretty scenery as we drove. We even stopped to see the ocean. When we stopped to eat we had no issues and I continued to follow my eating plan.

We pulled into Sierra Vista, Arizona late that night. We had stopped quite a few times along the way. We could have made much better time but we weren't in a hurry. We could see the main gate of the post but we stopped at a little motel right outside. We got our room key without any problems and within minutes I was bathed and tucked in bed. Tomorrow was the big day, the day we would see our new base in the light of day. I was so excited I could barely sleep.

Early in the morning I woke up to the offer of warm glazed donuts and milk. Daddy had gone down the street somewhere and found a bakery. We ate, and before I knew it, there we were driving up to the main entrance with its old, historic looking gates. Fort Huachuca was beautiful! The fort was established in 1877 and the Huachuca Mountains rested quietly, backdropped behind the old standard military buildings, barracks, and chapel. The sun shone brilliantly in the clear blue sky as I watched out the window at the picture perfect scenery passing by. It didn't look like the ugly place I had imagined. I couldn't wait to write Rhonda a letter and tell her it was actually pretty at Fort Huachuca!

We were fortunate to be assigned quarters at the base of a canyon in an area called Bonnie Blink. It was a beautiful new duplex with a wall of glass facing the canyon. 115–B Burt Rd. a stone's throw from our house, in one direction was the post cemetery, and in the other direction was a creek, actually the San Pedro River, with massive cottonwood trees forming a graceful canopy shading the babbling water.

I had so much fun living in Bonnie Blink. An old rubber tire hung from one of the trees, I would climb into it and swing from one side of the creek to the other. I skipped along the rocks in my bare feet, letting the cool water run between my toes. A few huge rocks as flat as tables were perfect for laying on and looking up at the sun through the dappled foliage of the trees. I'd walk up to the old base cemetery just because it was pretty and peaceful. I was unafraid and read the headstones one by one, in awe of the fact that some had been there since what I thought of as "the old times with cowboys and Indians." Many of the headstones were for small children and babies and I would place small wild flowers on their graves. I thought about the songs I sang in church with Grandma and I knew these children were all loved by Jesus. Until we moved to Bonnie Blink I had always thought a graveyard was the scariest, creepiest place in the world and now I played in one.

Life at Fort Huachuca was pretty nice. My parents had their friends and I had mine. Many of my friends were the children of their friends which made it easy to get together on weekends. Daddy barbequed and Mama would cook delicious dishes. The vinyl records dropping on the stereo provided music for dancing, laughing, and drinking cocktails. The kids had freshly squeezed lemonade and my daddy grilled hotdogs for us. We'd play croquet and badminton on the lawn. Sometimes everyone danced, and sometimes I just sat and watched Mama and Daddy. I always loved watching them dance and never tired of seeing them laugh and have fun doing this one sweet thing together.

I always loved watching them dance and never tired of seeing them laugh and have fun doing this one sweet thing together.

School was not so pleasant. Not because of the kids, they were all pretty nice. One of my teachers, who in my mind to this day is nameless, was horrific. I think I erased his name from my memory. When he stood in front of the class he ran his fingers through his red hair and wiped his brow with a dirty handkerchief. He had freckles all over his face and his arms and wore shirts that were a tad too tight, pulling the buttons. I remember all those details, yet he remains nameless. Each day he would greet the class with a joke. I usually didn't understand jokes, but I did understand the negative connotation, because he would always say something about a half-breed, then he'd look right at me and let out an evil snicker. This was a daily thing for months. He always had some little jab about a half-breed who couldn't get things right or something of the sort. One day he just couldn't contain himself anymore. He blurted out at me, "You're a half-breed and you're a freak of nature. You are one big mistake. You don't deserve to be alive. Your mother is white trash for having you!" I was mortified. I knew he hated me. He treated me differently than all the other kids. I had no idea how much he hated me until he said all those things. All the kids in class sat silently. No one knew what to do. I heard someone gasp. "I am not a mistake!" I cried. "Oh now she's going to cry. You are absolutely disgusting. Like I said, you should have never been born," he twisted his face in a sickened expression. I jumped up, ran out of the classroom, and ran all the way home. I cried until my parents came home that evening.

When they saw me with my eyes swollen and red faced and heard my story, Daddy went into a rage. It was one thing for people to

You are one big mistake. You don't deserve to be alive.

direct their prejudice towards him, but what this man had done was unforgivable. The next morning my parents and I were sitting in the principal's office as soon as the school doors opened. To our surprise, a few of my classmates had told their parents what happened and they were there to complain about it too! God helped me. I didn't even ask for his help but he sent it.

The principal and some other individuals brought my parents and me into the room with my nameless teacher. I think he was supposed to offer some sort of apology but it didn't happen that way. He stared at me. He stared at my mama and my daddy. His face turned very red, coloring in the spaces between his freckles until he appeared solid red. He reached for his dirty handkerchief and wiped his sweaty brow. He drummed his fingers on the table. We all waited for him to speak. This was his opportunity to clear things up, his chance to be the grown up in the room and explain himself. Finally, the silence burst, "Yes, yes I called her a halfbreed. That's what she is. She should have never been born!" Daddy jumped up from his seat, but Mama pulled him back down. The principal stood up, placed his hands on the table, looked that teacher squarely in the face and said, "That, Sir, just cost you your job."

To me the principal offered hugs and deepest apologies. To my parents he offered a guarantee that nothing like this would ever happen again. The teacher would be replaced immediately. In this day and time, the teacher's actions would be grounds for legal proceedings, but back then it was not an option, not even a thought. I do know Daddy literally wanted to kill the guy! I was grateful for the show of support. Kids and their parents stopped my parents in the hall to say how despicable the whole thing was. I was an emotional wreck and kept my head lowered so they wouldn't all see my tears. My feelings were still so hurt by the meanness of Mr. Nameless, but I was thanking God for all the kind and loving people in the world.

CHAPTER 4

Pointe Shoes and Déjà Vu

Daddy was transferred to Germany. We had to leave the beautiful place I'd come to love and call home. The giant moving truck and its team came to pack us up and I escaped to sit by the babbling brook in Bonnie Blink and cry. I was so torn, I never ever wanted to be away from my daddy. Of course being an army brat I had been several times, but I always felt I wouldn't survive a week without him. However, I was raised to be strong and I survived. I wanted to protect my daddy's heart, so I assured him that I would take good care of my mother in his absence and I would be fine.

There was a ban on family travel because of the cold war, so we couldn't go with him. Until it was lifted we would return to Massachusetts because Aunt Sigrid was there. The best part of living there was spending time with her, Claus, and Monica. The familiarity of being with them was a good thing and I loved them. Even though we didn't go back to visit often, our times together are some of my fondest childhood memories. Mama was happy to have her best friend and I was happy to just be free to be happy.

At first Mama rented an adorable little cottage on the outskirts of Ayer, Massachusetts, but night came so early in the autumn I became frightened. Every day for two weeks I stood in the middle of the living room frozen with fear until she came home. I'd stare out at the long, dirt road and the big, bare trees and what seemed like blackness all around us. I hated it! Mama was home by six but it seemed like midnight.

L-R - Aunt Sigrid, Claus, Monica, Norma-Jean, Mama

She promptly found a place in the center of town within walking distance to little shops and with neighbors all around us. I felt much better, but I still couldn't wait for us to leave that place. I was enrolled in classical ballet classes and piano lessons. Ballet was my thing. I don't know how I was graceful at the barre, but had not one bit of rhythm to b-bop. Twice a week I walked to the dance studio for my class and piano lessons once a week.

I had started to dance on pointe shoes which I hated more than anything. I should have loved it because of the satisfaction of reaching that level. I should have felt happy and proud of myself. I had achieved a new level of accomplishment that took years of dance training. My pretty feet developed bleeding blisters and ugly calluses. I didn't want to do it anymore. I didn't want to do any of the things my parents had worked so hard to give me. I wanted to defy everything.

My grades in school took a nose dive. I don't remember any of my classmates or even the name of the school. Mama forced me to go to a school end-of-the-year party. I wore a beautiful white chiffon dress and there was dancing. One boy asked me to dance. I waltzed with Mama all the time and loved to dance with her. Dancing with this boy was no waltz. I was tall and pencil skinny and his face came right up to my budding breasts. I was very embarrassed as he led me in an awkward box step. I was taller than all the boys in my class. All I wanted was to go home but I sat on a chair in dainty form watching others drink punch, eat snacks, and dance as I thought *This is so stupid!* My once in my crazy childhood shot at being totally sullen! Just before the party ended a teacher asked me to dance. *Oh God, a teacher.* I couldn't have been more humiliated but I got up and did my best. I think it was a pity dance; one I would have just as soon skipped.

When Mama and I could finally join Daddy in August of 1963 we couldn't fly to Germany like most families did because my mother was deathly afraid of flying. No way was she ever going to agree to get on an airplane. Instead, we went by naval transport ship, The USNS *Buckner.* We left New York on a beautiful August day full of excitement, people were waving, and the Navy band played *Anchors Away.* There were many other families on the ship with us as well as navy troops. Of course they kept us separated.

Every morning Mama and I would go out on the deck and watch the sea life; I loved watching porpoises swim beside our ship. One of the most beautiful sights of the trip was passing through "the white cliffs of Dover." Everyone on board stood on the decks and watched in awe as the captain maneuvered through the icy waters. We were so close it felt like we could touch the cliffs. I thought for sure when the

> *Germany gave me a sense of déjà vu, I kept telling Mama, "I have been here before."*

ship reached the Port of Bremerhaven that Daddy would be there to greet us. It was not so. He was in the field and I understood what that meant. We were on our own. We needed to get to Nürnberg and Mama had it all under control.

Germany gave me a sense of déjà vu. I kept telling Mama, "I have been here before." We had a very strange experience when I told her there was a pub down the street and around the corner only to discover that indeed there was one exactly as I had described it. Deja vu! I've continued to have these intriguing experiences throughout my life.

I also loved the special time I spent one on one with Mama in Europe. There was so much she wanted to show me. We drove around, exploring cities and villages and visiting countless museums and cathedrals. We would just get in the car and travel, ride the bus, or even better, the train. It was a magical time. It was like going back in history. Everything was so ornate and distinctly beautiful. I loved Europe.

One time just she and I went for a weekend retreat to Berchtesgaden. This was the place where Adolf Hitler had hidden and written part of *Mein Kompf*. It had been used as a camp for Nazi troops and in later years it's greenhouse supplied produce for Hitler's vegetarian preferences. Considering Mama's traumatic background I'm surprised that she took me there. But it was truly spectacular. It had been destroyed and rebuilt as an extraordinary resort. We went as a family to lots of beer fests and wine fests. Yes, my parents gave me beer and wine and no, I never got drunk or snuck around to drink. Under-age drinking is a big deal in our American culture but it wasn't in Europe. My parents were always very open about alcohol. They did their share of partying with cocktails in the mix, but in general weren't big drinkers. If they had a drink and I was curious, it wasn't an "Oh my God" moment, it was a "Here, take a sip" moment. I usually walked away with a frown instead of "give me more!"

Mama smoked cigarettes and Daddy smoked a pipe. I had no interest in smoking anything at all. I loved the smell of Daddy's cherry pipe tobacco but that's as far as it went. The smoke itself was just too disgusting. I vowed to never become a smoker, although I saw noth-ing at all wrong with drinking socially.

When we finally reunited with Daddy I was the happiest girl on the planet. We rented a small apartment from a German family upstairs in their home. We actually walked right through their living room to get to our apartment. Within a few months, quarters, that's what the military called living accommodations, became available for us on the base.

I loved living in Germany. It was beautiful and once again I had a true sense of belonging. My friends and I were all just a bunch of American kids living in a foreign country. It didn't matter what race we were, it didn't matter if your dad was an officer or an enlisted man, we respected each other and had fun. Daddy was transferred from Nürnberg to Bamberg during my freshman year of high school but I attended the American High School in Nürnberg. My friends and I rode the train to school every day. The bus picked up all the American students in our neighborhoods and took us to the train station. There were three to four cars just for us. What a blast we had laughing and talking as we rode that train day in and day out. We were rowdy, but we were good kids. If we weren't our parents would be sure to hear about it!

For the sake of continuity, my mother found me a piano teacher. She didn't know I was scared to death of this woman. She was an old German woman who lived in a building that looked like an old cas-tle but had been converted to apartments. The place had a sickening smell of mold and mildew. Her apartment was at the end of a long hallway that echoed as I walked through it; click, clack, click, clack my heels rapped on the old cement floor. Scared, I tried to hurry down the hallway, but always wanted to turn and run out of the building. I'd reach her door with my heart in my throat. The heavy steel knocker echoed against the ancient wood door adding to my fear. Finally she would open the massive door to allow me entrance. What a musty old woman in a musty old building. I felt guilty for disliking her. I had been taught to look for the best in everyone but couldn't get past the odors.

She had a huge orange tabby cat that sat on top of her spinet piano during my lesson. He would try to smack the metronome as it ticked back and forth. His fur was everywhere and I'd sneeze then lose my place. For this infraction she would smack the back of my hands with a heavy wooden ruler and yell at me in German, her spittle flying in my face. My eyes would fill with tears until I could no longer read the notes in front of me. I absolutely dreaded going there. One day, I finally told Mama I couldn't do it anymore. She didn't offer to search for another teacher. I think I had already broken her heart by hanging up my ballet slippers. The truth is, I loved the beauty of the piano music and would have continued lessons with a softer, kinder teacher. I left behind a lot in that old musty building. Now my mind is blocked and I don't think I can play a note, I feel robbed. Every now and then I dream that I sit down, open a keyboard, and out flows the music. In my dreams I play *Liebestraum no. 3*, *Clair De Lune*, Beethoven, Bach, and other beautiful melodies. Sometimes I even dream of playing boogie woogie with Daddy and laughing. Sometimes we're playing chop sticks but it sounds really, really good. But I awake to find it was just a dream.

> *Sometimes I even dream of playing boogie woogie with Daddy and laughing.*

Being Daddy's girl had many benefits. I learned to listen for the hidden message when he talked to me. He taught me that people say one thing and often mean something else. This taught me to really listen and focus when other people spoke to me. He bought me books and lectured me on the parameters of the world of men and women, sort of an early version of *Men are from Mars and Women are from Venus*. I was too young to actually date when he started explaining the finer attributes that I should seek in a man when the time came. He also made very clear the kind of person I could **not** bring home!

Some of the lessons Daddy taught me started with catchy phrases and action attached. For instance, he always said, "Put your best foot forward." Now how would I know which foot was my best? According to Daddy, either foot that you step forward with should represent you in the best way possible and dirty, scuffed, run over shoes do not make a good impression. They instead say, "I don't care much about my appearance so any old thing on my feet will do." Dirty shoes are fine for working in a dirty environment, but once you are out of that space you absolutely must change your shoes. Daddy said every man should invest in a good pair of shoes and a good suit. If a man owned a good pair of shoes and not the shoe shine brush, polish, rag to maintain them, he felt there was something very wrong with this situation. He taught me that a fine pair of shoes is to be maintained. According to Olden Jackson, a gentleman doesn't go in public with his shoes unshined, scuffed up, or dirty. Gym shoes, as he called them, were washed; boots for his uniform were always spit shined. So certainly, a civilian could keep a few pair of dress shoes clean and shined.

How did this lesson affect me and the whole put your best foot forward concept? Oh, how I love shoes! Flip flops, sneakers, lovely high heels, loafers......I love shoes of so many styles. I take such good care of them that they all look brand new. Yes, I have spent a life time shoe judging and shaming others. I have seen so many gorgeous, best foot forward men; but I really only liked their absolutely fabulous taste in shoes as they walked past. On the flip side, I must say I have seen a man with a gorgeous face and glanced at his feet only to be reminded of a gentleman according to Olden Jackson. Dirty, scuffed, ugly shoes are to this very day a number one turn off for me. My first thought on seeing this is *Let me buy you a decent pair of shoes!* I look at women's shoes in exactly the same way. I cringe when I see the total look accented with horrific shoes!

Daddy decided we were going to do sort of a remedial course on of all things the handshake. He had long ago told me that when I shake hands with someone I need to look them in the eye and give them a nice firm grip. When I say long ago, I was probably five. Some people believe that females should just offer a limp wrist, but that was not the school of thought my par-

> *Who knew that a good, firm handshake and a strong "Hello, how are you?" with a straight look in the eye is one sign of a good man?!*

ents offered. This was another of the attributes Daddy was encourag-ing me to look for in a future husband. No arranged marriage for this young lady, but years in advance of coming of age the requirements were being drummed in to my head. Who knew that a good, firm handshake and a strong "Hello, how are you?" with a straight look in the eye is one sign of a good man?! Lordy, don't let Daddy shake hands with a guy who offered him a soft grip!

While we're talking about hands, another pet peeve of Daddy's were long fingernails on a man. This was a red flag to him; in Olden Jackson's book, a gentleman keeps his nails trimmed and clean.

"Ladylike" was a word I must have heard ten thousand times. Chipped nail polish or dirty fingernails is certainly not *ladylike*. If your polish chips, take it right off. If you get something under your nails, use soap and water and the nail brush. Yep, my parents were making darn sure I was a stickler for good grooming. So hey, to the guy who worked on cars and didn't know the simple trick of a nail brush, sorry for judging you and thinking you were icky. I know that many of the things my daddy had as standards were straight up military training. There is nothing wrong with that as far as I'm concerned.

Our family's personal neatness culture extended to hair. Daddy had perfectly groomed hair and went to the base barber at least every other week. At night he slept in a stocking cap made from one of Mama's silk stockings tied with a knot at the top. This helped keep his pretty waves tamed. His hair always smelled amazing like Vitalis.

I would sit in the bathroom with my knees pulled up to my chest and watch Daddy shave. He would take that old bristle brush and whisk it around and around in the mug until he had a thick foamy lather, then slather it all over his face. Meticulously, he'd start on one side and make smooth rows removing the foam and rinsing it in a bowl of water. Miraculously his face would emerge smooth as silk and then he'd splash on Ice Blue Aqua Velva. He smelled wonderful and fresh. I loved to sniff his freshly shaved face. Daddy always smelled so good. Quite naturally, smelling nice was something I came to value; I loved a man who smelled good, just like Daddy. I loved my beautiful bottles of Chanel No 5 that Daddy bought for me, setting the standard for the rest of my life. To this day it is my signature scent.

So of course it was established that I had some very basic expectations from the people around me and I hadn't even met my first boyfriend yet!

CHAPTER 5

Toni, My Sister, My Friend

Toni and I were classmates at school and we became friends instantly. We have so much in common and yet at the same time we're polar opposites. She is the bravest woman I know! We've had so much fun together, but we've never had to be *having* fun, we were comfortable just being with each other. We were more like sisters. If you saw one of us, you saw the other. We even wore matching dresses, did our hair alike and ate the same foods. The original best friends forever!

Our fathers were both servicemen and my parents took us on trips together. The summer after we celebrated our 13th birthday together, they took us to Amsterdam and Paris. We

Norma-Jean and Eiffel tower - Paris

had a fantastic time and sang that summer's hit song, *Going to the Chapel* over and over again, driving Daddy crazy. The young soldiers in Paris flirted with us which also drove my daddy crazy! We just giggled about it all.

Toni was a part of our family and I became a part of hers. To this day we have always referred to each other's parents as Mom and Dad. She comes from a beautiful family; her mother and father were so in love and it showed. Her mother, coincidentally named Norma-Jean, always looked like a fashion model and her father James was always the perfect gentleman. He treated his wife like a lady. Toni's mom didn't work outside the home so she devoted her time to cooking meals and caring for her family and home. I admired that. My mama always looked lovely but, like I said, she really could have cared less about our house. Toni had two brothers and a younger sister, Tracy, who was the little darling of the family and spoiled. It couldn't be helped. She was a precious little doll and everyone doted over her, including me.

Toni and I had a party to celebrate our 14th birthday together; I'm ten days older. We had such a fun time! Our friends came and everyone dressed up for the party; we'd actually put on the invitation "dress up required". I still have the invitation and it was a day neither of us has ever forgotten. I had many friends in Germany; besides Toni, there were Grace and Ursula, both really sweet girls. I found Grace on Facebook a few years ago; she is still beautiful and still the smartest person in the room.

Toni earned a nursing degree as a single mom caring for her young daughter Dena. Nothing ever stopped her. After her divorce from Karl, Dena's father, she entered the military as an officer and was stationed in

Toni in uniform

some of the most dangerous places in the world, setting up field hospitals at the front lines.

To this day Toni remains the sister I never had, my friend, someone I can always count on through good times and bad. I can share my deepest thoughts, dreams, and joys with her. She is my chosen sister for life and nothing will ever change that.

⤳⤳ Jerry ⤲⤲

Toni had two brothers, Jerry and Eric. When I first met Jerry, her older brother, he didn't like me and I sure didn't like him. I thought he was arrogant and he thought I was the kid who hung out with "Bones"; that's what he called Toni. He ended up being my very first boyfriend!

L-R – Kenny, Toni, Norma-Jean, Jerry 9th grade prom

The four of us, Jerry and I and Toni and her then boyfriend, spent time going to dances at the AYA (American Youth Association) on weekends, playing tennis in the park, going in to town, eating bratwurst from corner venders, and sweet treats from local bakeries. We went on planned excursions coordinated by the AYA, and rode German trains to visit nearby towns.

Jerry was my date for the ninth grade prom. It was a big deal, it was basically my first real date and I was very surprised I was allowed to go. Mama sewed my dress, which of course like everything she made me, was beautiful. It was soft yellow chiffon with black polka dots and a full fluffy skirt. The dress had sheer long sleeves and I loved it! It looked just like one I had seen in a magazine. Mama could sew anything. We double dated with Toni and Kenny, but the guy she was really crazy about and spent the most time with was Bill. We all had fantastic times together.

Jerry played football and I cheered for the team. I was crowned Homecoming Queen and he was named King. It seems like simple fun now when I look back, but it was oh so serious then. Jerry was smart, sweet, and funny once I got past his cockiness. I really, really liked him. In fact, I told him I loved him. I wrote it on everything, I mean on everything. *Jerry and Norma, Norma and Jerry* like it was a mantra. We were so cool.

> *It seems like simple fun now when I look back, but it was oh so serious then.*

This young man also met every one of the standards Daddy had taught me were important. He never wore funky shoes; he owned nice dress shoes that he polished. He owned a suit, he cut his hair, his hands were groomed, he had a great handshake, he was respectful, and he always smelled like he just got out of the shower, except after playing sports. He loved God, he loved his family and he told me that he loved me! I really loved him. We were photographed together a hundred times. Him hugging me, or holding my hand, us looking goofy, dancing, looking serious, looking sad, riding the train, playing tennis, the two of us with Toni. I was his girl. He was my guy.

Now he would have made a great beatnik! Of course I had long let my beatnik family dreams go, or had I?

Everyone just knew that after graduation Jerry and I would go on to college, get married, have a lovely family, and be together forever. He was older than me and during the fall of his senior year in 1964 my daddy was rotated back to the United States. We were stationed at Fort Ord, California. It would be nine months until Toni's dad would return to the United States. So for nine months she and I wrote almost daily and Jerry and I did write every day.

Somewhere along the line I started thinking about what our parents had said about us being so young to be so serious. I started thinking about the football scholarships and the future Jerry had available to him anywhere he wanted to go. I also started giving a lot of thought to my life and what I wanted to become. There was so much I wanted to do for myself before I could com-

Norma-Jean and Jerry Homecoming Queen and King, 10th grade, Germany

mit to another human being. I knew I needed and wanted an education. My parents always talked to me about the value of an education. I wanted to travel and see the world and wanted to be financially stable. I knew I wanted one day to own my own home, marry, and have children. I knew that when I had children, I wanted to stay home and raise them. I wanted a full circle of family and friends that were loving and supportive. Toni and I planned to live near each other so our kids would grow up together. We said that when we were little old ladies we'd sit together in rockers on our front porches.

I had decided early in life what kind of wife and mother I wanted to be. Toni's mother, Norma-Jean Brown was my role model as a wife then and still is to this day. I always felt that being a mother was a calling, a blessing and honor, not everyone was meant to be one.

As I reflected on all my aspirations for the future and my parents' hopes and dreams for me and Jerry's parents hopes for him, I knew that there was no way a couple of kids could have a fighting chance at a good life without getting an education and obtaining some life experience. I felt the best way to do this was for me to break up with him and just concentrate on school, for a time anyhow. In my young mind it didn't mean I was saying "I don't love you." I was just saying 'I can't do this right now. Let's take a break." Actually, I was saying to Jerry, "I love you more." People say that a lot now. I truly wanted a great, happy, and blessed life for him because of loving him.

It was a very hard thing for me to do, but I told Jerry over the phone since we were maintaining a long distance relationship. I did not want to write a *Dear John* letter. I thought we would get back together one day, after other priorities had been met and fulfilled. Jerry was my first boyfriend. He was the first person, other than my parents, family members, or best friend that I ever said "I love you" to. But I wasn't even sixteen and I knew I had to give us both a chance to find what more there was in life.

So, I guess it would be predictable if I said I went on to finish school and then later we got back together again and Toni was the maid of honor for our wedding. But that isn't at all how things went.

CHAPTER 6

Not Everything was
Swell at Seaside

I was the new girl and arrived at Seaside High School expecting only good things and new friends. Daddy was stationed at Fort Ord and my parents bought a house in Seaside. We arrived in November so the school year was already in full swing. The school was a beautiful new facility set up on a hill with a view of the ocean. The student body was predominantly black but there were students of all races. I hated the fact that I had to leave Germany, where I had been so popular and loved everyone. At Seaside High the boys were much friendlier to me than the girls. I met many of the students and thought everything was fine.

I had only been there for a few weeks when I was confronted with my worst nightmare. One I could have never imagined. My hair was quite long, down to the middle of my back and I usually wore it pulled tight in a ponytail on top of my head and wrapped around into a fashionable bun or braid. I seldom wore it down because there was so much of it and by the end of a couple of hours it looked untamed. To keep it all tidy, it took a rubber band and a multitude of bobby pins. On this particular day I had a headache, so I skipped the hardware and wore my hair loose. I wasn't trying to make a fashion statement. I walked into the girls' bathroom and was suddenly snatched by my hair. Oh my God did it hurt. I was shocked, my knees shaking, heart pounding. Suddenly, a group of girls surrounded me, beating me with their fists, kicking me, and grabbing my hair. One girl pulled out a pair of scissors. I thought she was going to stab me. I was so scared I thought I was going to pee my pants. I was terrified of what they would do if that happened. Heart pounding, I cried out, "Jesus!" She spoke very improper English and sneered, "Oh yeah, you think you cute. You think you got some good hair. You all light skinned and stuff. You stupid b....!" I huddled in pain, trying to protect my head, shaking in fear. I couldn't see through the blur of tears stinging my eyes. Why would these girls attack me? I hadn't done anything to them, I didn't even know them. Why would they curse me? "Please stop, please!" I begged. They were in an evil rage, one girl pulled my hair to the nape of my neck and it was apparent they intended to cut my hair. I thought, *I don't care if they cut my hair, please God just don't let them stab me.* All of a sudden the bathroom door opened and all I could see was the large shadow of another girl. *Oh no... I thought, she is so big, I'll die right here.* I just whimpered.

I didn't know how to fight, I was defeated before it even started and didn't even try. "What the hell are you doing?" "Let her go!" The girls stood up and backed away from me. I dropped to the floor like a Raggedy Ann doll. "Cheryl this b.... thinks she's all cute and stuff just cause she's light skinned and got all this good hair. We gonna show her how cute she is all right. We beat her ass good! Now we gonna cut all her hair off." Cheryl said, "If anyone of you touches her again I will personally kick your ass. Now get out of here. Now!" She reached down to help me up. I was shaking

> "If anyone of you touches her again I will personally kick your ass."

and sobbing. "Girl look at you! You don't let anybody do you like that. You hear me? Nobody! You swing, you try to do something. You scream or if you can't do that, you run! Are you silly? You know me? I am Cheryl Parker. You don't have to be afraid of those girls. They won't be messing with you anymore." All I could do was cry. That day Cheryl became one of my dear friends. What a way to make a friend. We were friends until she tragically died in an auto accident years later.

After that awful day at school I came down with a serious case of the flu. I stayed home day after day telling my parents I was too sick to attend school. One morning after about five days of absence Daddy sat me down at the kitchen table for the confrontation I had been try-ing so hard to avoid. "You have no fever, you certainly don't look sick. What is the real reason you do not want to go to school?" It felt like the horrible day back at Fort Huachuca repeating again, except I was much older now. I was in high school and this time it wasn't a teacher who made me feel like a worthless person, but a group of students. I just couldn't go back. I'd rather drop out. I'd rather give up on all my dreams and aspirations than to be treated worse than a dog.

I hated being hated! I just wanted to stay home with the covers over my head. Instead Daddy marched me right over to the school. Wild things churned, flipped, and flopped in my stomach as we walked in the office. It was worse than butterflies. I thought I was going to vomit and was terrified. Daddy very calmly asked for my records, stated he was taking me out of school and didn't even make me give any explanations to the principal. I was so thankful to Daddy for handling it like he did.

With my records on the back seat of the car Daddy took me for a ride down the Pacific Coast Highway to Big Sur. We ate lunch and looked at the ocean, just watching the waves come and go. Daddy told me he wasn't sure he had handled the situation to his satisfac-tion. He told me he wanted to go back to the school and raise hell. He thought he would find the kids who terrorized me and confront their parents. No one treats his little girl like this and gets away with it. "Daddy, no, please I don't want any trouble. I just want to forget it. Pleeeeze Daddy." I couldn't hold back my tears. I was remembering the times I had seen Daddy in *Fight Mode* when we drove across the United States. I never wanted revisit those times. I pleaded more, "Daddy pleeeeze, please just forget it. Those girls weren't taught right. Jesus teaches us to forgive. I forgive them. I am okay." He let me have my way. Here I am over fifty years later and the pain is still very real although I still forgive them.

The next decision was whether I would go to a private school or give Monterey High School a try. I called Cheryl to let her know I had transferred schools. I also called my other friends from Seaside High because I had indeed made a few and wonder of wonders, my friend Grace from Germany was there. It was a small miracle to be stationed in the same place upon our return to the United States. She was surely the rising star of the school.

Right from the start Monterey High School felt great, I loved being there. There was no mention of my race, no mention of my color, no mention of my hair, no mention of my boyfriend or my parents. I joined the speech and debate team. I sat on the outside bleachers at lunchtime and on most days fed most of my lunch to the sea gulls. One day a sea gull bombed my head with poop and that ended my noon sessions on the bleachers. From then on I ate a box of junior mints every day for lunch. If I had to eat it by myself I was going to enjoy it.

...they just said racially charged words because they didn't have anything better to say.

Monterey High School had a great teaching staff as well as a student body that was diverse and accepting. I was friendly towards everyone and everyone seemed friendly towards me. If they had an issue with me they didn't show it outwardly. The student body was predominantly Italian American kids, some black, and a mixture of every other race you could think of. It always seemed odd to me that since Seaside was adjacent to the military base and therefore more of a melting pot than Monterey, nonetheless, I was treated better there than at Seaside. It left a huge question in my mind. One of my friends told me it didn't have anything to do with color or race. It was an isolated incident fueled by jealousy about me being the *new* girl getting attention from the boys. My friend said they just said racially charged words because they didn't have anything better to say. I hope that is the case. I have friends and family who graduated proudly from Seaside High School. Go Trojans!

Hilby Avenue, Seaside

My grandmother came to live with us right about the time I made the move to Monterey High School. It was a time of great change. Grandmother had dementia. She would look right at me from time to time and call me Billy. "Grandmother, I'm Norma-Jean." "Oh yes," she'd smile sweetly and fold her hands. Her pockets were filled with folded tissue. She would make stacks of toilet tissue and Kleenex, wrap them in a rubber band and stuff her pockets and her pocket book. Daddy had moved her from Chicago to be with him so she could become his dependent and receive better health care. I wished I had known her better. Although she was my biological grandmother I knew very little about her. Most of what I had been taught by a grandmother figure was from my self-appointed Grandma in New Jersey.

Grandmother's dementia caused her to wander and get lost. I thought Daddy would lose his mind the first time she wandered away. She also had severe diabetes and her already small frame was extremely thin. She would rock in her favorite chair and converse with Adolph, my deceased grandfather. I could see how much Daddy loved and cared for her and I tried hard to build the best relationship I could with her. I loved her very much.

Despite the way Grandmother and Grandfather had felt about my mother, Mama did her best ninety percent of the time to make her feel at home and welcome. She sewed for her and cooked nourishing meals. They didn't have much in common and at times I felt Mama was far too short on patience and understanding and even kindness. It became a sore spot between us and was one thing that I stood toe to toe and argued about with her. "Mama please be more patient. I don't think Grandmother can help the things she does." She then tried to be more patient and understanding.

Every Sunday morning Daddy would get up very early and stand in front of the living room window with his coffee cup while he played Mahalia Jackson on the stereo. Grandmother would wander out of her room and sit on the sofa entranced by the soulful worship songs. It was a sweet sight to see her frail hands pat to the beat. I'd join them until it was time for us to get dressed and attend church. Daddy played his albums every Sunday for as long as I can remember. Sharing this time with my grandmother is one of my few memories with her.

Note to my teenage self...........*Be involved with knowing my grandchildren whenever I have them.*

CHAPTER 7

Killer Smile

C harles Sims was quite the jock. The first time I met him he had just finished football practice and came strolling towards us. He was a sophomore at Monterey Peninsula College. My friend Lillian, also a student at the college, introduced us. I was just a junior at Monterey High School. Lillian told me he was a star player on the team and I could have cared less but when I saw him walking toward us I thought, *Oh, my gosh, this guy has a really nice build and a killer smile.* I looked away, embarrassed by my own thoughts; I never had those thoughts about anyone before! They certainly weren't fitting for a sixteen year old young lady! Shame, shame, on me! We said our hellos and he made a bit of small talk. He was smiling, looking at me the whole time while I was looking at Lillian. I was too shy to just stand there and stare back at him. After a few short minutes he said good bye, told me it was a pleasure to meet me, and with that he was gone. Lillian gushed, "He's so cute! What do you think of him?" "Uh I don't know. I just met him for two minutes. He's nice looking and seems very polite." I don't know how people expect you to form an opinion based on a two minute encounter.

Several days passed before I saw Charles again by sheer chance. Friday night Lillian and I went to the Monterey High football game. Turns out it was his alma mater. It was a typical Monterey night, cool and foggy. I was ready to leave as soon as we got there. Cool and foggy is not my thing, never has been. "Don't be such a party pooper," she chided. Then I saw him. Sitting there with girls surrounding him like he was King Tut with his harem. *Stupid girls! What are they thinking? What the heck is he thinking?* My mind was twisted with crazy thoughts. Lillian chose where to sit as always, she was bossy like that. We could see Charles from where we sat and she started going on about how cute he was. "So, if you think he is sooo cute why don't you go talk to him?" I asked. "He's busy." "Doing what? Nothing he is doing looks important to me! Watch this…." I go on her behalf, working my way over to where he and his

Charles Sims, Monterey Peninsula College football team

harem are sitting. The girls just stare at me standing there awkward and uncomfortable, but I still manage to smile. Charles looks at me and smiles like its Christmas morning, "Hey, hello," I said, "I want to talk to you." and he tells me to have a seat. I'm baffled, what should I tell him about Lillian? Do I ask him to leave his harem and come over where we are sitting? I'd have to go back and consult with her. I must look as stupid as the girls around him. "I don't mean right now," I squeak, turning and walking briskly back to my seat to tell Lillian I am ready to leave. All the way home I replayed the ridiculous conversation in my head.

I hope that boy doesn't think I was flirting with him because God knows I wasn't. Even if he was cute, I wasn't flirting with him. But, all those stupid girls fawning over him, what were they thinking? I couldn't get them out of my mind. Who does such a thing? *They should be ashamed.* I never did understand that whole picture I can still see in my mind like the flash of a movie reel. Blink and its gone. Close my eyes and it's there again. *Why sit surrounded by all those ridiculously silly girls? Was I supposed to meet him, supposed to intervene?* It would all make sense in the future.

Meanwhile, things were happening in the college locker room, not in the usual manner of locker-room gossip. It seems my name was floating around because of something I wouldn't do rather than something I would do. Usually, when a girl's name gets around it can tarnish her reputation. I guess this did in a sense, I was labeled as *lame* and *goody two shoes*. The guy who was talking a bunch of trash about me said, "She didn't know anything and I didn't have time to teach her." He had started talking about me because he felt rejected. He had invited me to lunch and Daddy gave me permission to leave the campus for lunch, nothing more. This guy picked me up and immediately proceeded to the local make out spot. I then proceeded to have a hissy fit and demand he take me back to the school right away, or I would tell my daddy. I was not about to park and neck with anyone when I only had permission to go to lunch. Knowing Daddy, I was probably being watched. The guy was furious with hurt pride and spread the locker-room gossip. He was a college jock and I was just a high school girl; he thought I should fall for him. But it sure didn't go his way.

Charles, of course, was in the locker-room listening to all of this. Turns out he had been dumped by two girls who wanted bad boys instead of him. I mean *bad*, as in jail bird bad. So he thought a good

> *It seems my name was floating around because of something I wouldn't do rather than something I would do.*

49

girl was exactly what he needed. Imagine that, Charles with the harem of girls sitting around him, dumped by anyone!

Homecoming was a big deal at Monterey Peninsula College. Lillian was waiting to be asked by a mystery man. She wouldn't tell me his name but she said I would be surprised when he asked her. She had a lot of guys so I might be surprised or maybe not. Anyhow, she knew any day now he would call. The young man who had been talking behind my back had a change of heart and called me to apologize. I told him, "Forget it, it's done, leave me alone, no hard feelings" and I hung up. My phone rang again, his friend this time, "He's really sorry, will you go out with him, give him another chance?" "Are you kidding me? No leave me alone! Forget it." About an hour later yet another call from yet another guy calling on his behalf, "He is a really good guy; will you give him another chance?" "No. Leave me alone. Forget it. He is rude and obnoxious and I will not!"

When the phone rang again I was quite agitated, "If you are calling for your friend just forget it! I will never go out with him again. Ever!" "Hey, wait a minute, I am calling for myself. Remember me? Charles Sims?" I apologized for being so snippy. My face burned red with embarrassment and I explained all the phone calls I had had that afternoon. Laughing, he said he understood. "I was wondering if you'd like to be my date for the homecoming." "I'd like that," I said. He agreed to call back and we'd work out the details.

When Lillian called later that day I said, "Lillian, just who is this mystery man? He better get busy asking you to the dance. Even I have a date already." "Oh? Who asked you? "Charles Sims" "You b....! You steal all my boyfriends!" Click.....dial tone. "Boyfriends?" I have no idea what she is talking about!

"Charles Sims are you now or have you ever been Lillian's boyfriend?" "Whaaat? Are you crazy? You better talk to Jimmy and Earl and those guys. They are her boyfriends!" Lillian had a reputation for being ridiculously promiscuous.

So, Charles and I began dating. At one point he had made a date with both me and a girl named Sharon. I told him to go ahead and go out with Sharon but if he did, just forget about me. He picked me up, and then drove to pick up Sharon, and he took us both to the football game. He sat with me. He paid her way in, but she sat by herself. I felt

I think this was the beginning of Charles weaving complicated webs for himself but I didn't see it coming.

like she was the stupid one. If he had picked her up first, there was no way I'd have ever gotten in the car with the two of them. Now that I'm more mature, I realize we were all stupid. Him for double booking himself, me for not getting out of the car when he picked her up, and her for coming with us. I think this was the beginning of Charles weaving complicated webs for himself but I didn't see it coming.

Charles remained quiet for all of our dating days. Or so I thought. I never heard one word of profanity and never saw him lose his temper. He showered me with lovely gifts for no reason or occasion; those are always the best kind of gifts to receive. He had impeccable taste! He could choose clothes for me like he was dressing a department store mannequin. They were always the perfect size and perfect fit. Every time. He took me to exceptionally nice and always respectable places and always, I mean always, treated me like a lady. I really admired his planning skills. He would sit down and plan out the most amazing dates. When we were together he pulled my chair out for me to sit, opened my car door, held every door open whether it be to a house or a public building, and helped me with my jacket or sweater. He did all the things a true gentleman should do.

We double dated a lot with his sister Linda and her boyfriend Ray. The four of us had a great time together. Right from the beginning we clicked. On our second date Charles, this God fearing gentleman, told me, "You're going to be my wife one day." I just laughed and said, "Well I don't plan on getting married for a very, very long time!" Years later, I'd find out that after he'd take me home from our wonderful and respectable dates he'd go to wild college parties where they'd get drunk and yell "Zulu" and the girls were fair game. I had no idea. What a surprise! The summer before we married, Charles and I went to Disneyland with my parents. It was a happy time together. Little did I know that months later we would be married.

L- Norma-Jean and Charles R- Norma-Jean and her parents, Alice and Olden Family trip to Disneyland 1966.

When I met the Sims family I fell head over heels in love with them. Every last person in the family had some quality I was drawn to. Charles had three sisters, LoVera, Jackie, and Linda. His cousin Verda was raised with him as his sister after her mother died. She is by far the hands down best cook in the entire family! Growing up she spent much of her time in the kitchen next to Mom Sims. When she grew up and married Les he was in the military and they traveled the world where she studied recipes of every culture. Her sisters Shirley, Barbara Jean, and Pat never lived near the Sims family but have been closely involved and deeply loved. So Charles grew up with four girls in the house. He also had three brothers, Fred, Emanuel, and Donald. Everyone was still at home except for LoVera, who was married and lived directly behind her parents with her husband Othell and four of the prettiest kids I'd ever seen. It was a full and lively house when everyone got together. Mrs. Sims reminded me of my Grandma, always cooking up things in the kitchen, always a big Sunday dinner. I enjoyed being invited to their home. The Sims had a loving family and it was great to be with them but I sure wasn't thinking marriage.

I remained committed to my future. I was crazy about Charles but kept in the back of my mind the reasons I had broken up with Jerry. My future! My future, my future! If it hadn't been for my thinking of my future Jerry would have still been my boyfriend. I definitely hadn't intended to start another relationship, especially at this young age. My education was dan-

My education was dangling out there in front of me like a brass ring to be snatched.

gling out there in front of me like a brass ring to be snatched. The world was a big place and I longed to see all of it. Yet, with each conversation I had with Charles he talked to me more and more about a future with him. "Yes Charles, well one day. You know when I've completed college and you've done the same. We're so young right now."

Charles was being scouted by colleges for his football abilities, particularly Oregon State. He was quite the athlete. His academics were lacking or he could have gone anywhere in the nation on a full ride scholarship. We started going to the library to study. I was trying so hard to get him focused. He would stare at me instead of the words in the book and put his hand under the table on my lap. He was focused on one thing. Me and what most virile young men are focused on, sex. Somewhere along the line Charles and I became sexually involved. We'd fool around and I would feel guilty. I felt so guilty that it's all kind of a blur to me rather than something sweet and special. He'd talk to me about it, then I felt safe with him. I trusted him. He was older than me by four years and I thought we were being careful. I'd fallen in love with him. So much so that I was willing to cut short the endless possibilities that were ahead. I was on an emotional see-saw. One day up and the next day I'd think about what I was possibly giving up and tell him we needed to refocus. He would refocus me all right, right back to him. And so it went. He'd ask me, "Do you love me?" "Yes." "How much?"

I never heard from Lillian again. If I wasn't at school, I was with Charles and if I wasn't with Charles, I was with my girlfriends. There were a handful of girls I was really close with, but I had many friends. Having a serious boyfriend took up a lot of time. I've always been one to really love my friends and while I was truly hurt about Lillian I hid it well.

Grace was the super-achiever of all my friends. We shared a similar background; we both came from bi-racial families and had similar life goals. Grace, however, was just a step away from perfect. She was beautiful, graceful, and incredibly smart. The more serious I became about Charles the more he pulled me in the opposite direction of Grace. We double dated to the prom and spent a considerable amount of time together, but eventually, I lost her friendship too. I hear she is a doctor now, a Stanford graduate. I still miss her after all these years. I mentioned that I found her on Facebook. Time has been kind to her,

Norma-Jean and Grace, double dating to the Jr. Prom, wearing matching dresses sewed by Mama.

she's still beautiful. I would love to see her again. Life is funny.

Then there was Mary. I never knew anyone like her. She was cute and bubbly and oh my goodness could that girl dance! We would spend hours in my room, her teaching me the latest moves and then I'd get to the dance and would not dance to save my life. I always felt like I was at that first dance party back in Massachusetts, I'd rather sit daintily on a chair and watch. When I did make a public attempt someone told me, "You dance like a white girl!" Translation: you have no rhythm. I do have white friends, however, who can certainly move. When you are young you process things differently. It wrecked my self-confidence. Later Charles told me the same thing. He said it with a big cheesy grin on his face like he was poking fun at me. That did it for me. My dancing days ended. For some reason he didn't seem threatened by my friendship with Mary.

One day when we were dating Charles asked his father to pick me up from school. I was so naive. When I saw him, I just waved hello, jumped in, slid right over on the bench seat so I was sitting right next to him in the Lafayette van and put my books on the other side of me towards the door. Well, the Monterey Peninsula is not that large and people can certainly gossip. Wouldn't you know that someone saw him pick me up and before long word went around that "Old man Sims was picking up a young girl at Monterey High School. Sweet young thing slid right in and sat right up underneath him." It is the funniest story, Charles and his dad

> *"Old man Sims was picking up a young girl at Monterey High School. Sweet young thing slid right in and sat right up underneath him."*

laughed about it forever. They had such fun teasing me. I never gave any thought that it didn't look right and he didn't think anything of me sitting next to him, I was just a kid. Charles and I moved ahead with our relationship and began to see each other almost daily.

One thing about becoming sexually active is that it changed everything. In addition to the new-found guilt, I used poor judgment. My parents trusted me. I trusted myself until I crossed that line. Now I jeopardized everything. Now I was telling lies. That's what I had become - a liar! I hated liars! I knew one day this would come full circle. One day I would have a kid that would look me in the face and lie to me. I knew I would be rendered helpless by my kid's lies just like my parents were helpless to mine. There wasn't a damn thing they could do about what they didn't know about. But I kept going with it. I wouldn't get caught. I thought I was so smart. I thought Charles was so smart. I was planning to go away to college after graduation. That was *always* my plan until I'd talk to him. He always changed it up and he confused me! Okay then, maybe when Charles graduated, if he did, jocks always did, because coaches always made sure they did, maybe we would be together.

In the back of my mind I still heard the self-lecture going on. I still remembered why I broke up with Jerry. I was too young to be serious! I had to remind myself. I had to tell myself over and over again *I have to get my education! I want to see the world. Not on the terms of the military, but on my own terms. I want to travel freely. I want financial independence. I want my parents to be proud.* I silently resented losing friends because Charles was not man enough to want me to become all that I had the potential of becoming. I wanted my future so bad, but I was lost. Nothing had changed except that I was messing around with a boy four years older than myself; actually he was a man. I was in love with a man who could take my thoughts and turn them around and make me think something entirely different in two minutes and then I could turn around and lie to my parents and friends. I didn't care about anything when I was with him. It was always the guilt and shame that came later when I had time to be alone with my own thoughts. Wow!

I woke up one morning and barely made it to the toilet. I threw up and threw up again! I thought I had the flu. It passed within thirty minutes so I went to school anyhow. Next day the same thing but it didn't pass, I stayed home.

I talked to Charles and told him I had the flu. He was always so sweet. He brought me flowers and 7-Up, magazines, and a pair of bright red Ked tennis shoes. The flu hung on for days. I was sick in the morning, noon, and night and didn't seem to be getting any better. To make it worse I had my period at the same time. I was praying to God asking him to make this horrible sick, dizzy feeling go away.

He granted my prayer. It passed okay. For about three days I was able to function normally, but then it started all over again. I convinced myself this was my punishment for being such a sneaking little liar! I woke up from sleep one day like I'd been struck by lightning. *What if I'm pregnant?* I got out the calendar. I couldn't possibly be. I just had my period and we hadn't fooled around in a very long time. I told Charles my fears. He didn't seem the least bit bothered by any of it. *Hmmm. I guess that he is just more mature than me.* I kept thinking about the consequences. Daddy always talked about the consequences of our actions.

Charles scheduled an appointment for me with his mother's gynecologist. *What was he thinking? Was he crazy? Was I crazy? Weren't there other doctors in town?* There were no home pregnancy tests back then. Today, there is no way I'd go there, but then I was just a naïve girl. I went for the appointment and Charles asked his Aunt Bessie to take me. "Really?" I don't know why he didn't take me himself. But I loved Aunt Bessie so I was happy she was with me.

I had never had a gynecological exam before. The room was cold and I felt vulnerable in my

> *"Young lady, you certainly are not pregnant. You just have the flu."*

bare feet and the little gown they told me to put on. I wanted to cry. I was alone, but I had to know for sure. I felt like Dr. Bradly was on a treasure hunt in my body. He dug and poked and prodded. He asked when my last period was. "Young lady, you certainly are not pregnant. You just have the flu." "But doctor, I'm so dizzy and I can't keep anything down." "Sometimes being dehydrated causes you to feel dizzy. Try to sip fluids and rest. It will pass. Just take it easy. You should be better in a few days." "Whew! Not pregnant." His words were music to my ears. I wouldn't do it again, ever. Okay, well I wouldn't say *ever*, but certainly not until I was married. This was just all too stressful for me, the lies, and the worrying. Important note to self, wait to have sex until grown and married! It was too late for that now.

I was sitting on my bed holding a cold washcloth to my face. Mama stood in the doorway observing me. "I think you and Charles have been playing tiddly winks and you are going to have a winky-tinky." I asked her to repeat herself. With her thick Latvian accent maybe I had misunderstood. Yep, I heard her right. She was off to work and I was left with her echo "a winky-tinky." *Did she mean a baby?*

That afternoon I was back at Dr. Bradley's office. He was annoyed, "Young lady according to your last menstrual cycle and upon examining you I find nothing to indicate a pregnancy. I have been the personal gynecologist to some very important people. Perhaps you'd like to check my references. Here is a prescription to help you with the nausea and a prescription for the pill." The pill. *Does he mean the pill? I can't take it without my parents' permission. He can't give me that without talking to them. But then I think, ha, he shouldn't even be seeing me without one of them knowing. I wonder about this guy. Scandalous.* I threw the prescriptions away. Later I wondered why. *Dr. Bradly might be a quack,* I decided not to go there again.

After about a month of battling waves of flu symptoms and losing weight I couldn't afford to lose, I wanted some answers. At the time I was 5'7" and 103 pounds. I was already skinny. Part of my school day was spent working in the nurses' office. I mustered up the courage to approach Mrs. Spindler with my dilemma. She was so sweet. She knew Charles because her husband Tor was his football coach at the college. Tor was built like a big grizzly bear and she was petite and slender. I told her everything and she listened with an open mind and heart. She told me flat out that I needed to get a second opinion. She recommended a doctor whose claim to fame was that he was Mamie Eisenhower's doctor. I'd have to wait weeks for an appointment.

I explained to Charles that I wanted a second opinion because, despite what Dr. Bradley, the quack, had said, I felt like I was pregnant. I actually had no idea what pregnant felt like but I knew I didn't feel normal. Charles said if I was pregnant he wanted to get married now rather than in a year or two after he finished college, which was my plan. I was very nervous. *We can't do this* I thought. A baby would change everything. My parents would just die of disappointment. What about the kind of wedding I always dreamed of? I wanted Cinderella and Prince Charming, a honeymoon in Paris or Tahiti. I wanted my baby to have a nursery with a big, bright, sunny window and wood floors and big rocker so I could sit, rock, sing, and read. When I had children I wasn't going to work, I was going raise my chil-

> *My education would assure their future...I wanted to take them from one corner of the world to the other.*

dren. My education would assure their future. I wanted to take my children to see the Eiffel Tower, to see the Pyramids, the Statue of Liberty, the Serengeti, and the Alps; I wanted to take them from one corner of the world to the other. I wanted us to go to museums and parks and have picnics and family dinners on Sundays. *Oh my God, what have I done?* I ruined my children's future. That's what I have done. I let myself *down.* What a mess! Charles was adamant about accepting responsibility if I was pregnant. *Responsibility! Hell, I don't want to be anyone's responsibility but my mama and daddy's.* "Norma, do you love me?" "Yes, of course I love you." "Then promise me that either way, you will marry me. It doesn't matter whether you are pregnant or not. Don't think about it. There is nothing to think over if you love me. Just say you'll marry me." I was young and confused. I couldn't answer him.

☙🕉❧

Halloween night on Hilby Avenue brought quite a few little trick or treaters. My job was to open the door and give them a hand full of candy. I was surprised when I opened the door and there stood Charles smiling and big wearing his college letterman jacket and a pair of jeans. "Trick or Treat," he said and I held out the bowl of candy. He grabbed a couple of caramels and sat down on the sofa. I plopped down next to him and told him I was surprised to see him. Mama came out of the kitchen to say hello and went back to what she was doing. We sat for a little while with interruptions from the little goblins. Charles said, "It's your turn to say trick or treat." I just giggled, "Oh my gosh, I've been eating so much of that candy, no more for me." "Give me your hand and say trick or treat and close your eyes." I gave him my hand and he slipped a ring on my finger, "I hope you like it." I opened my eyes and it was the most delicate vintage style white gold engagement ring. "I love it!" "So you will marry me no matter what? We are going to go ahead and get married right?" What a beautiful ring, what a surprise. *He really loves me. He really wants to get married.* "Yes, yes, yes!"

"Mama, look what Charles just gave me." "Is that an engagement ring?" "Yes, isn't it beautiful?" "Yes, Norma-Jean, it's very beautiful. Charles, you picked a very pretty ring. It's special." So after the trick or treaters were no longer coming we decided to go to Denny's to celebrate.

That's when things got serious. *When exactly would we get married now that I had a ring on my finger? What if I was pregnant? What if I wasn't? What about school? What about a wedding? Where would we live?* There was so much to decide. I had more than enough credits to be done with high school. That was from our military life traveling from here to there and accumulating extra credits. So I would opt for early graduation. I went for a second opinion with Dr. Genetti, but he also had said I wasn't pregnant. Therefore we would opt for the church wedding and pray the doctors were right, but in case they were wrong we would make it soon. As far as where to live, we found a nice one bedroom apartment in Seaside and

Charles, Seaside Police Department, 1967

began making plans to furnish it. We chose December 17th as our date. Close enough to Christmas that we could always enjoy our anniversary with the holiday festivities.

Daddy took the news fairly well. Every day he'd kiss me on my forehead and say, "Daddy's baby is getting married." He handled it better than I expected. After all, the news meant I wouldn't be stepping through the high school doors again after Christmas break. It meant the scholarship to Chapman would be foregone. But Charles was twenty-one and seemingly had a better grasp on life than I did. He had dropped his college classes and started working with the Seaside Police Department just like his Uncle CJ. My parents saw a responsible young man who showered their daughter with love and kindness and had the financial means to provide her with beautiful gifts. They saw in him a solid work ethic and they knew he had a strong belief in God. The thing nobody was really talking about was the possibility of a baby.

We always drank tea when there was something in life to sort out.

Mama was going to make my wedding gown. Invitations had been ordered. I had lost a few pounds from the constant nausea and Mama could tell. As she was measuring me I just had to talk to her. I couldn't keep all this from my mama. "Mama, remember when you said, 'I think you have been playing tiddly-winks. I think you're having a winky-tinky'? I think that's how you said it. Do you remember that day?" "Yes, Norma-Jean I know. I already know. You are having a baby." "No, no Mama. I have been to two doctors and both doctors have said I am not! But I am sick every day, I am throwing up, and I don't feel good. But Mama I still have my period. When a girl is pregnant she doesn't have a period, right?" Mama sat down with me and we drank tea. We always drank tea when there was something in life to sort out. She wanted to make sure I loved Charles. She acknowledged that although I was very young, if I loved him and wanted to marry him I would have her and Daddy's blessing and their help. They would always be there.

One way or the other I was marrying Charles. The flu didn't go away. Charles and I figured that I must be pregnant. I tossed and turned and cried at night. I missed Toni. She was my *best* friend. She was like my sister. I couldn't imagine my wedding day without her, but she wasn't part of the Sims family and if I dared mention her, Charles thought it was her brother I was missing. He was very insecure regarding the subject and would become angry. I decided to just keep quiet about it but I quietly resented it. I wish now that I hadn't just kept quiet about so many things.

Daddy's good friend Paul took me for a ride along the coast in his little red convertible roadster. He tried to get me to open up and talk but I was smarter than that. I knew he and Daddy had discussed me. In fact, I knew he had a bit of a crush on me, but if he ever made a move toward me Daddy would kill him. He was way too old for me, divorced and re- married, and smart in the ways of the world. He and Daddy were both veterans and drinking buddies. They marched in parades together as the color guard and spent hours at the V.F.W. He was kind of like a big brother. I gave him no information to take back to Daddy. I was happy and had no concerns about the future. Yes, of course I would complete my college education. Secretly I was feeling a little sad that I wouldn't be boarding that traveling ship for my studies with Chapman University. If there was anyone I would have confided in, I knew I could talk to Paul. He would always be dependable, but this time I knew it was a set up.

Charles hadn't even told his mother we were getting married! Why? He hadn't told her that he gave me a ring. Why? I have no idea. He was a grown man, free to make his own decisions. So I thought. Oh boy. When his mother and sister LoVera found out they came for a little chat with me and Mama. It wasn't so friendly and it wasn't something that made me feel really warm and fuzzy about our future. Although I was just a teenager, after that visit I told Charles in no uncertain terms where he could go and how to get there! I felt humiliated. Like I had come in and seduced this pure and innocent young man and stolen all the great opportunities from his wonderful life and now he was staring down the barrel of a shotgun thanks to me and my mama who must have orchestrated the entire thing - her being German and all. *Ha! She isn't even German. And what did that have to do with anything?* I was furious and although crying was what I 'd usually do, I didn't now. I told Charles I was going to go to New Jersey and have *my* baby, thank you very much and I needed nothing from him. Not now, not ever! "Whoa. Whoa. Wait a minute. My mother and sister don't run my life. I love them very much. But they don't speak for me or run my life. We planned what we are doing and that's what I want. Please forgive me. Let's put this behind us and start our lives together." Plea number one....

CHAPTER 8

Starting Marriage

I t was three o'clock in the afternoon on December 17th, 1966. At the corner of Fourth and Laurel in Pacific Grove cars lined both sides of the street and filled the parking lot of the newly built First Baptist Church. The pews were filled with loving friends and family as I walked down the aisle on my daddy's arm. He gave me away in pure Cinderella fashion just like I had always dreamed of. Every little girl's dream and more, it was an elegant wedding. I had it all; six bridesmaids, candelabras, the white runner, and of course beautiful flowers. Even LoVera softened her heart and blessed us by allowing her cute daughter Cheryl to be our flower girl. Cheryl cried because she thought Charles wasn't going to be her uncle anymore after he was married.

For me the most special person in the bridal party was Linda, pretty in pink as my maid of honor. She walked through the doors and down the aisle poised and lovely to a chorus of ooh's and aah's. She almost stole the spotlight!

My gown was gorgeous. Mama made it in a true labor of love and I was very proud. It was time. Everyone was in place and it was time for me to say, "I do." At 17, I was such a child bride, but I conducted myself as much like an adult as possible. I was happy to be marrying such a fine young man of 21. We were going to have a nice future together. As we stood before God and witnesses and repeated our vows. I believed in the sacredness of marriage with all my heart. I believed every word that Charles said to me when he promised to love and cherish me. He looked me straight in my eyes with the sincerest

Norma-Jean and her father, Olden Jackson, preparing to walk down the aisle.

smile in the world and I just knew everything was going to be all right. I had complete trust. No doubts. Note to self: *never, ever let my future daughter or granddaughter become a child bride! I don't care how happy they tell me they are.*

The entire day was a beautiful celebration of the beginning of our life together. We had a traditional cake and punch reception at the church after the wedding. Later that evening, while I was dancing with my godfather at an after party at my parents' home he asked me, "Are you sure you're ready for this?" "Uncle Chris, I've never been more ready for anything. Yes, yes I'm ready." But when it was time to leave the party I didn't want to go. Not because I was having so much fun but because I was fearful of being alone with Charles. I didn't know exactly what to do as a married woman. That may sound kind of odd, but the extent of my sexual experiences with Charles had been the fumbling of a couple of kids fooling around trying not to get caught. I could best describe it as a few uncomfortable quickies, never without clothes. So, my stomach filled with fluttering butterflies as I stood by the car with Charles saying goodbye to my parents. I was wearing the red, tailored going away suit Mama had

made for me. I looked very grown up, and sophisticated but I suddenly felt like a little girl. I wanted to stay with my parents and started to cry. My parents attributed it to my being emotional. After all, I've always been emotional. They never knew that I was so afraid to go. Yes, I was excited to be married, but I was also afraid because I realized I was really just a kid myself. I guess that is why Uncle Chris had asked me those questions. He knew I was just a kid. We were finally in the car and on our way and poor Charles didn't know what to think or say. His happy bride had turned on a dime. I couldn't quit crying. He kept telling me it was going to be okay and I just kept sniveling! We were headed for San Francisco but we were tired and with all the crying I was doing we only made it

Top - Norma and Charles with wedding party 12/17/1966. They were the first couple to be married at the church. L-R—Emanuel, Charles, Norma, Linda, Charles' niece Cheryl. Bottom - Olden Jackson, Alice Jackson, Norma-Jean, Charles, Airnet Sims, Emanuel Sims Sr.

about thirty miles from home. Neither of us had eaten much in all the excitement of the day, despite the abundance of food, so Charles made a quick detour to a corner store and bought a few things while I sat in the car talking to myself. *Stop crying Norma! What is wrong with you? Act like an adult.*

Our first night certainly was not what you read about in romance novels. Charles carried me over the threshold. That was nice. It was sweet. He was all smiles. I smiled at him. I was happy but cautious. Once we were in our room I immediately locked myself in the bathroom. I looked in the mirror. I looked awful. My face was red, my

> *I was excited to be married, but I was also afraid because I realized I was really just a kid myself.*

eyes were swollen, and mascara streaked down my face. I was a nervous mess. My knees were knocking and my hands shaking. I was in there thinking about what to do. *Take a bath? Take a shower? Take my time! Definitely take my time!* Charles knocked on the bathroom door and tried the knob. "Yes?" "Are you coming out soon?" I thought, *What the heck is his problem? I just came in here.* I decide to wash my face and wait a few more minutes to make up my mind about bath versus shower. He knocked again. "What are you doing in there?" and tried the knob again. *Oh my God! He is trying to come in here. Oh my God!* Not even my mother came in the bathroom with me because I was very modest. I didn't want anyone in the bathroom with me. "Norma, unlock the door. What do you have the door locked for? Let me in!" For me that did it. I can't trust him. I decide no bath, no shower; I unlock the door and stare at him. He stares at me like he can't believe it. I still have my suit on and my hair is still neatly in barrel curls atop my head. After we stare each other down for what seemed like a long cold minute, I smiled and walked past him toward the bag of food. "Oh my goodness, I'm starved. How about you Charles? Aren't you starving?" He moved the bag before I could take anything out of it. "I am trying to talk to you," he said firmly. "Oh you were? I'm sorry. What did you want to talk about?" *Ha, like I didn't see what was coming!* "I have a few things I want to say. Now that we are married, Rule #1- no locking doors behind you, Rule #2- no rollers in your hair at bedtime. Ever. Rule #3- I'm the boss and I love you." *Well I surely didn't see that coming! I thought he was going to talk about sex* "I love you too." We ate bologna sandwiches and chips. I took a shower and hoped he wouldn't try to come in the bathroom to join me or anything like that. We were both so tired we slept like babies. I was in my brand new granny gown, no negligee set for me. I felt warm and cozy, and safe. The next day we hit San Francisco and started our honeymoon and I never forgot the rules.

We had a wonderful time in San Francisco. We had been there so many times with Linda and Ray and it was truly one of our favorite places to visit. But this time was different. We walked up and down the streets, rode cable cars, and ate in China Town and on Fisherman's Wharf. We did tons of Christmas shopping and returned home on Christmas Eve.

We bought our first Christmas tree at a bargain price that night. It took up the whole corner of the living room in our little one-bedroom, $95-a-month apartment on Amador Street in Seaside. While we decorated the tree, we drank hot cocoa and played Christmas music, a tradition we would never abandon. Gifts were overflowing. We had shopped for everyone. I mean everyone, our parents, his sisters and brothers, his nieces, and his nephew. I loved his generosity. Mostly, we talked about the meaning of Christmas. We talked about our faith and our future. The next morning we made the rounds like Santa before joining the family for a huge dinner. It was a perfect Christmas!

The next few months were nothing less than wonderful. Charles came home to candlelight dinners and a little wife who was greatly enjoying playing house. I say *playing house* because I was, after all, only seventeen. I loved every moment of cooking and cleaning and waiting for him to come home. Life was good. His family was so nice and had finally accepted the way things were. My parents liked

Charles and were happy about our marriage.

A few months into our marriage Charles had knee surgery that required him to wear a huge cast for a couple of months. We talked

Charles came home to candlelight dinners and a little wife who was greatly enjoying playing house.

and laughed for hours every night. It felt like I didn't need another soul in my life. I was like Molly in the song *My Blue Heaven*, soon I'd have the baby and we'd be three in our own blue heaven.

Not only did I think our life was perfect, I wanted him to think *I* was perfect. So perfect that everyday I'd leave home to go across the street to use the bathroom! I guess it goes back to the modesty thing. Our apartment was tiny and our bathroom was in our bedroom. I was too embarrassed, too modest to go when he was right there just a few feet away. He wondered where I went each day, so one day when I left, he hobbled to the window, just in time to see me going into the ladies room of the gas station. He teased me about that for our entire marriage and my face never failed to turn red, even after thirty-five years.

June came and I was as big as a house! My 103 pound frame was now carrying 160 pounds. Charles bought me the most beautiful maternity outfits. I had spindly legs and arms and a big beachball belly, but I had cute clothes. What he didn't buy, Mama sewed. I continued to have "the flu" my entire pregnancy. At one point his Aunt Bessie took me back see the quack Dr. Bradley just to say to him as she pointed to my belly, "I just wanted you to see the flu you diagnosed." She smiled in a sweet coy manner. He knew what she meant. Aunt Bessie and I laughed our butts off.

ᘛ❦ᘚ The Sims ᘛ❦ᘚ

The Sims family was well rooted on the Monterey Peninsula. While they called *themselves* poor they demonstrated class in every aspect. I was a Sims now and just like Ruth said to Naomi, "your people will be my people," the Sims were now my people so I didn't have use for malicious gossip about the family.

They worked hard for what they had. They bargained with many of the people they worked for in order to provide more and it worked. People observed them with more, so much more than the average family, especially the average black family in Seaside. Sometimes this led to jealousy and gossip about them in the community. They were proud of what they had accomplished, as they should have been, but time after time I would hear them say, "We are poor and we had all these kids…."

The Sims' small house on Luxton Avenue was surrounded by a white picket fence and Mrs. Sims had planted lovely begonias, snap-dragons, petunias, and marigolds to border the lush green lawn. It was tastefully decorated and held luxurious things like many better off families owned, such as a silver tea service and fine china din-nerware. Mrs. Sims wore fine, name brand suits and pill box hats to match. She wore Italian leather pumps and matching handbags and gloves when she attended church. She was well read and subscribed to every black publication, *Jet* and *Ebony* as well as *Look*, and *Better Homes and Gardens*. She read books on flower arranging and home decorating and she loved cookbooks.

The girls wore beautiful clothes and their hair was always stylish. The same with the boys, they wore nice shoes, nice slacks, shirts, and sweaters that certainly didn't look like clothing *poor kids* wore. The entire family was well dressed and well groomed.

*Sims brothers and sisters, L-R—Donald, LoVera
Charles, Jackie, Emanuel, Fred, Linda*

CHAPTER 9

Oh Baby Charles!

O ver time Toni and I began to correspond less and less. I really missed her, but every time I mentioned her name Charles became angry. He couldn't seem to understand that she was family to me. The crazy thing was that he really liked her himself, but she is Jerry's sister and he just couldn't get past that. I greatly resented his attitude, but I let it go for the sake of peace. I always wanted peace.

Charles' cousin Diane and I became very close. At first she didn't like me as she had concluded that I was trying to entrap him. But after she got to know me, she realized I was a young girl like herself and there was nothing conniving about me. We really liked each other and became true friends, it was an easy friendship. She spent hours every week just hanging out at our place. Diane's mom, Aunt Bessie, joined us and often took us to lunch at Fisherman's Wharf.

Eventually the doctors confirmed my due date of June 24th. Well, we didn't quite know what to make of that for all the stressful days and for all those who would be counting on their fingers. We said to ourselves, "Let's see, we got engaged on October 31st and the baby is due June 24th." We scratched our heads and wondered, was I or wasn't

I pregnant when we married since the whole saga had begun weeks before he ever bought the engagement ring? We decided it didn't matter. It never did. It still doesn't.

Towards the end of May, he became impatient about the whole baby thing. *Let's hurry up and get this baby here.* He was just silly about it. He would put me in the car and go for long rides, but he'd choose the bumpiest country roads he could find. We rode over the entire Peninsula from Carmel Valley to The Highlands. That did not help his cause of trying to have the baby come ASAP.

On the morning of June eighth Charles woke me up to inform me that on this day I would be having the baby and therefore he would not be going to work. I told him he was off by about three weeks. It seems I was sleeping with my belly against his back and he could feel some contractions he hadn't felt before, therefore he concluded that it must be time. We called the doctor. He said he doubted very seriously that I was having contractions. It was probably just pre-term labor, no concern. If it got any worse feel free to come in and get checked. I thought he was crazy but as the morning wore on I truly did begin to have contractions that doubled me over in pain. By noon it was clear that maybe we should consider going to the hospital and not to the doctor's office. Charles left and said he would be back shortly. Oh my God! I don't know why he did that. He never had a sense of time, but I did what I so often did, I called his aunt Bessie and she was there in less than five minutes ready to go. I've been asked why I didn't call my mother, well, it was a Thursday and she was at work. She would have come but time was of the essence. Just as we were about to drive away he came back and innocently asked what the problem was. We did a quick switcheroo of cars and he got me there.

The Carmel Community Hospital was nicknamed *The Hotel*. It had a luxurious entry and a stay there was supposed to be as pleasant as a hospital stay could be. It was only a short ride from home; on the Monterey Peninsula nothing is very far. All the way there I kept thinking *I hope I get there in time*, because I felt like I was going to have that baby in the car. As a young girl, I was more afraid of the unknown to come, the things I had never experienced. First of all, *why is my baby coming three weeks early? Am I going to have the baby on my own, or am I still going to have a C-section? I heard they shave you down there, oh my goodness and they give you an enema. Double oh my goodness!* I was thinking about all of this on the short drive.

We hadn't done anything like Lamaze classes or birthing readiness. I don't know when those things started being offered, but no one offered any of it to me. Everything was happening pretty fast at first. Take off your clothes, put on this gown, get in this bed. In came a nurse, smiling and sweet, then another, smiling and sweet. Two or three, maybe four or more doing this or that confirming that *Oh, yes baby is indeed trying to come.* Clutching bed rails and gasping with pain, knees trembling, small body feeling like a freight train rumbling through, and then calm for a minute or two. And I thought, *How long before the doctor comes, how long before someone helps me have my baby?*

How long before the doctor comes, how long before someone helps me have my baby? Then, without warning, it begins again and I can't breathe, I don't know how to breathe. I am frightened and the nice nurses, they are nowhere to be found. There is a nurse so mean it oozes from her. She speaks harshly to me, even yelling at me until I can't hold my tears back any longer.

Charles held my hand and wiped my eyes with tissues, he looked so helpless I felt sorry for him. This was not the way we thought it was going to be. First of all, the doctor had said that my baby needed to come by C-section and I didn't know why that wasn't happening. We knew that childbirth involved pain for sure, but not the fierce, ripping, rumbling, destructive type of pain I was experiencing. Indeed there was a serious problem, I was hemorrhaging severely, and he was rushed out of the room to the waiting room with my parents.

My mother kept making trips to the bathroom and smoking one cigarette after another. The doctor came out to give an update. Mama said he said something like, "Just pray, we don't have her blood type here. We are getting it from the nearest blood bank. The baby's head is in the birth canal." She said she just couldn't hold herself together. Within an hour a highway patrol officer rushed lifesaving Rh-Negative blood through the door for me. They had rallied it from San Jose, 74 miles away. Meanwhile, my doctor had called in his partner to assess me and help. I remember him scolding him, "You really messed this one up; this is such a young girl." He came to the head of my bed and gently looked at me and said, "It's going to be okay, Darling. I'm going to deliver your baby." He asked for an instrument and then it was like I could feel his whole hand in my body for a second, grasping for my baby and he pulled him out of the space where he had been stuck for hours. He was free and alive and screaming! I remember the doctor showing him to me and realizing I had a baby boy. His little face was swollen like a prize fighter, the result of his futile hours of banging his little head against my pelvis, but we did it. I was elated, overcome with joy. Tears flowed down my cheeks and then the room went black.

When I woke up I was in a bright, cheery room and Charles was there. To this day I still have never understood what had gone wrong or why they couldn't have gone ahead and done the C-section. That's all behind me and all that matters is I survived and so did my baby! The associate doctor was literally my knight in shining armor and yet Dr. Genetti took the credit for another delivery. If I hadn't been so young and so naïve I would have sued him. But I certainly was very young and very naïve.

Diane Sims, high school, about the time we met, 1969.

Charles cried like a baby himself. He held his son in his arms and kissed his little fingers. He opened the blanket to count and recount every little toe and the hair, oh my goodness the hair, he ran his finger through it again and again. He was in love with his son but so emotionally wrecked he kept promising that this was it, never again would we ever have another child. Of course he had just had the dickens scared out of him.

Diane came to stay with us for a few days to help me out with the baby. All those sutures made for slow walking! We had the sweet experience of bonding even closer over this innocent and helpless tiny human being, my son, her cousin. We had a few good laughs as we approached him so gingerly, afraid of causing pain to his circumcision. He was just fine. As young women often do we made giggling noises and shrieking noises and the noises of ever so sweet sighs as we took turns cradling him and talked and talked. The place was filled with joy. It was great to have Diane there. What a perfect beginning.

When the swelling left his tiny face he proved to be a pretty baby after all. His daddy would brush and comb that head full of hair ten times a day and bring home a new outfit every other day. Before Charles Courtland Sims II could sit up by himself he had every boy toy made; balls, bats, footballs, bears, trucks, pull toys, and push toys. He was my parents' first grandchild and the first grandchild to carry the Sims name on his dad's side. He didn't have a chance and was hopelessly spoiled. If he wouldn't sleep we'd put him in the car and go for a ride. When he'd fall asleep we'd head home. If

Mimi, Charles, Oma celebrating Charles'
1st birthday, at home in Marina, CA

he woke up when we got home we'd turn right around and go ride some more!

We had baby Charles christened in the church where we had been married. I asked my godparents, Chris and Ina Lopes, to be godparents to my son. They were touched and honored. They had been a wonderful part of my life from the time I was a toddler.

CHAPTER 10

The Earth Shook

T hings were going along fine and we were really happy. So I thought. Charles worked in the wee hours of the morning at Fisherman's Wharf cleaning restaurants with his father and brothers in Lafayette Janitorial, the family business. His father had worked on the wharf since Charles was a small child. The business had provided a decent living for their family, but now his parents expected him to work in it and make it a more viable enterprise. The problem was there were more people depending on the business for a living. Charles was under pressure to obtain more commercial contracts and he did. They were busy all day with stores and offices. They also cleaned homes of movie stars like Doris Day, Clint Eastwood, and Merv Griffin.

However, Charles' first love was the Seaside Police Department. He became a police officer and patrolled at night, preferring to do that than anything else. Unfortunately, he didn't know how to tell his parents he didn't want to work in the family business. He was a good and dedicated son in every sense of the word and felt he couldn't possibly let them down. So understandably he was exhausted. His candle was burning at all ends and he was putting effort into something he really didn't want to do. He was lying to his family that he wanted to work in the business.

I don't know what happened. It was a seismic shift in my universe, as if my world literally veered off its axis! Every night after his shift Charles brought home his off duty revolver, a .357 Magnum. I hated that gun! I didn't want it in the house. However, we never spoke about it. I was afraid to. Then, he started staying out past his duty hours. He said he was working and I believed him. I always believed him. I wanted to believe him. Why wouldn't I believe the person I adored? Off duty officers covered a lot of things around the Peninsula. After parties even the local restaurants hired cops to monitor the after hour crowds. He did do that kind of thing sometimes, so maybe.... But something about him seemed different. I knew that he was under tremendous pressure. I think he didn't like being married anymore. Something had changed. He became very short tempered. His bouts of anger had intensified during our first year of marriage.

Charles told me he felt like he had a big debt to pay his parents. He was the eldest of the boys, but because they had been poor his parents expected him to accept responsibility for them. They said it was because they had given their kids more than most poor kids. There was that word again. Poor. It was true; they had given them much more than most of the kids in Seaside. They just had a lot of mouths to feed and clothe growing up. This was a sore subject with us; I told him that from my point of view none of us ask to be born, therefore I don't feel our parents should expect payback for raising us. Respect yes, payback, no. In some cultures children are expected to provide for the parents, it's a given. However, that's not a part of our culture so I really didn't understand.

I felt like my son and I had become heavy baggage for Charles... I was thrilled being a mother, it was my daily focus and joy, but I didn't

More and more I was praying for Charles because I didn't know what else to do.

know what to do to keep Charles smiling. He didn't send me constant signals that he was unhappy; I picked up on small things sometimes and if I asked him about it he'd always deny it. The Bible tells us that nothing can separate us from the love of God. More and more I was relying on my faith and trusting in God's love. More and more I was praying for Charles because I didn't know what else to do. I knew I was not separated from God's love, but I really needed his help *Lord, please give Charles some joy.*

The more I sensed something was wrong the less I was able to put my finger on it. I began to feel sad when I was with him...he basically ignored me when he came home and went straight for the baby. He'd hold him and talk to him and it was very clear how much he loved our son. He might ask me questions about our day, meaning me and the baby. I worked very hard at still trying to do the things I did before the baby came but it felt like he looked right past me or through me. I was fading, becoming invisible.

I saw a dark side. Very dark and very cold. I felt so alone and that was not what I wanted in my marriage. My husband was not being my friend. Sometimes I felt like when he came in the door the joy left, just evaporated from the room. I wanted him to be happy and thought maybe he'd find his happy go lucky side again if I was not there. I felt that I was his stumbling block, my baby and I were the albatross around his neck.

One day when he came home I told Charles I wanted to leave and that although I hadn't discussed it with them yet I was sure my parents would help me. He was furious, "You crazy, stupid, ugly b....! I HATE you. You make me sick. I'd just as soon kill you as to look at you. You are so goddamned ugly. Look at you! I hate your beady little eyes and your hair. I hate everything about you. Do you hear me?" I stood in the middle of the floor, frozen. I couldn't speak, couldn't move. He went to the closet, took his revolver out of the holster, and pointed it at me. All I could think of was my baby growing up motherless. I wasn't thinking *I don't want to die*, I was thinking *I want to see my son grow up! Surely he will not kill me! Should I try to plead or should I try to run?* All I could do was stand in that one small spot, frozen in time and space with no voice. He sat down in the armchair and leveled his grip and his aim. My shocked face broke and tears rushed down my cheeks as he began to mock me. He was half laughing at me while he was raising his voice. The baby woke up and started crying, he was teething and wasn't feeling well. "Please Charles let me go see about him." "No let him cry!" This was an absolute first. When our son cried *we* responded. The baby was crying louder, I knew he was in pain. I was too. "Please Charles stop this. Tell me - what is wrong?" ""Shut the f… up!" I was shocked. I had never heard him use that kind of language before. He took the bullets out, spun the barrel, pointed it at me, cocked the trigger, and clicked it. He was teasing me with fear. A smirk came across his face. He was enjoying my fear. There was a gaze in his eyes I had never seen before. I didn't recognize him. But I knew I should fear him.

He made me strip my clothes off and lay naked on the floor to further humiliate me. The room was chilly. He threatened to kill me if I moved or said anything. *Yep, he snapped*, I thought. *Dear Jesus, if I get out of this alive, this is truly the end! He has gone crazy under the pressure.* I heard him putting bullets back in the barrel again. My knees were knocking and I was so cold. I was thinking about my precious baby still crying. I begged, "Please don't do this, our child needs me." He yelled at me, "Shut up! F… you. I didn't say you could talk." God, I had never been more terrified. "Turn your face toward that wall. I don't want your ugly ass to look at me! " At that moment I think I hated Charles for what he was doing and yet I felt sorry for him because I knew it wasn't normal.

There is light and there is darkness. This was darkness—deep darkness of the scariest kind. This was an abyss of evilness and I felt betrayed and ashamed of his behavior. He was my husband, he had promised to love and cherish me yet he had just hurt me more than any other person on earth. This behavior did not show love for me and it surely was not cherishing. I felt as ugly and unworthy of being loved as he told me I was. *God where are you? Lord please help me! I heard* click, *spin one, two, maybe three times. Maybe he had me face the wall so I wouldn't see the bullet coming. Maybe I can run. Nonsense. No one can outrun a bullet and he's a marksman.* "Dear God, help!" I shrieked.

After what seemed like eternity, Charles laid the gun down and started crying. He was saying things like he didn't know why he acted like that. I didn't know why he acted like that either! I don't know what he was expecting from me. I just lay there. Naked, cold, and too frightened to move, I concentrated on feeling my own heartbeat. Just keep beating, that's all that mattered. He had threatened me to not move and I believed him. After a few minutes he got up, I prayed he wouldn't go near my baby. For the very first time I didn't trust Charles near him because his actions had just told me he could leave him motherless. He would give his son anything in the world, yet take away his mother. That I couldn't understand! I heard the door slam and tires screeching. I struggled to my feet, my legs shaking uncontrollably. I gasped for each breath and the next room seemed so far away. Trying to gain my balance, I finally managed to stumble over to my baby. I picked him up from his crib and held him close to my bosom, kissing his head and cradling his curly locks. His face was red, blue eyes pools of water, sleeper soaked with sweat, but once in my arms he calmed down and so did I. I was an emotional wreck. Charles had taken my heart, crumpled it, stomped on it, singed it with fiery words from the pits of hell, and thrown it back in my face. I was devastated and didn't have the rationale to understand what was at the core of his behavior. I dressed with trembling hands, then fell asleep exhausted with my baby in my arms, afraid to go and afraid to stay. I was just a kid myself, eighteen years old. I didn't drive so if I decided to go I would have to call someone. I was afraid to involve anyone else so I decided to wait.

The next morning I called Daddy to take me to a lawyer. He was blindsided as he had no idea we had any kind of problems but he agreed to take me. I didn't divulge any details that would stain Charles' image with my parents. I just said it wasn't working and I didn't want to discuss it further. Daddy didn't push although he was puzzled. In my mind the situation was going to come to an end and all I wanted was my son. I saw the attorney the same day and filed divorce papers, complete with a restraining order. I immediately withdrew the restraining order because I found out that it could really cause him serious problems with the Seaside Police Department. That was not my intention. I just wanted to guarantee my safety. A restraining order, or what is sometimes called an order of protection, is often no better than the paper it is written on. I had made up my mind, I was finished and all that mattered to me was to walk away with my son.

Charles begged me to reconsider; he would never do anything like that again. Plea number two....Most of his family blamed me for his behavior, what little they knew of it. I didn't tell them the horror he put me through. I figured they wouldn't believe me anyhow. He told them I had moved out and wanted a divorce. The general consensus was I should grin and bear it. They said he was too young for the responsibility. They said he was too young to be married. Things were really beginning to fall apart. I loved the Sims family like crazy and loved being a part of it. I didn't ever want to be apart from them and was so deeply hurt that any one

I hadn't been to our place in days. I was staying with my parents and was afraid to go home, afraid he'd show up there.

of them blamed me. Didn't they understand that I hadn't provoked him? If he wanted out, he could get out without the abuse. I would learn to hide any future incidents for the sake of peace.

I hadn't been to our place in days. I was staying with my parents and was afraid to go home, afraid he'd show up there. I bought new things for myself and the baby. He called and told me he'd left something on the doorstep for me. It was bags of new clothes for me and the baby. I couldn't sleep at night. I kept hearing his words in my head. They replayed like a stuck record. "You are so ugly I'd just as soon shoot you as to look at you. F... you. Stupid b....." Wow! How could he say that to me and then tell me a couple of days later that he loves me? I stood and stared at myself in the mirror. *Am I ugly? Why would my husband say that if he didn't think it?* When I was nearly asleep with my baby in my arms, I'd slip out of bed to go do a double check in the mirror. I felt like asking "*Mirror, mirror on the wall who is the fairest in the land?*" I knew I had joined the list of the ugliest in the land. My self-esteem plummeted with that incident. He said things in such a manner that I was left no other conclusion but he meant every word.

He started making his case for me to come back to him by talking about things he knew mattered most to me. Plea number three....It would be sad for our child to be raised in a home with divorced parents. *Could I tell him that I didn't love him anymore?* I don't know. *Could I?* He had been so mean and acted so crazy! I never could have imagined in my wildest dreams such behavior. Not from him. He was a great guy. Everybody loved Charles. But he had viciously hurt me. This was nearly unshakeable. It wasn't something new clothes, flowers, and dinners in nice restaurants were going to wash away. Underneath it all I was terribly hurt and trying to sort out what I really felt for him and what mattered most.

It took a few weeks to decide. I didn't want to say too much to my parents about him, they would never forgive him if they knew. My daddy would have ended it all for me right then and there. I felt alone. I didn't want to paint him as a horrible guy even if the things he did were horrible. That's just how I

I decided to give our marriage another try but I didn't fully believe him about the gun.

looked at it. I saw the things he did as completely separate from him somehow. I just could never bring myself to think of him as a bad person. I loved him so much and didn't want to let go of the dream of having our family together. He was working very hard to convince me to forgive him. Every other day he sent me flowers. He wined and dined me. But most of all, he was regretful and apologetic. He was making a valiant effort to win my heart back, and it was working, he was more like the old Charles every day. I saw him as a soft spoken, mannered gentleman. He said that this was a once in a lifetime event and he was never going to let it happen again. He agreed to leave his revolver at the police station if I came back home. I told him I never wanted it in the house again. I decided to give our marriage another try but I didn't fully believe him about the gun. When I first got home I searched the closets, the dresser drawers, the freezer, the bathroom—including the toilet tank. I checked between the mattresses in our bedroom, between the sofa cushions in the living room and every other conceivable place I could think of inside our home. I checked the glove box of the car, under the seats, and in the trunk. I didn't find the gun. I hated checking on him like that. I hated not trusting him, but I had to be sure. This routine repeated religiously every time he came or left home. I told myself just because I didn't see him walk in with a gun didn't mean it wasn't there. What mattered most to me, more than my own happiness, was my son's security. I had to be sure Charles didn't know I was checking on him, that would infuriate him.

I was emotionally bankrupt and not thinking clearly. I believed in dreams come true, fairy tales, and everlasting, true love. I wanted my dreams to come true. I wanted my marriage to work. I wanted my son to have a family. I was still just a kid and don't kids believe in fairytales…?

The sight of Charles with our son was the most beautiful thing. He was such a proud daddy and over and over again he told me that nothing, no one, mattered more than the three of us being together. I called off the divorce and tried harder at life. Each day I asked God to continue to guide and love us. For each day that was a good day, I said, "Thank you Lord! " I pulled joy out of darkness. Things seemed better and then......

CHAPTER 11

Trouble Named Carroll

Carroll Henry had been away in the service. To me he was mythical; I'd heard all kinds of stories about him, but never met him. Charles had grown up with him and he had a reputation for being a bad influence, someone Charles wasn't allowed to hang out with as a kid. Now here he was, back in town and sitting in our living room. Carroll wanted Charles to go with him to San Jose to see James Brown in concert.

Charles said, "I'll have to ask my wife about it." Carroll roared with laughter. "Sims, Sims, Sims, man, I never thought I'd see the day you would be hen pecked and asking a damn woman for permission to go someplace!" There was more boisterous laughter; Carroll was laughing like a hyena. Our place was so small I could hear everything they said from the next room. Charles just ignored the teasing and decided he didn't need to ask me anything. The two of them made their plans for the concert a couple days away.

I watched as Charles showered and got all dressed up, good smelling cologne and all. He was looking pretty good as they left in our sporty new maroon V8 Mustang. There we were once again, just my baby and me. I felt abandoned.

This was the start of something awful! Charles began to find every excuse to go out drinking and partying, it seemed the answer to his stress. He would pick a fight with me just so he could say, "I'm going out!" I grew comfortable with him being gone. I was used to being home alone, except I was never alone. Baby Charles was my constant companion and became everything to me. After a time I no longer felt abandoned.

I wasn't happy when Charles was gone, but I was in my own routine. I would play with my son until he was tired and then rock him to sleep. I'd do my housework at two and three in the morning. The bars closed at two and in the beginning he used to come home between two and three. Sometimes I'd fix him something to eat when he got home. Then, he started coming in later and later saying he had gone with the crowd to get something to eat. I began to find phone numbers on match books, napkins, and scraps of paper in his pockets, and I could smell perfume on his clothes. I said nothing, just nursed the hurt and pain.

He lost his wedding ring. I knew it was because he had taken it off so no one would know he was married. Again, I was beyond hurt but said nothing. A wedding ring is supposed to be a symbol of something everlasting and beautiful. The fact that his ring was something he'd rather not wear said a lot. I was determined I wasn't going to let him or anyone know what was bothering me.

We bought our first home in Marina just before Charles Jr.'s first birthday. It was a lovely home with a fireplace, hardwood floors, a sunny bedroom for the baby and a big back yard perfect for our German Shepherd dog, Shatzie. She often went on patrol at night with Charles and was becoming his constant companion. Sadly, she

Failure was simply not an option. I woke up every day focused on joy.

died from eating snail slug pellets in the yard. I thought he'd never get over it.

To look at us we appeared to be the perfect young family. But trouble was brewing. I could feel it in the depths of my soul. I refused to believe that we were going to fail. Failure was simply not an option. I woke up every day focused on joy. I had a will of iron and the determination to give my son the family he deserved to have.

We spent a lot of time with our families as we lived within minutes of one another in Seaside and Marina was just a few miles away. We talked to each other on the telephone daily. Since both my parents worked I spent a lot of time with Aunt Bessie just visiting, talking, and drinking tea. We both loved our cups of hot tea. She and I became very close and she and Uncle CJ loved to take Charles Jr. to the Naval Post Graduate School in Monterey. They always bought him new shoes because for some funny reason Aunt Bessie would always lose one of his little shoes.

CHAPTER 12

Shock and Grief

❦ Chuck ❦

One rainy November day in 1968 young Chuck Sims never made it home. He had just recently moved into his own place. We had spoken the day before and he was planning on coming by the following day to see Baby Charles. Ironically, my baby had many similarities to Chuck as a baby. I think that was part of why Aunt Bessie and Uncle CJ loved him so much. It was a well-known fact that my husband was their favorite nephew; he was Uncle CJ's namesake. On November 2nd Chuck didn't show up when he said he would. I had a funny feeling in the pit of my stomach, the way you sense something is wrong. It wasn't like him...but I figured maybe something had come up. Then came the call, "Chuck was just in an accident on Del Monte. He's gone. He's dead...," uncontrollable sobbing and then click. It was my brother in-law Fred. I dropped the phone and fell to my knees. "Dear God, No, not Chuck!" The Sims family was forever touched by this grief.

It was a horrific accident. My father in-law Emanuel and Fred were leaving the wharf and came upon the accident. "That's my nephew!" and they ran to him. I'm told that Chuck took his last breath in his uncle's arms. I'm thankful they were there. Uncle CJ was on a fishing trip at a lake. This was before cell phones so he had to be found and notified by the authori-

The promise of what could have been was stolen on a slick wet road in a fast car shortly after he turned eighteen.

ties. How do you break this heartbreaking news to a mother that her son, her baby, is gone? Aunt Bessie lost a huge part of her heart and soul that tragic day, she never recovered. Where there was once laughter and pride in what was to come for this beautiful young man, there was now a void. Chuck was beautiful in every sense of the word. He was funny, gentle, loving, kind, and giving. He had yet to find himself. He had ideas. It was 1968 and he was a young black man. The promise of what could have been was stolen on a slick wet road in a fast car shortly after he turned eighteen.

We were all living through a nightmare. For as much as we were grieving and in shock, there was no way to measure Aunt Bessie's infinite loss. Although she had other children and they too were drowning in grief she didn't have the strength to hold them up too, although she tried her best. It was impossible to fill the space left in her heart with Chuck's name on it. The

Uncle CJ and Aunt Bessie

91

sparkle left her beautiful eyes and I never saw them twinkle the same way again.

Chuck's funeral service was incredibly beautiful. The church was packed with grieving teenagers and friends of the family, as well as our large family. It was overwhelming for me, I can't imagine the depth of his immediate family's loss. I think they just went through the motions, sleepwalking, taking direction from nuns and priests and funeral directors and other family members. How could they do anything else?

The night we laid him to rest Diane and I sat in the dining room of their home on Broadway Rd. and got absolutely wasted just trying to cope and numb the pain. Diane needed that. She talked about her brother and we laughed and told funny stories.

I couldn't tell my story without telling how my personal life, as well as the Sims family had been touched by this beautiful soul. Rest in peace, Chuck. You are still and always beloved.

๑๏๛ Harriet Spurlock Jackson ๛๏๑

While I was lost in the cloud of sadness over Chuck's death, my beloved grandmother became ill with kidney failure, a result of advanced diabetes, and was in the Fort Ord hospital. The doctor told Daddy she had no desire to live. I knew this as I sat by her, holding her small, frail hand in mine. I kissed her palm and spoke to her, but she never opened her eyes. "Grandmother, I love you so much." She squeezed my hand, understanding what I said. "I want you to get well." She shook her head "no" ever so slightly. I cried, wanting more time with her.

This was my very own biological grandmother who was finally living with my family and surely could tell me so much, teach me so much. I didn't want anything from her but her love, wisdom, and knowledge about things only she could tell me. It was too late, she had dementia and severe diabetes. She had longed to be with her husband Adolph from the moment she had come to California. I knew she loved Daddy, but she loved and worshiped her Adolph, her beloved. I sat there for a very, very long time just taking in all I could of her. Looking at the way Mama had braided

Hattie (Harriet Spurlock Jackson), Charles Sims II, and Norma-Jean

her soft hair, studying her flawless complexion and full lips. I wanted to have an everlasting picture in my mind. It was the last time I saw Grandmother alive. Hattie Spurlock Jackson passed away peacefully on January 1, 1969.

I didn't accompany Daddy to fly her home to Chicago. I stood on the observation deck of Monterey Airport and watched as the casket was loaded into the cargo bay of the airplane and Daddy boarded as a passenger. I cried so hard everything in front of me blurred. Mama just held me and let me cry. Charles held the baby and we all waved as the plane lifted off. What a sad, sad day. I still miss her, am still sad, and have an empty space in my soul for all I didn't have a chance to share with her.

Wishing that things could have been different doesn't help after all these years. Instead, I thank God for what I did have with Grandmother and I know it taught me to embrace being a grandmother myself. I pray

I pray that my own grandchildren will come to me with questions...I will be honest and will try to give them a piece of myself that is not tangible, a bit of soul connection to last through generations.

that my own grandchildren will come to me with questions. I hope they have questions. I will be honest and will try to give them a piece of myself that is not tangible, a bit of soul connection to last through generations. I have so few stories of Grandmother to tell both my children and my grandchildren about Harriet Jackson, their great great grandmother.

One thing I know for sure is that she had one true love, my grandfather Adolph. He was her waking thought and her last thought every night until her last days. I also know she was a woman of deep, strong faith in God and demonstrated that until the end. I picture her patting her hands in rhythm to gospel music, smiling and finding solace in the words of praise. I have a bracelet that was hers, a dainty silver chain with a glass bulb holding in it a single mustard seed. In Matthew 17:20 in Scripture Jesus tells his disciples, "If you have faith as small as a mustard seed, you can say to this mountain, move from here to there and it will move. Nothing will be impossible for you." (Life Application Study Bible) I cherish my bracelet, the fact that she wore it, and what it meant to her. I hold on to the thought of her strong, deep, and abiding faith and hope that I am walking in her path. I hope my grandmother would be proud of the woman I am and the family I have created.

Adolph Jackson

CHAPTER 13

Double Trouble

Meanwhile, Carroll was like a bad virus that I just couldn't shake. Every time I looked up he was at our door. Now, don't get me wrong, I liked him, there were nice things about him and he made me laugh, but for the most part he shocked me. He came in the house loud, boisterous, and full of laughter every time. The problem was, he had no respect for marriage—not ours, that was certain. He also had no respect for my feelings. He constantly talked to Charles about making plans to go out to some great concert or some party, or talk about some fine woman he'd met. Although he had a good sense of humor, he was also rude and crude. I'd often be working in the kitchen and laugh at some of the unbelievable things he'd say. His attitude toward women was shocking. For example, he talked about his "night creeps." They were women he slept with who he said were "too ugly to be seen in public with." This was just another example of his disrespect for not only me, but women in general. In the same breath he would ask me what I cooked and would I mind getting him something to eat!

Many times I wished he would just keep on down the road. I was always nice to him and fixed him a plate of food, or as he called it, a "Sam which." I viewed him as a walking joke. Even though I laughed, he was just a big scallywag.

Later Carroll became an Oakland police officer and married. He asked Charles to take pictures at the wedding. Charles discovered after everything was said and done that he'd forgotten to put film in the camera. I thought to myself, *Serves those two right!*

I realized I couldn't keep blaming Carroll for Charles being in the streets. One day it struck me that even if he wasn't around things wouldn't be any different. I forgave Carroll although he never knew there was anything to forgive. I let it go.

There was a time that our house became party central. Records played on the stereo at full volume. Our collection included Otis Redding, Jimi Hendrix, and Janice Joplin; all had been headliners at the Monterey Pop Festival. Charles had worked off duty security for many of the concerts held there. I loved Janice Joplin and would've given anything to see her and the others perform. Lots of money was spent on vinyl over the years, everything from James Taylor to Funk, Jazz to Gospel, Carly Simon, Linda Ronstadt, Al Greene, and Freddy Fender. I later fell in love with anything Marvin Gaye; romantic and political messages filled his lyrics.

Music saturated our house much of the time, but once I put Charles Jr. to bed, I tried to maintain quiet. That is until the word got out. After the club would give a call for the last round of drinks, Charles would announce on the P.A. system that there was an after-hours party at our house. People would drop in whom I didn't even know. They'd roll up the carpet and dance on the hardwood floors; the noise was impossible to contain. My son would sleep right through it all. Crazy thing was, Charles would often ditch us to go out for a meal, leaving me to greet strangers at the door, all of whom I let in to continue partying. So many times I resented this. One time I asked a guy to please not smoke inside my house. He replied, "This b.... is crazy!" I knew this had to end. A party every now and then was fine, but nearly every weekend was just too much. Disrespectful strangers in my home was not something I could tolerate. I was not happy about so many things.

༄༅

I had found a job working at United California Bank. They were ultra conservative in every way. We were only allowed to wear beige, brown, gray, navy, or black. Our hair couldn't touch our collar. Hose was a must and no dress could be above the knee. No problem, a piece of cake. I decided to let my hair grow so I was pulling it up every day and twisting it into a chignon. To my parents' dismay my after work and weekends wardrobe had begun to reflect my core values.

> *To my parents' dismay my after work and weekends wardrobe had begun to reflect my core values.*

The hippie culture of Haight Ashbury in San Francisco with its free love and hallucinogenic drugs was a big thing, but I had no desire to be a part of it. I didn't want to join the Hare Krishna's. I just wanted world peace and love. Live and let live. I changed my appearance entirely on the weekend. I let my hair down and didn't put any moisture in it so it was quite bushy and dry looking, the humidity from the ocean added plenty of volume and if I braided it when I washed it, then let it loose after it dried it was huge. My jeans were deliberately ripped and had patches; they were most likely hip huggers, usually accompanied by a halter top. The look was often completed by a jean jacket covered with pins, earth shoes, and jewelry full of love and peace signs. I even braided brightly colored cord into my hair, but only on the weekend. This was all at extreme odds with my weekday attire and attitude at the conservative bank. They would have never allowed such a show of personality and expression for the state of the affairs of the world and I hated working there with all my being.

Although my parents were used to seeing me dressed prim and proper, with no hint of a tear, rip, or patch, I was too young for old lady brooches. They didn't get why I wanted to wear slogans all over myself, especially being a young mother, but when we talked about it over tea, like we talked about everything, they came to an understanding of sorts. Instead of little Norma-Jean growing up to be a beatnik, I'd made it after all to what I thought was a really cool place. It was a statement after all. They understood so much. Daddy was also against the war in Vietnam and even his beloved Eartha Kitt spoke out against it. I also sympathized with the Brown Berets movement of Chicano activists who organized anti-Vietnam demonstrations in Mexican American communities.

I discovered that while I hadn't grown up to live the life of a beatnik as I'd dreamed, I fit the hippie definition in many ways. I was vehemently against the Vietnam War! I collected anti-war and anti-establishment buttons and loved all things *PEACE*. I did have buttons that read "make love not war," but I didn't take them literally. I was *not* in favor of free sex and I was *not* in favor of psychedelic drugs. I was for just being free to be whoever you felt you were free to be. I was not opposed to marijuana at all, nearly everyone I knew smoked it. Charles kept a cigar box in the headboard of the bed and occasionally smoked a joint. I had tried it once or twice and it wasn't my thing at all, I preferred wine.

In April of 1968 Martin Luther King was assassinated. I remember crying and didn't understand how this could happen. I was alone with my son and just held him and kissed the top of his head about a million times, running my fingers through his soft curly hair. My tears soaked his little head in a baptism of grief, just like they had with my little dog Cookie so many years ago. The world can be so cruel. I wanted a better place for him.

> *In April of 1968 Martin Luther King was assassinated. I remember crying and didn't understand how this could happen.*

I had taken my first African-American studies classes in college and I was *not* radicalized, although Charles thought so. I was willing to protest, use my voice, and use my home. I was willing to raise my fist and say, "Black Power". Charles and I were in a tug of war. I saw the "pig" (police officer) in my home as thoroughly white washed and he saw me as being completely brain washed. He was furious and made me withdraw from my black studies class.

If you've ever been around a group of hippies, you know they are definitely not racists. I never had been racist and wasn't starting then. I hated the idea of the police taking dogs like our German Shepherd and turning it on a crowd, making people run for their lives, rolling tanks in, and using deadly force against people who expressed dislike for war. I didn't really like that cops were being called pigs, I respected them. One day a few black students were at our house and we were discussing some ways of peaceful protest, taking the struggle to the streets. Charles told me he wanted me to ask them all to leave. He drew a line in the sand.

Charles was extremely conflicted, not just about the political scene. He had discovered a new love and it had a grip on him. He discovered that he loved white women—the blonder the better. The whiter and wilder the women the better he liked them. Thinking about the struggle of our black brothers and sisters was not high on his agenda. I always wondered what it was that drew him in that direction and away from me, even though I myself have a white mother. I would not be bleaching my hair to make it blonde, nor staying out of the sun to avoid becoming darker. What you see is what you get. Perhaps that was the answer to why he was so specifically attracted in this way…the intrigue of someone so utterly different than what was in front of him.

CHAPTER 14

My Baby Girl

We decided to do what most couples in love with their children do. We decided to try to have another one. I knew we had some problems but I honestly thought having another baby would bring us closer together and we would be just fine. I couldn't imagine it any other way. I wasn't seeking counsel from anyone, surely older more mature people would have told me to wait.

Getting pregnant was not a problem but it turned out that carrying a baby was the challenge God set before me. I experienced three devastating miscarriages, all in my second trimester. I was an emotional wreck. In my heart I blamed Charles for one of the miscarriages after he had flung me against a wall in a rage. He said it was not his fault. He pointed out that I had lost two other babies. Maybe, just maybe, he was right. I had doubts. How sick was I to be willing to try again? I nearly lost hope of having another child. Charles kept encouraging me saying that more than anything he wanted another baby with me. I believed him, or I guess I wanted to believe him. His words were a contrast to his actions. He went out all the time. That didn't matter to me though, I figured once a baby came he'd be home with us. When I say he was out there, I mean he was really out there. I suspected what he was doing, but I didn't know for sure and I couldn't prove a thing. So, why would I want to make waves? Maybe I'd just wait and try again for another pregnancy at a better time. I prayed about it and made a life changing decision for myself. I would wait to have another child. Plea number four....I ignored.

A few months later when I woke up feeling like I had the flu I was nervous. After waiting an appropriate time period to make sure it wasn't the flu I went to see my doctor. He confirmed what I had feared, I was pregnant again. I was not at all happy about it, I had been careful. How could this have happened? I didn't want to be pregnant and was convinced it would end in miscarriage. I felt I couldn't have a successful pregnancy. I told the doctor I just couldn't go through another loss. I told him my marriage was not solid and I didn't think it was the right time for a baby. He said he understood completely. He told me we could just schedule an abortion before I would lose the baby. He said it would be the same thing as having a D&C, the same procedure they had done after the miscarriages. It felt like a sensible option. I would head off the pain. It never dawned on me to think, *Who does that? What doctor in his right mind is going to make an offer like that?* On one hand it was sensible, on the other it went against everything, I mean everything, I believed in! I didn't know for sure that I could ever abort a baby, but I didn't want to get all the way past my first trimester to be disappointed again.

My doctor knew me though. I guess he was looking deeper at my soul than I could ever realize. He fooled me. He gave me a bogus date for the procedure. I went from day to day in extreme emotional pain. On the day I felt that first little quiver that did it for me. There was no way on earth I could think of not having my baby. When I called the office to cancel the procedure I found out that I was not scheduled for anything more than a checkup. *Thank you Jesus!* I had been duped. My doctor knew that I just needed to get past that big fear date. I made it and was on my way to a healthy pregnancy. I was filled with hope. I prayed I would carry the baby all the way. Charles said he was happy too! What more could I ask for?

What I didn't know was that Charles wanted a family just as much as he wanted his freedom. One day he seemed happy, the next day he seemed miserable. I didn't know what to think. I rubbed my belly every day and night. I talked to the baby, *Mommy loves you, you are precious. Keep growing. Be healthy, I'll protect you.* Four year old Charles kissed my belly and told me, "I only want a baby sister, no brother." Charles once again bought me the most beautiful maternity clothes. What he didn't buy, my mother sewed. He showed concern for how I felt, but he left me home alone with our son when he could have been there. We had great days filled with fun and laughter and then I had lonely days and nights. I was fearful of sparking arguments and just wanted to get through the pregnancy with peace, joy, and a healthy baby!

> *Mommy loves you, you are precious. Keep growing. Be healthy, I'll protect you.*

Charles Sims II, age two

I prayed a lot. Charles Jr. would find me on my knees and bless his heart he would want to pray too. I guided him gently in prayer. He wanted God to bless everyone and named all his relatives one by one, asking God for specific things for family members. He not only wanted them to be blessed in general but he wanted them to have nice things and good health. He prayed for our new baby and always said, "Thank you for my baby sister growing healthy in my mommy." Telling him we should just be happy that he had a brother or sister coming was not an option for him to consider. I was thankful for this determined and loving little boy.

When I couldn't say anything else I'd just say, "Thank you Jesus!" He picked up this phrase too.

Charles waited until I was well into my pregnancy. I was huge. He'd been out one night late and about three in the morning slipped into bed. After a while he said, "Are you asleep?" "No." "I have something I need to tell you." My heart flipped over and then flipped again. I think I knew what was coming before the words rolled off his tongue. "There is someone else I'm involved with, her name is Kathy and I love her." I lay there, stunned. I threw the covers back and in a split second I was in the middle of the living room, hysterical! "You son of a b....!" I yelled. For the first time in my life I was angry enough to hurt someone. He tried to calm me. "Don't you touch me." I was seeing pure red, like a bull when a red flag is waved in front of him. "Why? Why? Why? Why would you want another baby with me when you have someone else? Let her have your baby!" I rubbed my belly in apologetic gesture to my baby. I wouldn't want the baby to feel unwanted, unloved.

I hated Charles right then with every fiber of my body. I thought about all the nights he was gone. I wondered how many other women there were and what their names were. I wondered if Kathy was exclusive and if she was I wondered what it was about her that made her so special. I paced the floor and wrung my hands. I cried. I sobbed. I was sick, just sick. I thought I was going to throw up. I couldn't even look at him, couldn't be in the same room with him. I checked on my son at least fifty times before dawn. I didn't want him to wake up to all of this. I finally had to get out of the

> *I forgot about the milk. I walked in the house with the sweater box tucked tightly under my arm...*
> *Love is patient...*

house and decided to go to the store for milk even though there was a nearly full carton. Any excuse was better than none.

As I was getting in the car I noticed a beautiful copper colored foil gift box behind the driver's seat. I opened it. There, lying gently folded between sheets of exquisite tissue paper was a very soft, very expensive alpaca wool cardigan sweater. It was indeed beautiful. I know class when I see it, this was no bargain store find. I could have never bought such an expensive gift. Inside the box was a scroll tied with a ribbon. I opened it with shaking hands. It was a print of First Corinthians 13:4-13. I went ballistic. I forgot about the milk. I walked in the house with the sweater box tucked tightly under my arm. I set it on the couch and looked at it. I ran my finger up and down the smooth, cool foil. He was in bed. I stood over him. "*Love is patient, Love is kind.*" My voice was cracking and getting louder with each word. "*It does not envy.*" Let's just skip to "*It is not self-seeking.*" Ha! What a joke. I tore up the scroll. I threw the pieces up in the air and they fell like confetti at a parade. Before I knew it I was striking him in the face over and over with my fist. He pulled the sheet up trying to shield himself from my blows. He yelled, "You're crazy! Settle down!" I looked at him with fire in my eyes. "Don't you ever tell me what to do ever again." My fist hurt and I was tired. I stepped back. "I hate you! How could you do this to me?" He got up, showered, dressed, and left. I hung his precious sweater carefully on the best hanger in the closet.

I called Mama before she went to work. "Please come and take Charles for the day." I put on a good act when she came and told her I was feeling very sick. I didn't mention my broken heart. I think she sensed something but didn't push. I hugged my son, gave him bunches of kisses, and told him I'd see him later. I was relieved to have him out of the house. I didn't want him to feel my pain.

I then packed up Charles' belongings and set them on the front porch. I was done. I finally had enough. The sweater was still hanging in the closet and every now and then I walked in, pushed the closet door open and stared at it. It was a foreign object. By the end of the day I couldn't take it any longer. I went to my sewing box and got my shears. Pushing open the closet door, I took a solid deep breath and began at the cuff working upward. I cut that precious sweater into strips, leaving it hanging only by the shoulders. Whew. It felt good. It

> *By the end of the day I couldn't take it any longer. I went to my sewing box and got my shears. Pushing open the closet door, I took a solid deep breath and began...*

felt too good. I let out so much rage. Finally, I closed the closet door and walked away. In the kitchen, I brewed a cup of tea, finding familiar comfort in the ritual. I kept returning to the dark hollow of the closet to gaze at the destruction I had wreaked. I couldn't believe it. I called Reverend Nance and told him I felt complete shame for what I did to that stupid gift. He told me I should be thankful because if I hadn't destroyed the sweater and let out that rage, I might have hurt Charles instead. He prayed with me. I felt some solace. Some. A small measure of the guilt lifted from my shoulders.

That same day I called Linda. Never mind that she was his sister. She was also one of my best friends and like a sister to me. In my state of mind I had to have support. Toni was far away; too far to help. I knew I'd be okay. Our home in Marina was long gone and we were living in a home my parents owned. After the baby was born I'd finish my education so I could provide for my kids. I told myself I didn't need a man. Especially a lying, cheating, conniving, and abusive one. I was done! My kids would be my joy. Linda came. She has always been there. She let me cry, rant, and just talk it out.

Then the phone calls started coming. "Is Charles there?" Charles' mistress had gone too far by calling our house but she really overstepped her bounds when she tried to have a conversation with my son. The telephone rang and he dashed for it, hoping it was his daddy. I heard only one side of the conversation. "Yes." "No." "I don't know." Something about the way he was holding his shoulders and casting his glance toward the floor away from me told me he was nervous. Someone was asking him questions, that was clear by his answers, but who? "Sweetie who are you talking to?" "Kathy." I took the phone from his small hand and without a word I hung it up. She had some nerve. I thought to myself "What a b....!" She continued to call for days, looking for him, asking questions, trying to talk to *my child, my son.* I wondered if she even knew I was pregnant. When she finally left us alone I can only imagine it was because she heard from him and he filled her in.

I tried to be joyous. I read that a baby feels everything the mother feels. I didn't want to make my child sad and angry before it was even born. How awful that would be. I was very stressed out but I had to get a grip. The next few weeks were hard. My parents moved to the Reno area because my father accepted a position there. My mother transferred too and in the blink of an eye they were miles away. I decided to put on the best front anyone had ever seen. I pulled out a different dress every day and did my hair and makeup. I was going to look my best regardless.

One day Charles showed up and wanted to talk to me about a great plan he had. I was vulnerable. At a different time and place I probably would not have agreed to any of it. He thought we should leave the Peninsula because so much had happened. A fresh start somewhere and we could really make it work. He loved me so much. He was willing to move to an apartment in another town just so we could have a fresh start and keep our family together.

Before I knew it we were living in San Jose just off Stevens Creek Blvd.. Charles Jr. called it *Stevens Queek.* My hormones were still raging and my heart was still broken but no one knew how I felt. I didn't talk about it. I still had some bad vibes and I feared if I spoke about them they might manifest into something real. I had no idea what I was doing. I wasn't in my right mind. My parents were far away and now I was far from friends and the rest of the family. I was further away from my doctor and hospital. It was a stupid decision. I had no idea we were also closer to Kathy, who was a student at UC San Francisco. Charles continued to commute to work on the Peninsula. All I had managed to do was remove myself from the home we had lived in and place myself in an apartment. The house had plenty of room and a big back yard. The apartment was just that, an apartment. I was by myself most of the time with a temper tantrum throwing son. He was my best friend. We read books and went for nature walks and had long talks. When he was upset or angry I couldn't do a thing with him. I was not the disciplinarian. He got away with so much. But he was just a little boy feeling the weight of his parents' messed up relationship.

He was the smartest child and asked tons of questions. He was stuck on "Where do babies come from? How did the baby get in your tummy? How is it going to get out?" I bought him a book from Time Life for children. It had pictures that looked like paper dolls but used the correct anatomical names for body parts. Baby Charles, as he was affectionately called, waited until we had company for dinner to show off his skills. The couple lived in our complex and I was trying to make new friends, so I invited them over. After dinner he wanted to help clear the table and scrape the dishes. As his proud Mama I pulled his chair up to the sink to let him help. As he began to scrape the dishes he belted out a song. In his loudest, most enthusiastic voice, to the tune of *Oh My Darling Clementine* he sang, "Oh vagina, Oh vagina..." Oh my gosh, I had no idea where that was coming from. I ran to him with my face flaming, trying to hush him up. The couple just sat looking shocked. Surely they were wondering what kind of people we were that this very little boy was singing such lyrics. Not only singing but belting it out like it was our family anthem! I wanted to ring his precious little neck. He clarified it with showing me the garbage disposal opening and saying it was a hole just like where the

Baby Charles, as he was affectionately called, waited until we had company for dinner to show off his skills.

babies came out in the book. So much for giving too much information to a preschooler. I'm sure if we had been in the company of family everyone would have had a good laugh, but I was trying to make some new friends.

I needed to go home to family support and familiar surroundings. My parents had found a tenant for the house so we couldn't move back there. Charles and I found the cutest little place. It was bright and sunny with French doors off my son's room that led to a very nice court yard where he could ride his tricycle and play safely. I liked it. It only had two bedrooms but the baby would share a room with us for a long time.

The house was perfect for my son. What we didn't notice when we first toured it was that everything was scaled down. The sinks were just right for him, the stove, the countertops, the door handles. I didn't even realize the home had been customized for a couple who were little people and the realtor hadn't bothered to mention it. I couldn't believe I had been oblivious to the scale of things. Oh well, spoiled as he was why not have one more thing just right for him? I still liked the place! At 5'8" counters that were perfect for my son gave me a good laugh after we moved in and had the startling realization! I thought it was hilarious. Even the shower in the bathroom was designed so we had to duck down or the water hit us at just about the waist, but for my son, perfect! My husband didn't complain and we made the best of the cute place.

I felt like my parents' career advancements came at a difficult time for me but I never told them that. I wanted only the best for them. They had a new home and new friends, but they called every day. Near the end of my pregnancy I was experiencing some complications that landed me on bed rest. Mama saw that as an opportunity to come and get her grandson, "Booby" as she called him. They kept him until I had the baby. She had put him in a day care center that he enjoyed and each day they reassured me that everything was great. I had no doubts.

Three weeks early to the day I went into labor. The birth of our daughter turned out to be one of the absolute best moments in life that Charles and I have ever shared. We had hoped for a girl. That was for two reasons, a boy and a girl would be very nice and the other reason was because baby Charles was hoping for a baby sister. It would be wonderful since a brother was not an option for him. In those days people made predictions about the gender based on how you carried the baby and who you were talking to. High for boys, low for girls or some said vice versa. There were no ultrasounds to allow parents preparation time. The normal color for a layette was yellow. We had everything yellow. When our baby pushed her way into this world the doctor commented we had another football player based on the wide shoulders. As he pulled out the rest of her tiny body he corrected himself, said, "A little girl football player." Charles and I both cried and laughed. The moment was a perfect union between two souls expressing pure joy. Regardless of all past pains and wrongs this was a new beginning. Her new life would be just the tonic our aching marriage needed. We would keep our family together, Charles and I and our son and his new baby sister!

The birth of our daughter turned out to be one of the absolute best moments in life that Charles and I have ever shared.

We named her Alisa Airnet after both of her grandmothers. Let me explain that. My mother's name was pronounced Alisa but spelled Alice with an accent over the "e" in Latvian. When she came to the United States she started going by Alice instead of constantly explaining. Charles' mother's name was Airnet. She had been named by a French woman and the true spelling of her name was Airnet with an accent over the "t", pronounced *Airnay*. But I just went for simple adaptations of both names in hopes they wouldn't be butchered.

Speaking of family names...Airnet's brother was James Brazil Myart. "Brazil" was a nod to family roots in that country. He was a tall, attractive man with a flair for design and fashion and could sew anything. He always told me to spoil myself and invest in one quality piece of clothing that would last for decades. He was gay and lived with his partner in Los Angeles. My children learned acceptance by interacting with him although their grandfather Emanuel poked fun at James behind his back every chance he got.

Alisa was a beautiful baby. The nurses thought she looked like an Indian papoose. Her locks of hair were long and had grown from the back of her head around her neck, tucked tightly under her chin. The nurses took it upon themselves to cut it. They stated it was unsanitary. I was furious but like most of my anger it was gone in the blink of an eye. The nurse apologized, I forgave her. I was not going to let anything spoil this newfound contentment.

Bringing Alisa home was sheer bliss. My parents brought Baby Charles home from Nevada and we were all together at last. When I placed his baby sister in his arms he grinned his little sideways grin and his eyes twinkled with delight. Daddy got the camera out and took pictures, preserving the moment forever. To this day it's one of the sweetest pictures I have. There are very few of us all together, this one is priceless. I prayed he would grow up watching over his little sister and they would be close to one another from the cradle to the grave. One time when she was crying a lot, he did ask, "Do we have to keep her?"

Charles sweetly stayed close to home for a week or two, then slowly started going out little by little. I began to embrace the sad darkness of my old thoughts. The Peninsula was not the best place for our family. I turned to my comforter Jesus. I prayed. Before I knew it there was a miracle breakthrough.

*Charles, Norma-Jean, Charles II, Alisa
(3 days old), Seaside, CA*

CHAPTER 15

The Biggest Move

My parents offered us an opportunity of a lifetime. They said if we moved to Nevada they would help us buy a brand new house in a subdivision near them. We took them up on it and I counted this as a joyful blessing.

We moved to Sparks, in the Reno area, when Alisa was just an infant. We stayed with my parents for a short time while our house was being completed. Thanks to our jobs and my parents' help we were doing well financially. We were able to choose the flooring and light fixtures as well as the paint colors. We chose yellow for the exterior with white shutters. It was a classic two story house; the only thing missing was the white picket fence. We furnished it in style from front to back, top to bottom. It was so much fun. We shopped at Bruner's for all new furniture, we decorated, and we worked in the yard. We put our stamp on it. The house was in a great neighborhood and was a perfect place to raise a family, I loved it and felt so blessed. I had my son, my baby girl, and my husband. Finally, life felt really good.

Charles went to work as the first black correctional officer for the state of Nevada. The department wanted to make it an inclusive environment. However, some of the other officers weren't on board. I experienced some harassment and ugly calls late at night while Charles was at work. In spite of this, much of life was good.

My ultimate dream was to stay home and raise my children. However, there were times I needed to work outside the home to bring in additional income. We used a variety of different childcare options to manage during these times. The first job I found in the Reno area lasted all of half a day. I went to work for a company that made vending machine sandwiches. They immediately put me in charge of egg salad. They placed me in front of huge pots of boiled eggs and told me to start peeling. Some of the eggs had cracked and there was a slimy film floating in the water, not to mention the overwhelming sulfur odor. I couldn't take it. I was gagging and thought for sure I would throw up in the pot! When I had my lunch break I left never to return. I didn't even collect my pay. I just wanted to leave. My thoughts went directly to that college education I so greatly desired.

I went home and actually had a good laugh about the place. I wanted to stay home with my baby girl but there were so many things we planned to do with the house and we wanted to put our son in private school. A good job would be wonderful. I decided to pray about it and just see what would happen. I applied for a job as a cocktail waitress at a local casino. I knew nothing about it. I had never done that kind of work. When I came home with the fishnet stockings and the low cut top complete with push up bra and ruffled panties, Charles said a booming not only, "NO" but, "Oh, Hell NO!" "But I can make good money in tips." "I could care less! Take it back immediately!" So I did.

Then a friend told me about a job at a natural hot springs/ hotel. I went for an interview and was hired on the spot. The place had a breathtaking view. It sat on the Truckee River and wild horses

I applied for a job as a cocktail waitress at a local casino. I knew nothing about it...When I came home with the fishnet stockings and the low cut top...

came down to drink the cool water. I've always loved trees and the grounds around this beautiful hotel were scattered with towering, magnificent examples. They paid me very well and I worked a flexible schedule. It was a great job. I loved it until they got busted for illegal activities that had been going on long before I ever came to work. The whole place was shut down for a time. I was one of the few employees not arrested and could have gone back when it reopened but I didn't.

During this time I was caught in a very peculiar place emotionally. We were far from all of the good things, the positive parts of our life on the Peninsula. I especially missed Sunday dinners with the close-knit Sims family. We would all get together and cook and eat and play games and just have a great time being together. I missed my nieces and my nephew. It was strange being so far away from everyone, I felt out of the loop. Our long distance phone bill was crazy. Back then there was no such thing as unlimited long distance, we were charged for every single minute. But we could pay our bills and our mortgage.

Back in Seaside my son had always been with his cousins, who affectionately called him Baby Charles. I wanted Alisa to have that relationship with her cousins but I knew in the long run I wanted this house for my children. It was a hard choice but I wanted them to have a home to grow up in. Charles was just learning to spread his wings. He learned to ride a two wheeler; he could skate and play baseball. I also took him for tap-dancing classes, which he loved. I was happy to let him explore any activity he showed interest in. His favorite song was Don McLean's ode to American pie. One year his little preschool has a Christmas program. Charles was very proud and all dressed up. The children were singing *Go Tell It on the Mountain* and when the music stopped Charles was still singing; he belted out the last line with his arms flung dramatically out. His voice cracked and the audience was delighted. Even now I still cry when I hear this song.

I did finger-painting and crafts with neighborhood kids who had become his friends. My kids were my true blue friends. Their smiles brought me priceless joy. It was in this house that my daughter took her first steps and we celebrated her first birthday. I thought I'd always live there, but it wasn't meant to be.

Out of thin air Charles decided to give up his job and our home and move back to California. He watched a Bing Crosby golf tournament in Pebble Beach on a small black and white TV while he was working in one of the prison towers during blizzard conditions one evening. He said snow was not his thing. *Now you tell me.* He planned to go back and run the janitorial business. No retirement, no paid vacations, no sick days, and no insurance was enough to keep him in Nevada. He just wanted to go home. I couldn't believe it! How could he make this decision? I missed everyone too, but I needed and wanted stability for my children. I too genuinely missed every

Norma-Jean and Alisa, 1st birthday, Sparks, NV

aspect of being with the Sims family; the noise, the laughter, the affection we had for one another.

I stayed in the house and tried to go through the motions of raising my children alone. I tried to tell myself it was in my best interest to hate him as much as I loved him. Of course, I could never hate anyone, let alone Charles. But I tried to identify my feelings. I couldn't love him. I really didn't want to say I loved him. That would mean I should be with him and what I needed to do was put my children and their needs first. They needed

Later I would realize his impulsiveness was a symptom of mental illness.

a stable home. I felt let down, betrayed and as usual pretty insecure about how Charles really felt about me. Later I would realize his impulsiveness was a symptom of mental illness. He had made the decision without consulting me or considering me or the children at all. *Who is Bing Crosby to me?* I didn't care about the damn tournament and the beautiful sweeping golf course by the sea. I cared about our children and their future. He walked away from us, just up and left for golden beaches and warm temperatures.

I forced my mind to pick myself up every day and smile for my babies. Every day I made a mental checklist of the things that brought me joy. I even counted them. Number one, my babies. Number two my parents. Number three, a beautiful home for myself and for my babies. I counted my joy every day and yet I felt crushed and abandoned somewhere deep in my soul. I sure didn't want to let my parents down again. I didn't want to stick them with a house when all they ever did was try to help us. Their generosity was a life line but so was the love they gave me.

I tried not to discuss Charles with my parents; I didn't want to be in the middle. I had spent too many days defending my mother's good name with Charles and defending why I was still married to someone who could up and leave me and his children on a blustery snowy day. He just packed up his stuff in our brand new car and drove away without a word. No wonder I felt betrayed as he kissed me and the kids goodbye. His actions showed me where his loyalties were. *What the hell was wrong with his parents that they wouldn't say for once, "Charles, you need to stay there and take care of your family!"?* Both my parents were supportive, just reacted in different ways. My mother was furious. My dad was gracious and said, "It's all right" trying to reassure me.

Part of me wanted to skip backwards in time to days when life was easier and more promising. I never wanted any division with his parents or his family. God only knows how much I loved and missed them all. So I swallowed those thoughts and didn't speak, instead I called often and stayed in touch. No one ever asked about Charles, our relationship problems were an unspoken thing within the family.

Once Charles settled in back home in Seaside it took a while before reality hit him. "Norma how could you do this to me? I miss you. I miss my children so much." I know the last thing he ever wanted was to lose his children. He was in no danger of losing them. I was not about to try to use them against him. Never! I simply wanted to provide stability for them. I knew if I stayed, I could do that. He called me over and over with the same question. Why was I doing this to him? The truth was I didn't do it to him, it was his choice but I couldn't make that argument stick although I tried.

One day we talked for hours in a marathon telephone conversation. He tried to convince me that the place for me and our children was back on the Monterey Peninsula with him. He had been faithful during the short time we lived in Nevada, but in the dark corners of my mind I feared that on the Peninsula he would return to his cheating ways. I didn't talk about it. I didn't even want to acknowledge my thoughts. I just wanted those dark thoughts to evaporate. Poof and gone! But when I was alone they crept relentlessly back into my mind. I pushed them aside again and again, proceeding with the slightest sliver of caution.

Charles had a way of convincing me that I was the root of every problem in every situation. I didn't seem to have the wherewithall to throw off this huge heavy blanket of guilt and stand up for myself. I was always swayed. I was always the guilty one. I need to try harder, I need to give more, I need to do more, and I need to be different. I was not enough, not ever. Not really. In my desperation, I accepted the guilt and the challenge to make life better for myself and my children. I would try.

This meant placing my parents in a truly bad position. I knew they would be disappointed with me. It was so hard for me to walk away and leave them holding the bag

I didn't seem to have the wherewithall to throw off this huge heavy blanket of guilt and stand up for myself.

with that new house mortgage. Charles promised that we would help them with the house until it sold, but that didn't happen. Daddy gave me his blessing and told me to go. He said everything would be all right and he and Mama would visit often and send for us to come for visits too. So against my better judgment, against that constant small voice in my head, that voice that had actually begun screaming like a siren *Don't go!*, I packed up my children along with my hopes and dreams and moved back to California, closing the book on a life in Sparks.

ᖋᗄᕲ A Day in the Life in Pacific Grove ᖋᗄᕲ

Days in Pacific Grove became filled with activities for the kids. We had been married here in this little town on the Monterrey Peninsula, our church was here and in many ways it was good to be back. We didn't see Charles much as we were all busy.

One typical day in 1973 I was driving Alisa to dance class and we were running behind. I finally spotted a parking space in front of Holman's Department Store a few minutes before her ballet class started. I reached for her in the back seat and she instinctively jumped into my arms. She didn't want to soil her pretty pink ballet slippers on the sidewalk. Her class was held upstairs in a studio kitty-corner to the store. "We have to hurry baby so you won't be late." "If I am late I will make them start over." I laughed, "It doesn't work like that." Wrapping her arms around my neck, she pulled my face close and kissed me on the lips, "Understand me Mommy, if I say start over, they will!" I believed her.

"You sound like elephants. No, no be graceful little ladies."...She stopped and glared at him...

I climbed the stairs two at a time and puffing, set her down at the top. We were early! She ran to charm her teacher, an old Russian man with so many years of ballet under his belt I couldn't understand why he was still doing it except it was obvious he loved it! His rumpled appearance, unkept shoes, and potbelly contrasted sharply with the bevy of little girls in his class. "We were going to be late but I didn't want us to be, so as you can see we aren't. We are early! Do you want to see me do a plie or an arabesque?" I took a seat and watched. She was full of wonder, so determined and intense. She was also witty like her big brother. She could be an angel and a brat at the same time. I often wondered how she would be when she grew up. During class the burly teacher rumbled at the little girls in his heavy accent. "You sound like elephants. No, no be graceful little ladies," he barked. She stopped and glared at him, big brown eyes sparkling. I knew what she was thinking from the expression on her face. She continued on displaying her grace. After class she extended her tiny hand in a gesture, "Did you hear him Mommy?" "Now say goodbye." "Bye!" She jumped up to my hip and wrapped herself around me. "I hate being called an elephant." "I know baby."

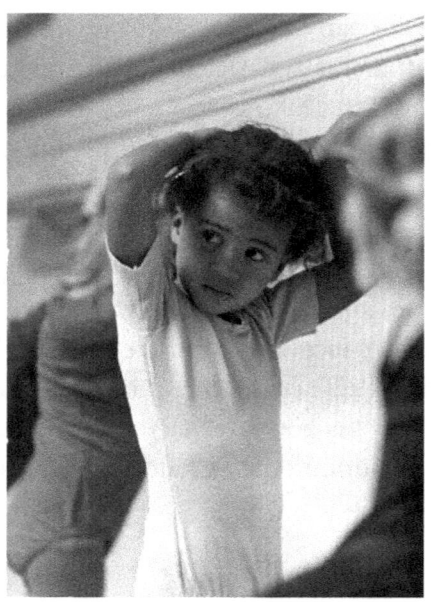

Alisa giving "the look" to her ballet teacher

*L—Alisa age three, R—Alisa and Charles after
Uncle CJ had given Charles some coins.*

CHAPTER 16

Changes and More Changes

The next few years passed like a super train barreling in and out of stations. My life held mostly stressful days, sprinkled in between with unforgettable, incredibly wonderful ones that left me in awe. The kinds of days that make you put your hand over your heart and just say out loud from the depths of your soul "oh wow." I'm not sure why but I always managed to go through the motions and act like everything was peachy-keen. I wasn't happy, but I wasn't particularly unhappy either.

I suspected what was happening when Charles was away from home but when it came to dealing with it, I found it easier to stay in denial. Over the next few years Charles became known as *Good Time Charlie.* That nickname really hurt me but I laughed and acted like it didn't. Weekend nights were always his party nights, but on Sunday morning he'd take his family to church. He was appealing to

> *He was fun to be around and whenever he told a story people listened... Our children were being raised with a scrambled double message.*

everyone, the *sinners* and the *sanctified*. This went back to his upbring-ing. The Bible says, "Bring up a child in the way he should go and when he is old he will not depart from it." Well, Charles had certainly been brought up in the church. Although he was the life of the party, any party, out in the world, he still clearly loved the Lord and enjoyed church. He appeared to be an all-around great guy. I don't think I ever met anyone who didn't like him. He had a lot of personality and could work a crowd or a room with just a few people. He was captivating and well spoken, people were drawn to him. He was fun to be around and whenever he told a story people listened, like E.F. Hutton. He was always very animated and made people laugh, so of course they liked him. They loved him!

Our children were being raised with a scrambled double message. Their daddy was *Good Time Charlie*, the party guy, and the ultimate family guy all in one. His message to our children was, go to church, read the Bible, and always do what is right. He was the stern discipli-narian in our home yet, as the children were growing up they were keenly aware of their father's other side. In many ways he was the best dad around. He was more than proud of his children. He never carried a picture of me in his wallet, ever, but he did have pictures of the kids. He never missed a parent teacher conference, a pediatrician appointment, a birthday party, a play, a recital, or a game. True, he was often late, but he would show up. In fact he always had time to fit in playing with his children when they were very young. He insisted I read to them and with them, something I wanted to do anyway and was committed to. He knew it would make them better equipped to get through school and later in life. He was acquainted with our kids' friends and most of their parents. He took our children on outings, to the zoo, to the movies, to the park and shopping.

He taught them the importance of being generous and the impor-tance of helping others, especially those less fortunate. He also taught them how to choose gifts for me. No matter what we were going through, whether we were together as a couple or apart, he gave me lovely gifts and so did my children. They learned from him to do special things for me on holidays like Mother's Day, Christmas, and my birthday. I was the recipient of many truly nice gifts even when it wasn't a special occasion. Our children always had nice clothes, nice toys, and nicely decorated and furnished bedrooms. It was important for him to provide even when it was extremely difficult to do so. He always tried.

Charles found time to coach Pop Warner youth football before our son was old enough to be on his team. His dedication to serving youth and the community was honored by various organizations. He even served on the board of directors for the kids' figure skating

Alisa, age four, Charles, about 30, Baby Charles (family nickname), age eight.

club. He did all of that and still found time to work in his parents' yard and help them do the heavy cleaning in their house. Often it was a joint effort with him and his brothers.

He was juggling many responsibilities and relationships. The problem is that even the best juggler drops things once in a while. It's a stressful occupation that requires concentration. There is a big difference between juggling balls, apples, or oranges and real life relationships. Unfortunately, the more responsibility he tried to handle, the shorter his temper became. He would often revert to the man who had an inability to control his anger. The time between his "blow ups" as I secretly called them, was getting shorter and shorter. I became more nervous with each one and didn't know what to do as I never knew what he was going to do. I knew something was wrong, but what? I was so insecure as well as extremely co-dependent. I always thought everything was my fault. Always, always, always. Charles often told me this so I came to believe it. *Maybe if I tried a little harder. Maybe if I kept things a little better.* I started transferring my feelings onto my children although I never meant to do that. "Don't upset Daddy." "Make sure you clean your room so Daddy won't be mad." I made the children nervous and I think unintentionally caused them on some level to fear his presence. I did respect him. Maybe part of the respect was fear. Maybe a large part of it was fear, depending on the situation.

I realized some of the feelings and reactions the children had were because of the harsh, belittling way he disciplined them. Charles and I had never seen eye to eye on discipline matters. By the time baby Charles was two he was the temper tantrum champion. The little guy deserved a crown or a heavy weight belt, to hold up his tiny fist in victory. This child displayed more temper than anyone I had ever seen. I had no control over him. Perhaps because I was so young and didn't know how to deal with some of the issues of life, I found a friend in my son. In him I found joy. He was my adorable baby and I often let him call the shots. I didn't like seeing him upset. I liked him to be happy. Had I been more mature I would have realized the need for boundaries with children. I let him have his way about most things and he became very spoiled. It was so much easier than seeing him turn red, scream, sweat, and throw himself around beating his fists. If he didn't want to go to bed I didn't make him. He would generally exhaust himself but I would be exhausted too.

When his daddy was home it was a different story. The days went smoothly. He didn't throw any of those temper tantrums because he knew from experience that kind of behavior resulted in serious consequences. From the age of two until he was 18 he knew his daddy would

I did not grow up with that type of discipline and cringed at the very thought of it.

whip his butt if he acted like that. Charles had grown up in a home where his parents whipped the kids with belts or switches. He felt if children acted up or disobeyed they deserved a good whipping. He had no problem with it and neither did his family. However, I did not grow up with that type of discipline and cringed at the very thought of it. I had to walk outside and down the street out of ear shot when he disciplined our kids. Sometimes he would leave welts on them. I'd cry, sometimes more than the kids. I'd talk to myself when I was walking down the street so I wouldn't hear my babies cry. *This is what slave masters passed on to us. Whipping to keep you in line. They whipped their slaves; I'm not whipping my children!* Call it whatever you like, spanking, whipping; I wasn't in favor of it. It seemed so cruel, so inhumane. I begged Charles not to use this form of punishment but he was not hearing me. He was old school in that regard and if it had been good enough for him and his brothers and sisters, it was good enough for his children.

I read Dr. Spock for advice on how to help me raise my son. I read Dr. James Dobson's *Disciplining the Strong Willed Child* for my daughter. I had been one of those kids who was very easy to discipline, so it was hard for me to fathom having a child that needed that much discipline. But my children were challenging. Sometimes when they were younger their dad would stand them in the corner. That form of discipline seemed more acceptable to me. Or, taking something away, or sending them to their room. As the kids got older more forms of discipline were implemented. Alisa as it turned out, loved being sent to her room. There she could read, which was what she liked to do more than anything. She and Charles both talked very early. Spanking her did not deter her from speaking her mind. Her outspoken nature was challenging. She always managed to say the most inappropriate things with full use of her extensive vocabulary, regardless of the consequences. Her daddy thought the fix for her was the same as he used on her brother from age two on. He felt she needed a good spanking for being defiant in her speech and thought. Not so! It didn't work.

I'm not totally one hundred percent against spanking, because there were times that although I thought I never would, I did spank them myself, usually one or two smacks on the bottom with my hand. I found other ways of disciplining them to be more affective. For example, Charles was crushed if I told him I was disappointed in his behavior. He would cry and promise to be good. The funny thing was I thought I'd try that tactic on Alisa. I was answered with a very sharp look and a stern, "Well I'm disappointed in you too!" *What the heck?*

Another time Alisa walked into the kitchen one morning, looked up and clasped her little hands together in prayer. "Good morning, God," she said sweetly. Then, she put her fists on her hips and glared at the ground, "Good morning, Devil." When I asked her what she was doing she explained, "Well, we have to say good morning to both of them."

Unfortunately, I think I made the mistake of being more friend than mother. Once that is established it is hard to shift. Although I was known for my abundance of patience, I did have a boiling point. When I reached it, I spoke through clenched teeth, usually in a hushed tone that let them know I had enough and I meant business. As my son grew taller than me, I would grab his arm and poke him in the middle of his chest with my finger and tell him, "I am still your mother."

All I ever really wanted was for them to live up to my expectations for them, like always acting well-mannered and respectful. I taught them many things along the way and hope I instilled a love of family in them by example. I truly loved our family. My children had wonderful grandparents, aunties, uncles, and their first best friends, their cousins. God gave me my children. I adored them and wanted them to be loved by others. I used to tell them, "Don't go acting up, I want other people to love you too."

Because my children had so much freedom with me, as they got older the word NO was a challenge for them. They questioned my authority, my motives, and showed me that they did not respect my discipline methods at all. They laughed at me often which infuriated me. I wanted control, but like I said, the transition from being more a friend to the mother in charge was difficult. I missed that window of opportunity. I can't repair what is done.

My children did receive constant supervision and direction and most people said we had great kids; they showed respect and knew their manners. Their father used profane language, mostly when he was angry, which I hated, but kids still pick things up. I see the use of it as ill-mannered and wanted my son to be a gentleman and my daughter to be a lady. I think profanity takes so much away from a person. So when my kids used bad words I'd march them right into the bathroom and wash their mouths out with soap. I understand that as the culture is changing the use of profanity is growing. However, I think when a person allows themselves to enter a profanity laced rage they have lost the opportunity to sanely express themselves. A person's vocabulary should be more than a few heated recitations of empty words that only hurt and don't serve to show any intellect. My children were my reason for getting up every day. My *joy* was in being a mother that could raise kids to be proud of!

During the first few years of Charles' and my relationship, things were predictably the same and yet there was always an undertow of tension and mistrust. I never knew if he was being honest with me. *When you're not here, what is up? If we move into this house how long are we going to stay? If I write a check for groceries is it going to bounce?* I was embarrassed but kept my doubts and questions to myself. I tried hard to avoid this riptide that I knew was always there. I knew what it was capable of. It pushed us apart

> *When you're not here, what is up? If we move into this house how long are we going to stay? If I write a check for groceries is it going to bounce?*

in separation and pulled us back together again countless times. I would go along until I felt like I was doing something I didn't believe in anymore. I was discouraged by the constant financial struggles and instability. I hated having to move from house to house because we would get so far behind in the rent. Charles had impeccable taste and we always lived in nice places. In fact, some of our homes were incredible! I can appreciate good taste, class, and beauty when I see it as much as the next person. Did I want to live in a nice home? Absolutely! Did I want to be constantly uprooted? Absolutely not! We lived all over the Monterey Peninsula in a variety of houses, apartments, and a condo. Charles never moved us into a dump. I know he tried very, very hard and wanted the best for us always. I loved the attempt, but the letdown was painful. What do you say to two little kids? Here we go again……. "It'll be fun, it'll be exciting." Even they had doubts after a time.

CHAPTER 17

Faith Questioned

I respected her opinion. So that dark day I asked for it and felt my heart shatter.

Let me back up. Charles had been trying hard to convince me that he wanted the best for us. I pondered his words and tried to put them and his actions in perspective. One day my mother-in-law and I were having a discussion, just like we often had, talking about marriage and family life. The children were quite young and I was very upset and was seeking her guidance. She was the spearhead of our Marriage and Family Life group at church and did a wonderful job. Asking for her opinion that day turned out to be a huge mistake. Her answer shattered my heart. She told me that all the problems I was having in life were because I had a lack of faith in God. *Are you kidding me? Where was that answer from? How could she say this to me?* I had soooo much faith in God! I didn't want to cry, but I began to weep. I needed to get home.

I took my sobbing, heart shattered, crushed self, collected my children like claimed baggage and went home to the sanctity of my bathroom. Door locked, still weeping. The kids tapped on the door with worried voices. "Are you okay Mommy?" "Yes, I am fine." I lied, trying to protect them. I cried a river. I cried like the dam holding everything back had failed.

Children have needs so I pulled myself together enough to come out of the bathroom, not wanting them to witness me in this state. Hiding the crumpled wad of tissues in my shaking hand, I dabbed away the tears when they weren't look-

> *"Are you okay Mommy?"... I lied, trying to protect them...I was utterly destroyed.*

ing. Faith had brought me through everything. Faith was what made me want to keep trying. Determination to make everything okay for my children brought me out of that bathroom but I couldn't hold myself together. I was utterly destroyed.

I couldn't stop crying, although I desperately wanted to, so I called Aunt Bessie. She came right away. She made me tea. She tried to talk me down off the imaginary cliff. When she realized this was no ordinary day of crying, no ordinary case of the blues or hurt feelings, she called for back-up for the kids. Then she wrangled me to the car and headed for the emergency room. Sweet Aunt Bessie knew me so very well, she could always make me feel better about anything with shared stories and a cup of tea. She understood deep in her soul that I needed more than that this time. Much more. The doctors gave me an injection that made me drowsy but did nothing to stop the tears. You would think I would be all cried out. I wasn't.

The one person whom I considered kind, loving, understanding, and most of all an expert on family life, had broken my heart with those few words. I felt so unworthy. Unworthy because she said it was my fault, that if I had a larger measure of faith I wouldn't have this life I was living. The doctors admitted me to the hospital. *Who gets admitted to the hospital for crying? Crying!* I will tell you. People with mental issues! Yep, that's where they put me. They put me *there* in the psychiatric ward and drugged me and I finally slept. That's what

I always pray for when I'm having a bad day, is sleep. The Bible says *weeping may endure for a night, but joy comes in the morning.*

The next day I woke up in my right mind, tears stopped, although my emotions were torn and ragged. I wanted to get the hell out of there. I looked around at the other patients. *Oh my God. Let me outta here.* But no. I had to do something they called "group." And I had to talk with a doctor, one on one. All I wanted was to get back to my kids. After three days of being with people who were talking to themselves and answering themselves, watching those who stared with catatonic eyes, after three days of having senseless conversations with strangers, I finally went home. I never told the family what had sent me spinning. And they never asked. Mom Sims never brought up the topic again and never asked why I had left crying that day. I didn't want anything to jeopardize my relationships. Not my relationship with Mom, or anyone else in the family. Besides that I knew everyone would most likely agree with Mom. So I moved forward, but every now and then I still think back on that day. I will never let anything take me there again! I am eternally thankful for Aunt Bessie who was there to take me home.

The next day I woke up in my right mind…I looked around at the other patients. Oh my God. Let me outta here.

❧

I stepped back into my life and continued trying to make it work. I fell into a troubling pattern with work. I would get a fantastic job and work for several months to a year and then trouble would arise. I signed with a modeling agency and was doing well, making great money for our family, but trouble met me there also. Trouble for me was Charles' "extreme jealousy". He made accusations at every job I ever had. The script never varied, it was always that some man on the job wanted me and was making advances. When I say, "some man on the job," it could have been any man according to Charles. I must have been interested in everybody according to him and everybody must have found me attractive to the point of lusting after me. His obsession with this was nerve wracking. It became miserable for me to go to work and come home to be interrogated. I quit many a decent position because I couldn't handle the accusations and being kept up all night arguing about it and trying to defend myself. The script was repeated endlessly for hours and I would become exhausted, knowing I wouldn't get any sleep those nights.

Things became more financially stable with me working steadily but it was an incredible challenge. I went back to school because I wanted to further my education so I could earn a good income that would help our family. But trouble met me at the door step of the school as well. As soon as I'd complete my first assignment Charles' accusations would start. "What did you do to get an A?" Then he would demand I drop the class.

As soon as I'd complete my first assignment Charles' accusations would start. "What did you do to get an A?"

Most of the time when I was separated from Charles I would find a job and also take classes. Before I left the Reno area I took a class in medical assisting to provide me with a good employment skill. which it did. My motivation was twofold. I wanted to provide for myself and my children and I was exercising a bit of defiance. It was sort of like showing him what I could do. Of all the things I really desired it was a college education. This was not college but it gave me some solid ground to stand on. I was proud of having taken that class and found a job working for a podiatric surgeon in Monterey.

Dr. Smith was a bright young doctor who taught me so much and gave me a great opportunity, offering to pay my college tuition, but there were two problems. The first and biggest was that he didn't keep his comments or his hands to himself and he expected gratefulness for the opportunity he was presenting me. I said, "It is not okay for you to touch me!" He downplayed his actions. Today this experience would be a part of the #metoo movement. The second problem was that I realized I really didn't enjoy dealing with other people's feet as much as I thought I would. If people came in with horrible, stinky feet, which happened often, I'd make up a story about the doctor running late and stick them in the whirlpool with lots of sudsy disinfectant. I couldn't see making a lifetime career of it. So, adios Dr. Smith.

I wanted to go back to school but Charles was completely against it. He saw no value in it. I had finished the short course in medical assisting but it truly wasn't what I wanted. I had chosen it solely for stability. I was more interested in humanitarian issues, particularly black studies. I think I turned Charles off to the idea of me getting an education because of this focus. He was greatly influenced by his uncle CJ who was more old school in his approach to race issues. He didn't want to make any trouble. The black power movement was sweeping across America at the same time as the civil rights movement and this passive girl was all too happy to raise my fist and say, "Black Power!" I was passionate about people and their rights. I wanted everyone to vote. When my son was just a tiny boy back in Seaside I would strap him into the baby seat on the back of my bicycle and go door to door doing voter registration. I went to hear Black Panthers activist and author Angela Davis speak. She is currently a Distinguished Professor Emerita at the University of California—Santa Cruz. I had a mind of my own and when I expressed interest in anything other than the house, the kids, or our family Charles tried to shut me down. I had to live with the consequences of unsteady income. I have seen more utility cut-off notices than I care to think about. Coming home at the end of a day and finding a tag on your door is humbling, humiliating, embarrassing, frustrating and I could go on and on.

One consequence of having so many addresses is that I can't remember them all. I do remember the places I liked best. I loved living in Skyline Forest where home was a beautiful condo. The forest was our back yard, yet we were close to everything. We had to move from there for the same reason as always. The day we moved I lied and said I was having a stomach ache. I locked myself in the bathroom and tried to hold back the tears. I splashed cool water on my face to tamp down the redness and just tried to pull myself together so my kids wouldn't see what a weepy mess I was. I hated it. We had received an eviction notice for not paying the rent in a timely manner. I was mortified. Of course I never told anyone the reason we were moving again. We just packed up, moved, and got settled in. It was almost second nature. Of course, as I always did, I pulled myself together, put a smile on my face, and said, "Let's get this show on the road."

Charles was not a lazy man by any stretch of the imagination. He was a hard, hard working man, creative and with an entrepreneurial spirit. The problem was working in the family business was like taking a pie meant to feed six people and trying to stretch it into enough pieces to feed twelve. It just becomes untenable. But everyone was counting on him. It was "The Family Business." There were days when money poured in and days when things were so lean there wasn't enough to go around. Charles didn't have the education and knowledge to keep a steady helm. He relied on bookkeepers who I knew were double dipping, secretaries who were not needed, and not enough grasp on the money coming in and going out. When you are the boss, you pay everyone else first and then you pay yourself if there is money left. He often had to take advances from the bank until he couldn't. There were times money was so good he could walk into the car dealership and drive off with a shiny new red Porsche. Just sign here.

> *...working in the family business was like taking a pie meant to feed six people and trying to stretch it into enough pieces to feed twelve.*

Everyone on the Peninsula knew the Sims family had money. But they didn't know the deep down dirty truth of the struggles that Charles and I were going through. He was an enterprising man and most of the time he worked his butt off. There were times much later in our relationship, when the children were older, when I worked and he didn't. Lafayette Janitorial had contracts to clean nearly every restaurant on Fisherman's Wharf in Monterey. They had held these contracts since he was a toddler. He took that part of the business over from his father early in our marriage, handling this workload in addition to his job on the police force. In the wee hours of the morning he, his brothers, and his brother-in-law Othell would be at the various restaurants, Lou's Fish Grotto, Angelo's, and Shakes, among others, cleaning, vacuuming, mopping, and walking the catwalk above the ocean washing windows before they opened. Then they would take a break, drink coffee, and eat sourdough bread with the Italian owners. "Hey Charlie, You're looking good today." They all loved him. In fact, everyone loved Charles. From there the vans would head to Carmel or Monterey to clean stores before they opened. One of the restaurants they cleaned was The Spinning Wheel Steakhouse in Carmel. Later the company hired crews to do the residential cleaning. He also created a landscaping company that installed and maintained residential and commercial landscaping over the entire area. He was a hustler. Then he reached out to get the government contracts. Where did all that money go? What happened? How could we possibly struggle when money was coming in from so many multiple sources? I was always broke, even when he had a pocket full of money. It was a form of control.

Where did all that money go? What happened? How could we possibly struggle when money was coming in from so many multiple sources?

I watched as life just unwound financially and otherwise. Charles worked harder and harder trying to create and build a dream for his parents and his family to be proud of and for all of them to benefit from. Each time he stumbled it frustrated him. He was hard headed and didn't want to listen to advice. His sister LoVera told him he needed to take some business management courses and he became belligerent towards her and ignored her counsel. I tried to convince him and got the same response. He was buckling under pressure. It was too much. Things began to fall apart and contracts were lost one by one. The writing was on the wall.

By this time his brothers had relocated to manage government contracts up and down the California coast. Jackie was married to Fred and wasn't onboard with going down with the ship; neither was Emanuel's wife LaVerne. Both wives were always extremely stable and best friends who had grown up together in Paso Robles. I was kind of jealous of them. They had independence. They always had money of their own, could go places without asking permission, and they had a career path. I was proud of them even if I envied them. They rarely included me in anything, but I understood why.

I would have loved to have become a teacher. When I tearfully told Bertha Hutchins, one of my favorite professors at Monterey Peninsula College, that I was withdrawing from school, she asked me to promise her I would write. I did promise her and over the years have done a lot of writing, mostly privately in my journals. Until now. Now I am telling the story of my life experiences and how I am able to count it all joy. I want other people, but especially my kids and grandkids, to know that despite circumstances, there is always *joy* to be found.

About those journals I have written in over the years—they were of great help to me. I spent hours, usually late at night, journaling about my feelings. My journals were like a close loving friend in whom I could confide with no judgement, no shame, and with whom I could share my greatest joys, sorrows, disappointments, hopes, and dreams. Now the thing about those journals was I spent a great deal of time and energy trying to keep them hidden because of the things I said about being abused. I knew if Charles ever read them, he'd probably kill me. I poured out every emotion from how much I loved him to how much I desperately needed to get far away from him with my children. I was always so torn about sharing my feelings of betrayal in words. It was right there in my own penmanship on the often tear stained pages of my journals. I set fire to those damning little books several times through the years of our marriage, in the fireplace or the barbeque pit. I would wait until no one was around, pile them up, douse them in lighter fluid, and strike a match. I just stood back and watched all my words go up in smoke. Proof of the ugly abuse gone in the wind. I'm sad that the lovely memories I had also been sure to write down were now gone as well, but they are forever in my heart. I felt relieved that there was nothing tangible to find, no written evidence to hide. I could only hope to erase the bad memories from my heart.

So many times I wrote, "If something bad happens to me, please know that if you're reading this, it was Charles." I'd write, "Today I have bruises on my wrists

> *I just stood back and watched all my words go up in smoke. Proof of the ugly abuse gone in the wind.*

and I am so happy that I didn't see my parents…Today I have a migraine because Charles was so angry and when he lost his temper he grabbed my hair and slammed my head against the wall." I'd plead with Charles not to do these kinds of things in front of the children. "Please don't throw things, it frightens them, Please don't Charles, Please don't, Please don't." And yet he would continue throwing things. My emotions would ebb and flow like the waves of the ocean. I would write more in more journals to soothe my aching heart and then on any given day, I would set a fire, watch it all go up in smoke and try to start the next chapter in a new journal praying it was all going to be much better.

⁓☙ Carrying On ☙⁓

So there was no career path for me to walk, no walking across the stage to accept a hard earned college diploma, but we always were striving for a better situation than the one we left behind us. I always saw the glass as half full and not half empty. That gave me what I needed to stay strong and carry on. We appeared to be the perfect family. Our children were beautiful and smart. We made an attractive couple. No one outside of a few close family members knew the struggles we had in our relationship or financially.

I have no particular talent but do many things with enthusiasm. I can't carry a tune but used to sing my uninhibited heart out with my babies; it gave me great *joy* to teach them all kinds of songs they still know to this day. I'm artistic enough to have done years of crafts with my kids, my nieces and nephews, and many neighborhood kids. I've read more books than a librarian and written volumes in my journals, for all that I am grateful. I do wish I could have done more. I wish I could have given more. I wish I could have been more prepared for the role of motherhood because I was preparing two people for their journey into the world. I don't think enough thought is given to that before we start having babies.

There was a time that nearly the entire Sims family lived on the Peninsula. When I say the entire family I mean of course Charles and I, his parents, my parents, his brothers and sisters, his Uncle CJ and Aunt Bessie, and their family. Only Linda and Verda had moved away because they both had married and their husbands were in the military. The Sims family was well known on the Peninsula. In the early days they were never known for financial standing but rather for being a hardworking, respectable Christian family. They were known to be kind and popular in the community. They were known for giving back to the community by way of volunteering for various causes and events. Charles' parents were admired for having done such a great job of raising their kids. Not one of them had ever been in any sort of trouble. They were happy although they weren't well off. On each child's birthday there were no fancy outings or gifts, Mom prepared their favorite dish and baked a cake, cobbler, or pie, whichever was their preference.

Then they saw the house on the hill, Mescal Avenue to be exact. Mom wanted that house so badly. Her sons wanted her to have it. She deserved to have a beautiful home. So they pulled it off. It was a brand new home at the top of the hill in Seaside, just drive straight up Broadway and take a right before the old Fort Ord gates. The house sat back from the street across from the park. The living room had a huge picture window with a view of the bay. Mom chose a $3000 bright yellow sofa from W&J Sloan Furniture in San Francisco. She had divine taste! I can't imagine the price of that sofa in today's market. The windows were dressed in floor to ceiling sheer drapes and the room looked like a designer had pulled it together. This was years before *HGTV* but *Better Homes and Gardens* could have featured the house. The guys planted a front lawn and lots of flowers in the flower beds because Mom loved gardening. The yard was kept perfect with the help of her sons. The house was kept clean with the help of her sons. They came regularly to wash the windows, mop the floors, scrub bathrooms, and clean the oven. The entire house was beautiful and lacked for nothing. Of course, as our finances were helter skelter, there were quite a few discussions about some of the expenditures on Mom and Dad's behalf. When I say discussions, sometimes it was very hard to say nothing. I wanted them to be happy and well cared for, but not at the expense of my children.

Robbing Peter to pay Paul often meant we gave to keep Charles' parents going, or to satisfy their desire for something special. Then I had to borrow from my parents to keep us afloat. It was a vicious circle. We just kept going around and around, masquerading as if all was normal, but nothing had ever been

We just kept going around and around, masquerading as if all was normal, but nothing had ever been normal.

normal. I loved our life and I hated our life. I loved the people in my life. I didn't want anyone to ever be denied good things. I wanted everyone to have a good home, a nice car, food, clothes, health, and most of all love. I didn't want anyone to have stress and worries. I wanted his parents to have what they deserved. It was just hard on my little family to give up so much for his parents to be able to have that home.

The house was a great gathering place for "The Family" and was often busting at the seams with noise and laughter and fun! The family was growing with so many new nephews and nieces—Adrian and Sherrie, Stephanie, Kim, Stacy, Aaron, and Kelle. We were together all the time. Our children played in the park across the street for hours on end. They had weekend sleepovers. They played board games with their grandmother. Their cousins were always there with them. We all cooked in the kitchen together. Love filled that house. Babies took first steps in that house. Cousins took communal baths together in that house. They played hide and seek in every nook and cranny of that house. We all loved the house on Mescal. It felt like home. When we were all together having fun there was nothing that made me happier. This was my family. But then…..

I was learning some hard and painful lessons about life, love, and friendship. My friend Toni never did live close to me, but she was one person other than my mama and Daddy who offered *unconditional* love. She was one person I didn't pretend with. I missed her more than she ever knew. So often there were days when I would wonder if life would have been better with Jerry. After all, he had never said one unkind word to me. There were days I wished I could go back and change it all. There were days I thought I had made a huge mistake. But then Charles would be there and he was persuasive. I did love him so much. I knew our relationship was sick and I was also aware of the fact that it should end, but I just kept on loving him. I couldn't shut it down.

In all of our residence hopping we lived in almost every town on the Monterey Peninsula. Although we were always members of First Baptist Church in Pacific Grove and Reverend Nance was our Pastor, Charles attended the AWANAS children's program at a local Baptist church when we lived in Marina. He had a great time there on Wednesday nights and learned a lot about the Bible.

I was Den Mother for his little Cub Scout Troup and became the neighborhood arts and crafts and snack mom. We lived directly across the street from my sister-in-law LoVera and her family. The kids could play all day with each other and then retreat to their mutual homes or spend the night for endless fun if that's what they wanted to do. We had a good time together.

I was close to my sisters-in-law and knew that I could confide in them about anything. LoVera and I would sometimes talk for hours. I think early on she understood that Charles was dealing with mental issues but what could she do? She tried to always give him sage advice but I was the one more apt to listen to her. Sometimes she would admonish me, getting after me like I was one of the kids. To her I was like a kid and it took years before she saw me as an

The Sims—Emanuel Sr.,
Donald, Airnet

adult. One time I was at her house late one night before Alisa was born. I was crying and she ordered me to get to bed and get some rest. She was no nonsense, treating me like a little sister. When Charles Jr. was sick with spiked fevers as a baby she would just whoosh in and take charge. As the oldest of the Sims' kids she was bossy and loving. She and Charles Sr. didn't always get along. I formed a close bond with her children that is uniquely different and extremely close. I remain especially close with my niece Cynthia to this day.

My youngest brother-in-law Donald and I always had a special bond. I volunteered at Special Olympics and other events for him. Mom would tease me that if he were on the same level as Charles he would give him competition for my affections. It became a family joke. Everyone understood how crazy I was about Donald and he in turn loved me.

In the summer of 1975 I had to have a partial hysterectomy. Because of my young age the doctors left my ovaries. It was still a difficult thing to have to endure at that stage of my life. It wasn't that I was going to have any more children, I was not, it was just the idea of it and then the long recovery. I was always worried about leaving my babies. I checked out of the hospital on a bright sunny morning A.M.A. which means "against medical advice." I wanted desperately to get home to my own bed and my children. Before the end of the day I was readmitted to the hospital and back to the operating room because I was hemorrhaging. It was a stupid error on my part and the insurance company refused to pay the bill although I was readmitted on the same day. Needless to say the hospital bill was enormous. We never were able to pay it.

Charles and I separated again months later and I moved in with Diane, his cousin. She and I and my kids got along great and enjoyed an easy lifestyle. We tried to keep stress to a minimum. She was pregnant with Cira and asked me to be her coach for her baby's birth and of course I enthusiastically accepted the challenge. We went to birthing classes together and although her boyfriend Chris was more than willing to be there, to do anything, Diane was independent as all get out. This was her baby, on her terms. That's how she wanted things to go.

Diane never passed any judgement. She loved me dearly and also understood Charles well and loved him with all her heart. She and I had each other's back and shared much laughter and comfort. She lives life on her terms and I admire her fearlessness. We remain close friends right to this day.

When it came time for the baby to come, odd circumstances unfolded. Diane had been in labor for some time and it was clear she was nearly ready to deliver. The nurses moved her into the delivery room, complete with mirror so she could view the birth if she wanted. Then protocol would tell you that they attended to her, checking and monitoring. That's not what happened. They all took a break... together! Yikes. The two of us were alone in this room and her small body was stressing as the baby was ready to come. No nurse in sight, no doctor in sight. I stood by her

The two of us were alone in this room and her small body is stressing as this baby was ready to come. No nurse in sight, no doctor in sight.

head and she gripped my hand like an arm wrestling champ. She wasn't looking in that mirror but I was and I could see dark hair crowning. *Oh my God!* There was a surgical bucket at the foot of the table. *Oh dear, I have to catch the baby or it'll fall in the bucket.* A million thoughts were running through my head as well as joy and fear. I was calling for the nurses but my voice didn't carry to wherever they were. We had done a lot of things together but I didn't like the odds of me and Diane bringing her baby into the world by ourselves while we were in a damn hospital. Suddenly, here the doctor comes running in pulling a surgical gown up over one shoulder. He said something like, "Hey, are we ready to do this?" I don't even remember him telling her to push. He caught the baby. I said, "Are you going to charge full price for that, Johnny Bench?" He knew what I meant and I don't think he was amused, although he smirked. "She's a girl!" What a beautiful baby girl. She was perfect. The staff treated Diane with kid gloves until she was released. I heard that a few heads rolled because of that incident but I never verified.

If I was going to be Godmother to Cira Jalene Monet Sims I would be required to attend classes since I am not Catholic. Diane had been

143

raised Catholic and gone to Catholic schools. Of course she would baptize her baby in the Catholic Church. I was touched, honored and more than happy to go to class and it did give me a better understanding of Catholicism. Diane is Godmother to Alisa so what a perfect covenant we had between us and our beautiful baby girls.

The whole time I lived with Diane I was still seeing Charles. It was more like he was a boyfriend than a husband. The fact that we were separated again was just an unspoken reality. The kids and I still got together with the rest of the family several times a week. I worked for Lipscomb Realty in Monterey and loved the cute little office. Gabby, one of the women in the office, was really cool and I admired her for her independence and style. She had a softness about her that made her approachable and likeable, yet she had a tough business woman side that took no crap!

My boss was another story. At first I wondered if he was schizophrenic. I think he was an alcoholic as well. He could be pleasant and agreeable on any given day, with a sunny persona, and then in minutes he could turn dark, angry, or gloomy. He could also be vulgar although I sincerely doubt if he remembers any of the inappropriate things he said to me or anyone. He had a genuinely nice wife and two adopted children. He had money and a car he liked to race, both at Laguna Seca Raceway as well as on the streets of Monterey. It was kind of a footloose crazy guy kind of thing. That was an interesting job!

CHAPTER 18

Oak Hills

Charles and I decided to move to Oak Hills for yet another new chapter in our life. He reasoned that maybe the next few years would be better than the last. This would be the ideal place for our family to start fresh. It was a beautiful, peaceful community and we leased a spacious four bedroom home with a huge backyard perfect for the kids. The house was only a couple of months old and had never been lived in. I loved it there, enjoying the rolling hills dotted with huge oak trees and green fields planted seasonally with strawberries and other crops. During strawberry season the aroma of berries filled the air and in the early morning fog hung over the fields leaving a crisp mist in the air as the sun rose. It was simply stunning.

I continued working at the real estate office although it was a long drive. One day after my boss came back from lunch inebriated once again and acting vulgar I decided I had had enough. I grabbed my purse and keys and rushed out the door disgusted and mumbling under my breath. I was too nervous and afraid to look back. His loving wife tried to convince me to stay but this wasn't a one off. It was a pattern and I was done.

When we moved to Oak Hills in the late 70s and I was determined to live our life to the full potential I knew was there for us. To accomplish this I did lots of creative budgeting like making casseroles we could eat on for a few days. We'd go to the park and pack a lunch instead of stopping for burgers. I made birthday presents and birthday cakes in special shapes. Sometimes I'd send in just half a bill payment until more money came in.

Our young kids were in grade school and involved in lots of extra activities that involved commuting them around the Peninsula but it was well worth it. With the loss of my income our financial struggles began again. We shouldn't have had any struggles as the janitorial business now had government contracts up and down the California coast thanks to Charles and my mama who worked hand in hand helping Charles write contracts and bids. Unfortunately, the business was complicated and there were a lot of people involved. Lots of money in and lots of money out. The same old story.

There was always the God sent help from Oma and Opa as my children called my parents. They were living back in Sierra Vista and both of them worked on the base at Ft. Huachuca in government positions. They gladly helped pay for music, ballet, and martial arts classes, and when Alisa fell in love with figure skating they helped with that too. Charles Jr. also joined her on the ice for a time. They were so cute. They skated

Alisa and Charles during skating days.

146

separately and they skated as a pair competitively. He quickly grew tired of the fancy costumes and choreography and drew a line in the sand. He wanted to switch from figure skating to hockey or just do Pop Warner football. After he took a nasty spill in a pair of rented hockey skates and I saw the pristine ice stained crimson with a pool of my son's blood, I was more than willing to have him hang up his expensive figure skates and play football.

Keeping Alisa on the ice was costly. It required two pairs of custom boots, fitted with Sheffield steel blades, one for doing figures, and one for skating free style. Oma spent hours sewing competition outfits but there was always the expense of proper skating attire for practice. There were early morning sessions, coaches to pay, and extensive travel expenses. She was a real hot shot on the ice and we kept her skating until she developed a bit of an attitude and her heart wasn't in it one hundred percent. That's when I said, "If you aren't going to give your all, I am not going to sacrifice my all for you to have this bad attitude." She adjusted that attitude and continued to skate for a few more years, doing quite well.

CHAPTER 19

Oh Brother!

When I say *Oh brother* I'm not using it as in *Ah my good-ness,* I mean it literally! Oh, brother! I have a brother. Miracle of miracles for the only child who spent so much time daydreaming about and wishing for a big brother; I actually have one! I was told time and time again that I would never have a big brother. What an unrealistic expectation. Perhaps if I had been wishing for a baby brother my parents could have pulled that off. But I was unreasonably uncompromising in my dream, I wanted a big brother, period.

I was twenty four and we were preparing to move from Skyline Forest to Oak Hills. All was as good as it ever got. My father called to tell me that he had received a phone call from a man who was related to Mama. *That's so cool.* "Who is he, where did he come from, how did he find your phone number?" Questions and more questions raced through my mind. I nearly dropped the phone when he said, "He thinks he is your mother's son."

I nearly dropped the phone when he said, "He thinks he is your mother's son."

Wait a minute; did Daddy just say what I thought he did? My mother's son—as in I have a big brother? Hallelujah!!! Thank you Jesus! My prayers were answered just like that. In a split second of time an impossible dream came true. Don't ever tell me not to believe in miracles.

All the other words floated up into space and I heard only what I needed to sift out of the conversation. Daddy, on the other hand, needed to talk some more. He had never heard my mother mention a son. He was blitzed. Mama wasn't home when the call came. Daddy would wait until she came and talk to her about it all. I hung up the telephone on my end with a great big, *Yessss!* Hours later Daddy called me. There was a lot to say, a lot to wrap my mind around. Like a script from a movie, tragic story to happy ending and everything in between. Where to go from here was another question.

Mama admitted to Daddy that she had had a baby boy. She was traumatized about sharing this news. *Oh my God, can I believe it when I hear his name?* What name did Mama want me to name my son? Andrew! The name I told her absolutely no to. The name I rejected because I wanted to name my son after his father. I would have been naming him after my big brother whom I had never met because I never knew he existed. My head was bobbing like a bobble head doll, spinning like a whirly gig. Ears perked up, I listened to Daddy for more information. There were so many details to process. There were so many missing pieces.

Apparently Mama said she thought her baby was dead. There had been a bombing of the place he resided in after being taken from her. She was told he was gone forever. It never crossed her mind that it could be a lie. She knew he was gone. He was dead because she believed there was no reason to lie. She had seen firsthand what bombs did. The war was awful and unthinkable and impossible to understand. Why would anyone lie to

> *Apparently Mama said she thought her baby was dead...She was told he was gone forever.*

her about her baby? What was to be gained? The answer is clear to me as it became clear to her; it was to protect her precious baby's where-abouts. The goal was to keep her away. She had indeed been kept from him for a lifetime. She told me her last memories of him where so precious and yet so painful. I guess she tucked him safely in her broken heart along with other tragic memories of the war. Now she was opening her heart and talking about something that was silenced in her soul and never allowed to slip past her lips. The revelation was like a tornado. You could only truly understand the gravity of finding out that her Andrew was alive if you heard it from Mama. Her accent became thicker, stronger, and she rode the wave between elation and anger at being robbed of her child.

This is my mama's story to tell us. We wanted and needed to hear it. *How could she have never spoken of it?* She said there was too much pain. It was done, it was over. She told us her baby boy, blond hair and big bright eyes, happy little baby boy, was taken from her. No, snatched from her, stolen from her, ripped away from her. She was robbed of the one and only good reason she had for living before she was placed in a concentration camp. Some would call it a work camp. The papers that I now have in my possession, neatly saved, and tucked away, say that she was in a labor camp.... *Oh my God*, I thought of all the times I rubbed Mama's legs, felt the shrapnel under her smooth skin. I know now that the war had done more than leave her with physical wounds. The wound of losing her child was too much, too deep, too grave for her to even speak about. How many times she must have cried silently. There was a really empty part of her soul that was in so much pain over all of this. Her mother and brother gone, loss of everything. She never had the opportunity to go back to her homeland. At one point she had wanted to return to visit but was told she might not be able to come back to the United States if she did.

Daddy was in shock, but he was always a greatly loving soul. He was looking for clarity and I understood. Daddy said Mama had poured herself a big glass of straight vodka when she got the news.

Of course she did. I would too if I was in her shoes. *Who took the baby, how did he live, how did he find her after all these years?* These were all legitimate questions. Mama said he must be an imposter, someone from the Soviet side of the world, or someone from the Nazi regime looking to do harm to her new life. Once before, years ago when I was a child in Sierra Vista, someone had contacted her using the American Red Cross. They claimed to be her brother whom she knew to be dead. Elated at the possibility of a miracle, she sent gifts, wrote letters, and couldn't spend a day without thinking of how they could reunite. Sadly, it wasn't true. She eventually found out that people in high places do follow your life if you are born in a place like Riga, Latvia, marry in Germany, and come to the U.S. Perhaps she knew things she shouldn't know. Her dream of being with her brother again crumpled into thin air as she learned the truth. Security clearances were not all that easy to come by, but Mama had one and so did Daddy and they both worked for the United States Government. She was intensely upset at the news and feared that their clearances and jobs might be in jeopardy.

She couldn't take the risk that her son wasn't telling the truth, she wanted to see him. She would go alone. They worked out a plan for recognizing each other. He would have a ski parka over his arm, she had a leather hand-tooled pocket book she would carry over her arm. Mama said she needed nothing to make him stand out from the crowd. When she saw his face, she instantly knew it was him. Her Andrew. He was all grown up and so handsome. He grew up to be a good looking man, tall and very European, Her baby did live. He did survive. He looked exactly like her. He knew her and she knew him. I wish I could have been there to witness their reunion, but I think God allowed it to work according to his plan. They needed to have that moment in time privately without

Mama said she needed nothing to make him stand out from the crowd. When she saw his face, she instantly knew it was him.

distraction. I'm so thankful to know this was one of Mama's most *joy*ful moments in life.

How can you recapture a lifetime? Like the saying goes, "You can't put the genie back in the bottle." She would never have the opportunity to guide him, teach him, and comfort him as mothers do with their young children. All of that was gone. All that remained in front of them was a chance to bond. The chance to make the best of a life-time of lost time.

I understood how this had jolted Mama and Daddy. I really did. But my daddy was so loving and understanding. He had no anger about her keeping this to herself, only *joy* that she was now free to talk about it no matter how difficult and *joy* that she had the opportunity to know her son. This would complete her and he wanted her to be complete in every way. That's just the kind of man he was. He wanted to get to know Andrew too. As for me, my parents were telling me to slow down, calm down, let things unfold. I went to bed thanking God for the miracle and woke up thinking I couldn't wait to see Andy as he was called. I learned that he had children. "Oh my God, I am an Auntie!" Then there must be a wife, I had a sister-in-law to top it all off. The most incredible th ing of incredible things that had ever hap-pened to me was unfolding like a flower blooming in spring. I couldn't wait to see what was coming.

I first met Andy when he drove to Sierra Vista with his new fiancée Cindy and some of his children. I learned he was divorced, but I was happy to meet his new love. I would still get to know the mother of my nieces and nephew. I flew down with Alisa and Charles. It's all a blur, I guess sort of like being drunk, having such

Norma-Jean and Andy, long lost brother and sister.

a great time but blacking out or something. I remember flashes. I remember the kids playing on the monkey bars in the local park. His kids and mine. I can see the kids swinging, kicking feet to go higher, laughing, running, and playing chase. Thinking it was the coolest thing ever for them to meet each other. I remember Andy throwing a football nearly the full length of the cul-de-sac to my son. My brother was very athletic. I remember posing for pictures with him, Cindy, and me. I remember gazing at his face thinking he was so dang handsome. I had so many questions floating around up in my head. I couldn't ask them all. I couldn't put words to my thoughts. It was if I were thinking in another language that I understood but couldn't

Lisa, Kelli, Norma-Jean, and Cindy, Sierra Vista, AZ

speak. Like when you hear someone speak in Spanish and you comprehend what they are saying, but you can't answer in anything but English. It was like that for me. I rejoiced in the joy in my mama's face. She had her two kids together and grandchildren from both of us. His children were beautiful. Daddy seemed to be so happy too. I have pictures from that visit, but still have blank spaces in my memories of the day.

After Cindy and Andy were married he was stationed at Fort Ord. Oh my goodness, was God watching over me or what? I had the opportunity to get to know my brother and Cindy better. We spent a lot of time together and I cherish those golden days.

I got to know Andy's ex-wife pretty well too. She filled me in on some of the past years and sent baby pictures of the children to Mama and me. She sent pictures of Andy riding a motorcycle, skiing, and playing with his babies. She sent pictures of him in his military uniform, both his dress blues and fatigues. I was so grateful. Their divorce was extremely contentious, lots of bad blood between those two, but she was gracious with us. I knew not to bring up the past marriage with my brother. When he mentioned Judy it was not endearing. I will say however, that they did have a beautiful family together, it just ended badly.

Andy and Cindy

Mama came to a place where she began to open up to me about the past, Andy's father, life in Riga, life in Austria, life in Germany. The camp, how she got there, how she got out of there. She shared her feelings about the whole sum of her life and finally having her son in her life after all those years. She had been traumatized in the past, that's for certain. Although she had been mistreated and abused, she was a very strong woman with great determination. There was nothing in her that hinted of any love for Andy's father. It was long gone, although she had once loved him very much. She blamed him for having her baby taken away from her and seeing to it that she was encamped. She said she couldn't and wouldn't become affiliated with the party he had joined. The vast political differences between them were like the parting of the sea, her on one side and him on the other, but he had the upper hand.

My brother had spent years in an orphanage. Miraculously, he was taken from there by his own father and brought to the United States. He went to school, graduated, and joined the military. He traveled to Europe while serving in the Army, where he began his search for his mother who he thought may have died in the war. He searched death records and marriage records. Bada Bing, Bada Boom, Alice Erika Tenis married Olden Jackson, U.S. Army. There was the clue!

By this time he had enough rank and pull to go through the necessary channels to locate my father. After all, there were only two Olden Jacksons in the Army. Of course the proper channels can give you name, rank and serial number of one of their own. In this case, name, rank, address, and phone number. So he found his mother after a lifetime.

The story that Mama told me varies from the story that Andy had been told and even the information he said he has. I am positive he loved his father. I am glad he loved his father. For me, if I had ever been able to speak to his father, I would have told him I was robbed of the chance to grow up with my only brother. I am sad about that. I would have asked him how he could love my mother but love the political party more. It just makes me sad to think of him, to know he came to the United States with my brother and lived a nice life.

I would never really have a deep conversation with Andy about any of my thoughts, questions, and anger because it was all water over the dam. No point to it. I had tried a couple of times and he told me that Mama had put him in an orphanage and left him there. He has the papers to prove it. I don't want to see the papers. During the war, papers were required just to move around in society. To go from one place to another you had better have your papers on you. I think many papers were made for many different purposes. I know my brother feels the papers he has are legitimate. But, you know I was raised by a loving and compassionate mother whose only lie she ever told me was one of omission. I truly believe in my soul that she was heartbroken and couldn't talk about her baby being taken and him dying without her comfort. I think she probably wished many times that she had died with him. But he isn't dead

I decided long ago to just accept the blessing, count it as joy and move on. Perhaps one day I will write it in a novel and present it from Mama's side...

and this is a subject that I don't discuss with my brother. There are so many versions of truth, as they say, there is yours, there is mine, and the truth lies somewhere in between. So, I decided long ago to just accept the blessing, count it as joy, and move on. Perhaps one day I will write it in a novel and present it from Mama's side based strictly on the things she told me. No one can dispute what she told me. I can't dispute what anyone else has been told. It's their truth.

My love for my brother has gone through different phases, I suppose like most siblings, albeit a bit late. For a time we were very close and in contact a lot. Over the years we have drifted further from one another, but he remains in my heart the big brother I always wanted and God sent to me. If I ever have a problem I feel I could count on him. If I needed to talk, I know he would listen. If I decided tomorrow that I want to go visit him for a week, he would welcome me. Yep, he is my big brother.

Years ago, Andy gave me a beautiful gold cross with a tiger stone on a gold chain. I wore it often and cherished it as the first gift he ever gave me. It was delicate enough for this super girly girl, but sturdy enough not to break easily. My heart broke when someone stole it from my nightstand. We had a house full of people during one of those parties and I had left it on my nightstand. I can't say carelessly because it was in my own home and I often took it off right before bed. I cried about it then and it still brings tears to my eyes when I think about it. I loved that tangible symbol of my brother's love for me. I imagine someone pawned it. Who would ever wear a stolen cross? Talk about bad karma!

Just writing all of this about my brother makes me miss him more. It makes me think I need to go visit him. I think I will very soon! I love him so much and am thankful for my nieces and nephews. The strange thing about family is the love you feel for the unknown relationship. I am just now at a place in my life to be able to travel and visit and form the bond. Years of financial instability made it impossible before. That's the sad truth. But if you want to do something and there is still life in you and the ability to do it, you should! I have felt some embarrassment about all the years that have passed like water under a bridge with no face to face visits, no holidays, no summer get aways, no packages sent to nephews and nieces with love from Auntie. But I was so often hanging by a thread both physically and financially. This sounds like a barrel of excuses but I'm stating truth and whispering hope in the wind in saying that I am still here and have a family that I would love to know better. So I will. I am planning to make some more memories.

I believe in miracles. I wished and prayed for a brother, a big brother, and I have one. His name is Andrew Tenis. I call him Andy and am so proud of all he has accomplished and all he is. He is ten times smarter than I could hope to be. Just like everyone else I hold dear, he has lifted himself up with a high degree of education, as has his wife Cindy. He had a distinguished military career and retired as an officer, then went on to retire again from a prestigious position in the civilian sector. My brother has settled where he can ski and play golf and is still mentally as sharp as a tack. I think, considering the beginning of his life story, whichever version you choose to go with, he has done exceedingly well for himself and should feel proud. I know Mama was so proud of him although she didn't have the opportunity to raise him, guide him or tell him how much she loved him. I love him, my *big brother.*

Pat, Sister of My Heart

They say God watches over fools and babies. Well, I'm not a baby and I don't like to think of myself as a fool, but the Lord always knows what I need in my life. I needed a new friend.

The U-Haul truck was parked across the street. I knew someone was moving in but I was busy. I'd meet them later and give them a chance to get moved in, then introduce myself. Alisa came bolting through the door. Pulling me by the hand she chattered, "Mommy, Mommy please come! You have to meet them! They are so nice!" Her big brown eyes sparkling with delight always helped her make her case. I laughed, "Oh, okay, okay I will come."

She was right. Pat and Scott looked like they belonged in a Norman Rockwell painting. The perfect couple. I knew the moment I met Pat that she was my friend. It was like a prearranged meeting with someone you've known for a very long time but never met

Pat and Scott Green

158

face to face. It was kind of like meeting a pen pal or a phone buddy for the first time. She became my heart sister and we've shared every life milestone together.

Pat is one of the warmest and bubbliest people I've ever known. Whenever she comes into a room she transforms it. God had sent me a friend who added a spark to my life that had been missing for a long time. Scott was much more reserved but we fell in love with him too. He was a hard worker, gone all day, only to come home and work in the yard, the garage, or some other chore. He was always busy. Our family loved the Greens.

Pat was busy too. She actually had to keep a careful social calendar so she could know where to fit in visits with friends and family. I never had to be fit in, she always had time for me. We spent so many days together and talked and talked and talked about everything under the sun. Family, politics, religion, or sometimes gossip, we talked about it all. We were soul sisters. I can't think of anything we weren't in sync about. Well, maybe this one thing—Pat has rhythm! I have never been a great dancer even back in my school days when my friend Mary tried to teach me the latest dances like the bebop and the jerk. We joked about Pat and her dancing and say she must have some ethnic blood in her somewhere. She is a wonderful dancer. In fact, when she gets out on the dance floor people stand back and watch her!

She is also an accomplished fitness teacher. She owned her own fitness company, Body Focus, and has appeared in fitness videos. She's even been featured in a book, *Body for Life*.

Pat is a beautiful soul. She loves to help others and as a child of deaf adults (CODA) she serves as an

Norma-Jean and Pat "twinning"

interpreter for deaf students at schools, hospitals, churches, wherever she is needed.

People often commented that they thought we were sisters. It is flattering to me because I have always thought she is beautiful. We both have dark curly hair, dark eyes, and olive skin. I suppose that's enough similarity to make people think we are somehow related.

Our children became what I call "interchangeable kids." My kids were at home at her house and her kids were at home in my house. If my kids needed discipline when they were with her and Scott, they got it and the same went for her children when they were in our home. Mostly what the kids got was love and a strong sense of what friendships are made of. Pat's son Brian began calling Charles Sr. "Big Bear" when he was little. And the nickname stuck. We thought it was hilarious because to a small child his big cuddly frame must have seemed like a big teddy bear. Our kids were so cute together.

It is no accident that our paths crossed. Pat would turn out to be an *angel* God placed in my life.

During the summer of 1976 I was preparing and getting last minute things together to go on our annual trip to Los Angeles. This year it had been postponed several

> *It is no accident that our paths crossed. Pat would turn out to be an angel God placed in my life.*

times, in fact some bags had sat packed and ready to go for weeks. I was very excited and anxious by this time and was determined that nothing would stop us. For as long as I can remember Charles and I had taken the kids to LA for a terrific summer vacation. It was another thing we did as a family even if Charles and I were separated.

We always stayed at the Marriott in Culver City for several days. During the years Charles' sister Jackie and her husband Aaron lived there, we would also stay a few days with them in their Spanish bungalow style home. Jackie is a formally trained artist and teacher and displayed much of her colorful artwork in their tastefully decorated home. They joined us on our adventures with their adorable little son Aaron, nicknamed "Boo-Boo."

We usually left on July 5th and would be packed and ready to go the day after the family's annual 4th of July celebration at Balado Park in Hollister. We planned our trip around the days the Dodgers played at home. We would go to the games, eat Dodger dogs, frozen malts, and peanuts, sing with the crowd, and cheer our favorite players on to victory. When we weren't at Dodger Stadium we were at Disneyland.

As I was packing my arm brushed over my breast. I felt something wet. I pulled up my shirt to see where the wetness came from. As I pressed my hand against my breast blood trickled out. I looked closer, thinking perhaps I scratched myself. No scratch. I didn't know what to think, this was strange. I called my doctor and was told to come right in. Pat kept the kids. A thousand thoughts ran through my mind on the drive to see my doctor in Pacific Grove. The doctor looked concerned as he pressed and probed his way around my breast. He examined the other side, discovering that blood was also being excreted from that nipple. He sent me immediately to Carmel Community Hospital for some further testing. Of course we didn't go anywhere that day, nor the next.

When I got the news from my doctor with a prognosis of cancer I was outraged. I acted so out of character, in fact, I flat out acted crazy. "If you think you are going to get money out of me to pay for another year at your cushy country club, you have got the wrong girl! I know how you doctors are. Oh, oh maybe you have in mind to buy another Mercedes Benz. That is your car in the reserved space, right? Oh no, I don't believe a damn thing you are saying and I don't have time for all of this. We were supposed to go to Disneyland two days ago. Instead here I am wasting my time with you!!" "Calm down Norma, I know this is hard to accept but I assure you I am telling you as frankly as I

"Sveetie face za facts, if you don't do something you probably will not see your next birthday."

can what is going on." I stormed out of the office. I didn't want to hear another word out of his mouth. "Damn liar. You can't trust anyone these days."

I don't remember much about the drive home. After steamrolling into the driveway, I called my parents. They convinced me to come to Arizona and the next day I was on an airplane to Tucson. They had set up an immediate consultation for me at the University Hospital. More probing, sticking, and prodding called testing! The results were the same. In a thick German accent, with strong "v's" where a "w" should be, the doctor in charge of this little team looked at me and said, "Sveetie face za facts, if you don't do something you probably will not see your next birthday." Tears flooded my eyes and spilled like water over a dam. How could I have breast cancer? I was so young. This would be my second major surgery in less than a year. I had already had a hysterectomy. Now they were saying I needed a bi-lateral mastectomy. This was not easy for me. I glanced over at my Mama sitting in the corner chair clasping her purse as if someone was going to snatch it from her. She took off her glasses and wiped her tears. I reached out my hand to her. She stood and came to me. Her touch comforted me.

With the hysterectomy I had had no choice but I had my two lovely children and felt I had some compromise by the fact I got to at least keep some part of me called ovaries. But no one could see that loss. When it came to breast surgery I was giving up a visible part of me. I told my parents if I was going to have surgery I wanted to go back home where everything was familiar. They agreed and I flew home but they drove out a few days later. The doctor offered us an option that made me feel so much better about the whole thing. Reconstruction using silicone filled implants. Medical technology is so much more advanced today but back then it was a horrendous ordeal at best. These were possibly first generation implants. Insurance would pay for everything except reconstruction which they deemed as cosmetic. Daddy took out his check book. "Thank you Daddy!"

Charles and I were living together at the time and my parents offered him all the help and support with the house and children he might need. When I came home from the hospital a neighbor came by to visit. She was a Jehovah Witness and as soon as she began telling me why I shouldn't have received the blood transfusions Mama showed her to the door. She was fiercely protective of me.

Several days after I was released from the hospital my parents returned home. I was in pain, I was depressed, my weight dropped, and I looked pale and sickly. I was fearful of being left alone. I could barely take care of myself, let alone my very energetic children. Charles needed to return to work. Pat was the angel God sent. I needed help dressing, bathing, and changing dressings and she pitched right in. She fed my children when Charles was gone. It was August and school was out so they were home all day. She made me I don't know how many cups of tea and offered words of encouragement. "Norma-Jean you are looking so much better today." If I hurt, she seemed to hurt too. If I cried, she cried with me. When we laughed, we both laughed like no tomorrow. How can you thank someone for loving you unconditionally? I wasn't giving, I was taking. I was running on Grace, Mercy, and Faith. She bolstered my faith. I believed I was healed. I believed in a matter of time I would be running around with her and the kids.

Norma-Jean and Pat wearing their breast cancer awareness shirts.

We'd be back at Dennis the Menace Park and going to lunch. Gratefully, I counted on her coming across the street every day. I counted on her to brush my daughter's full head of gravity-defying hair. There is no

163

way to sum up all the little things she did. Fold laundry and have the kids put it away, unload the dishwasher, change the linens. It's too much to list. During this time Pat and I bonded more and more.

Pat was someone I admired and wanted to be more like. Just like everyone loved Charles Sr., everyone loves Pat! I have never met anyone who doesn't fall in love with her. I've always felt undeserving of such wonderful friends and family, a negative side effect of low self-esteem I guess.

On the Jackson family tree I am the only offspring that has not accomplished something great. Victor is a doctor, Robert is a lawyer, Edith was a school teacher, and Billy is a college professor. My closest friends have college educations and successful careers. It always seemed to me like someone was achieving something in life. They are going for it, grabbing the golden ring. Sometimes I would wonder why I have never been a great achiever and I feel sad and disappointed. It makes me feel like there is something I still need to do. I had too much time for reflection over the years. I still reflect, but I have come to accept who I am with less self-loathing. I think that's a good bit of positive progress.

I did heal from the cancer as time went by, regaining my strength. It was a difficult time but love and my faith in God brought me through. My family has always loved me and I owe them a great debt of gratitude. And to my sweet friend Pat who cared for me on a daily basis and also loved me unconditionally, how can I ever begin to say thank you?!

Little did I know that as that crisis ended more hard times were in store for me, but my spunk and spirit were revitalized and I had found happiness in my restored

Norma-Jean and Pat

health. I wasn't perfect, but I had joy. I had my parents, I had Charles, and most of all I had my children who were the center of my life. I had my dear friends Toni and Diane and now I had Pat and her family. This gave me real joy and a sense of contentment. Nothing was going to rock my world in a negative way.

CHAPTER 21

Cheating

We moved twice that next year, just different houses on different streets. Our children were enrolled at Prunedale Christian Academy and this was a very good thing for both of them. Charles was self-confident and proud that he could name all the books of the Bible by memory. Hallelujah! He could recite verses and interpret their meaning. The teachers were strict enough but not so much as to crush his inquisitive spirit. Alisa was able to learn at her own pace and for once she was being encouraged to speak what was on her mind. She tested as an academically gifted child. They were both being taught in love and were well behaved and well mannered. I think the influence of the Christian school also helped with respectfulness. I was thrilled.

Charles Sr. was working hard but earning less. Even though he had many times referred to my mama as a b.... behind her back, which would bring me to tears, when it came to writing contracts and proposals, he turned to her. She kept helping him. This disrespect just broke my heart because I would never in a million years call his mother out of her name. My mama would do anything that she felt benefitted me and the children. In the long run her work benefitted many people as government finance was her field of expertise. Contracts with the U.S. Government could be extremely lucrative.

Charles stayed away from home most of the time and I was lonely. He'd drift in and out, I always felt he was coming home only to see the children. He had no ups or downs when it came to loving them. I would threaten to leave him for good, but I never ever used the kids against him, they were not pawns.

During this time the Sims family, became scattered. Emanuel and LaVerne moved up to the Sacramento area for Emanuel to oversee the government contract at Herlon Military Facility. Fred and Jackie left the Peninsula around that time too. We all seemed to be going in different directions.

When I realized that once more we were going to have to move for money reasons I said "ENOUGH." I called my parents and told them the kids and I would be coming to stay with them. Charles begged and cried and promised to set it all right if only. Yet another plea! To me it was just one more straw on the overloaded camel's back. I had become self-aware enough through the years to realize that I measured my self-worth by how he treated me. When he treated me poorly, I felt unworthy, when he treated me well, I thought I was okay in the universe. I had always wanted to believe in both Charles and the dreams he so eloquently wove for me and our children. Not just for us but for the entire Sims family. As the eldest son he was viewed as the savior of the family and reluctantly played the role as he carried this tremendous weight. I'm exaggerating but I was guilty of believing in him almost as much as I believed in Jesus.

He was like a drug and I was an addict. I couldn't understand myself. Why were the children and I always swallowed up by opium dreams and empty promises that always left me picking up the pieces

> *He was like a drug and I was an addict. I couldn't understand myself...always swallowed up by opium dreams and empty promises.*

of my heart and life trying to put everything back together again? I was tired of the games. I was so damn tired of loving him. I was tired of loving him and him loving everyone else and not being man enough not to make a stand. Right from the day he said he wanted to marry me, he didn't have the guts to stand up to his mother and say, "I asked Norma to marry me." She had to find out second hand. I still get angry when I think back to that. I want to say, "Damn it, Charles, stand up for yourself, and stand up for me IF you really choose me!"

The kids and I lived in Port Orchard, Washington for a little over a year. My parents had both taken jobs at Puget Sound, yet another career advancement for them both, and purchased a beautiful home, so we moved in with them. I was doing better. I didn't plan to go back so I only brought priceless things with me, like photo albums and the kids' most prized toys and possessions. I enrolled in college again. Daddy and I actually took a couple of Black study classes together. I was making A's and working in a local bank. My children seemed to be well adjusted, although they pleaded to go visit their dad. They asked regularly and I promised they could see him soon. It became my standard answer.

With a little help from my daddy I was able to purchase a new car. Charles called nearly every day; he was having a tough time coping with our absence. Friends began to fall away from him and the number of government contracts reduced. I felt terrible hearing all of this. I hadn't stopped loving Charles, I wished I had. I was trying to kick my addiction and codependency and I resented him. I had discovered his involvement with his secretary prior to my move. When I thought of him being with her I hated it. I hated what he was doing and I hated her. I was obsessed about it. What was it she had that I didn't? She was part of the reason I left. I thought, *Our bills aren't paid but you can take her out, I have never ever been to a happy hour.*

Charles came several times to visit; our kids were always our common ground. We had a great time taking them for ferry rides and pizza. After he'd return to California they would have it rough for a few days. On his last visit he convinced me to give it another try. I was hooked again. Like the alcoholic to the bottle or the junkie to the drug. It didn't make sense even to me. But I was going to do it; I was going to go back with him against all odds because I loved him.

We actually had nothing much to go back to except for Charles. He had traded his car in on one for his parents, our house was gone, and the bills were unpaid. We returned anyhow. I had saved money and a brand new car. I paid the bills, we rented a decent house, and we were all together again. Once more I was counting my blessings, looking for *joy*. I was positive I would have it this time.

Within weeks I discovered the secretary was driving my new car! I was furious, but instead of lashing out I swallowed my anger. My children needed stability and I wanted to give it to them even if it killed me. I tried to maintain the façade of a stable and happy environment even as I choked on seething words that I wouldn't verbalize. I just couldn't wreck it for my kids one more time.

> *Within weeks I discovered the secretary was driving my new car!*

I actually found myself babysitting her children while she was at work and keeping them while she escorted my husband to happy hour. Their happy hours were some of my most unhappy hours. I loved her children but felt used. I was out of control. I began drinking wine to help me pass the time. My kids were of the age that they played by themselves and kept busy. No more tending to them minute by minute. However, I watched the clock minute by minute. I felt stupid and crazy, so I poured a glass of wine and stopped watching the clock. I could hear my children begin to talk about me to each other, "Mama is acting crazy," "What is wrong with Mama?" They saw me pour one glass of wine, then another. My son was 12 years old at the time and knew what was going on. He was like a hawk and became very protective of me and Alisa. He was a little man carrying a big weight on his small shoulders. I'm not sure why, but I kind of let him dictate how he wanted things to be. Someone had to be in control and I knew I wasn't capable. I felt as if I was spiraling out of control. I told no one. Not even Pat! I was a secret keeper. I was a liar just like in the early days of my relationship when I started lying to my parents, "Oh yes, everything is fine," "Oh I'm good." Hell no, I was not good! I was coming undone day by day. This little boy, this man-child looked over me. He made it well known to me that he wanted his family to be together and any intruders, like this secretary, had to go! So we tried to work it out by talking about it.

He became so overprotective of me that even when I went to the hairdresser he would hover. My stylist, Clifford, had been Charles' football teammate from high school. Then he went into the military; he jumped out of airplanes and was one tough guy. At some point he had an epiphany. He desired to do hair. He could do hair like nobody's business. My hair always looked great when he styled it but that was as far as my interest went. Clifford began to morph into a different person, becoming more effeminate in his behavior. Believe me, there wasn't anything I had that would interest him. That didn't stop my son from hovering, listening to every word spoken between us while I was at the shampoo bowl. He viewed him as a threat and stood guard, listening to every word spoken while Clifford nipped and primped his mama's hair.

Through those years of trying to be the best everything, the best daughter, the best wife, the best mother, and the best friend, there were also days along the way that I am not proud of.

I have been apologizing to my son forever about a very inappropriate outburst I had during those years. I honestly don't exactly remember his age, but oh do I remember the events of the day. I remember my behavior and I will never forget the look on his face. I was then what would be called today a micromanager. I hovered over my children and insisted certain things be done a certain way. Remember, I am the girl who grew up in a house that I cleaned. All was in disarray unless I created order, all except for the drawers and cupboards which my mother kept neatly in perfect order. No wonder I wanted to have it my way, including perfectly organized dresser drawers and pantry shelves.

On that infamous day I was doing laundry. My son was tasked with putting away his folded laundry. I taught him to neatly put undershirts in one drawer, underwear in another, socks in another, that was the rule. It was a simple task, even for a child. He was hasty about doing this, I suppose he wanted to go outside to play or something. I went into his room to add a few additional pieces. When I opened the top drawer there they were—underwear and socks stuffed haphazardly into the drawer with undershirts. I proceed to open the underwear drawer and the department store picture-perfect piles set a few rows wide had become one big jumble of underwear. "No, no, noooooo, this is not how I have taught you to keep your things." My mind kicked into high gear, zero to one hundred in ten seconds. I yelled for Charles to get in there. I was determined to show him that this was not acceptable under *any* circumstances. The more I talked to him about it the angrier I became. "What is your excuse?" I demanded an answer. He had none. In a fit of rage, I yanked the drawer out and threw its contents on the floor. I did the same with the second drawer and then I did the unspeakable. Full speed ahead I reached crazy! I went full metal jacket on my poor child. I tipped over the dresser. I must have had an adrenaline rush because it was a rather heavy piece of furniture. He was staring at me like a deer in the headlights. Having never seen this kind of behavior from me before his brain was calculating what to do, what to do that wouldn't push me further. My brain was calculating, trying to re-shift, lock and load with love and patience instead of anger.

I crumpled to the floor, exhausted, confused, and ashamed. I don't know why I snapped over something like that.

My mind was going like a siren, "Just get out of here!" I screamed at him. "Go to your grandmother's house before I hurt you." Never, ever

171

had I been so upset with my son. Over his dresser drawers, of all things! Are you kidding me!? He ran out of the house.

I crumpled to the floor, exhausted, confused, and ashamed. I don't know why I snapped over something like that. Not true, I do know why I snapped. I snapped because of one word, pressure. Pressure to keep it all together while time after time after time things spun out of control. Pressure to not do anything to set Charles Sr. off. Pressure to at least have order in one thing, even if it was just neatly folded stacks of clothes in a dresser drawer. Pressure to at least keep all my soup cans in the pantry lined up perfectly. These were all things I knew I could control on a daily basis and I did. Up until then.

During one of our months-long separations, I met someone. How could I allow this to happen after being on the receiving end of Charles' shenanigans? I'm not proud of it, but it's a part of my story. I actually had a restraining order against Charles, which was violated every time he came to see the children, but I was fearful of him after an afternoon of physical abuse at his hands.

I was working at John Gardner's Tennis Ranch in Carmel Valley. It was beautiful and I loved working there. When people come to play tennis they are happy, not rude, angry, or uptight. So there I was, working at this wonderful job minding my own business. I was happy to be on self-sufficient street once more.

He had a membership at the ranch and came in to play tennis on a sunny afternoon. He was as cheerful as the sun outside, I could see kindness in his eyes and his smile was contagious. He was not trying to flirt, he was just engaging. He was an officer stationed at the Defense Language Institute, or DLI as the locals called it. Ironically, my husband drove a corvette and so did he, the same year, different color. He was unmarried and successful..

I was married but separated. He asked me out several times, but I declined. Then, one day he asked again and I accepted. Just dinner, nothing more, is what I agreed to. The kids were at Auntie's house and he met me on time with flowers in hand. We went to eat and lingered over dinner with casual conversation and scrumptious dessert. He was very sweet and I learned a lot about him. I liked him, but nothing could compare to what I felt for Charles. He, as it turned out, had quite a crush on me. I couldn't understand what his attraction was. I didn't feel pretty, I didn't feel smart, and my personal life had been a hot mess for years. Not one month, or two, or six months, but *years*. I continued to see him every time he came to play tennis. He would linger in the pro-shop talking with me. *Flirting with me.* We had several more dates which I always kept discreet. I didn't know what I was doing, where I was going with my personal life.

One day he told me he wanted it all. He expressed that he wanted me, my kids, and my life to join with his. He wanted to take me away from all of the stress and the drama and make a new life together. How sweet is that? It had me running scared. I talked to Paul, my friend and confidant, and the one male who always had my back, other than my daddy. Paul was always there with sage advice, steady as a rock. I talked until I knew what I had to do. The answer became crystal clear; there was no way I could continue seeing him under any circumstances. It would be awkward at work, but I could do it. On a personal level it was unfair to him. I was starting something before a proper ending. Either divorce and move on, or work things out with Charles. I didn't know what to do about my marriage but I knew I couldn't give someone false hope. He had never met my children and I wouldn't have let him near them unless I knew for certain that I had moved on and he was *the one*. I had been too hurt by Charles and his involvement with other women. I knew I couldn't be the hypocrite. So just like that I put an end to it, happy that I had never climbed into his bed. He was hurt and I was sorry for that, but it would have been much worse if it had gone any further.

꩜

On the note of "happy hour," one day I decided to host my own while I was in charge of my children and yes, you guessed it, the secretary's children as well. While the four kids played, I walked across the street since my husband and she had my car, and purchased the largest bottle of wine I could find in the neighborhood convenience store. I went home, did my makeup, did my hair, got dressed up, and sat in my bent cane rocker to enjoy my wine in solitude. One glass after another I drank it down, trying to come to terms in my mind with why I was always left behind. *Was it my appearance? Was it my personality?* The more I thought about it, the less "happy" I felt. The kids came into the living room every few minutes with questions. "What are you doing?" "Why are you dressed up?" Charles Jr. zoomed right in on my emotions and placed a comforting hand on my shoulder. "I'll watch everyone Mama, don't be sad."

> *On the note of "Happy Hour," one day I decided to host my own...I walked across the street since my husband and she had my car, and purchased the largest bottle of wine I could find...*

By the time Charles Sr. walked in the door I was toast. He was angry! "Oh, you want to drink by yourself, let me help you!" He poured more wine in the glass and forced it to my lips. "Drink this if you think you're grown." "Damn it," I said, "I am grown and I can do as I want!"

He then made the brilliant decision that we should all go get pizza. Pizza! Oh my God I wasn't ready for food, but he insisted. So off we all went, girlfriend included, to the pizza parlor. One whiff of the cheese and I was in the ladies room hurling up the cheap sangria wine I had so carefully sipped for the last few hours. Oh well, revenge

174

is bittersweet. As I realized I had made a bit of a mess in the very clean restroom, it also dawned on me that my husband would be entering this building far before opening hours and *he* would be cleaning the restroom since this was one of his contracts. Touché!

I wish I could say as I'm writing this that happy hours ended, or that I was invited to start coming. That never really was the case. It was something that would become an important part of Charles' lifestyle and remain so, no matter where we lived, no matter for whom he worked, no matter what he drove, no matter whether we were together or apart. He was going to happy hour!

CHAPTER 22

Goodbye California

L ife on the Monterey Peninsula should have been great. It is, after all, one of the most beautiful places in the world.

One day I sat on a huge rock overlooking the ocean, watching the waves breaking fiercely upon the shore. I was close enough that the spray was blowing sea water mist in my face, my hair was damp and I no doubt looked wild. I knew I should back up because I don't swim and a huge wave could knock me off into the water. For a split second I thought about just walking right into the surf and letting it sweep me away. Just a split second. I loved my children too much to leave them motherless. I felt so empty and yet so full up to the top with everything. Nothing had gone the way I had imagined my life to be. Constant stress, constant worry, feeling unloved and unworthy of anything better was just a part of daily life. *How could that possibly be* I wondered?

I had reached the point of not wanting yet another separation from Charles. I didn't want to listen to any more of his stupid pleas with me to believe him, or trust him, or continue loving him. Every time I went through that I gave up a little bit more of myself and I gave away another piece of my kids' peace of mind and stability. I know I put my kids through all of that to try to bubblegum my failing marriage together. I finally concluded that I was the only one who could really be strong enough to give them what they needed. I didn't know exactly how I would do it, but I had no question that it was my duty. I had them; I had to take care of them. I wouldn't walk myself into the sea; I wouldn't give in to being a doormat. I could and would show them I had *always* been fighting for them and I would continue. Over my dead body would anyone other than me be raising my kids! I turned away from the sea, and got back in the car and headed home with a new resolve riding shotgun.

My kids were at Pat's house and she looked at me questioningly when I got there. I didn't say anything, not even to her, my dear friend, about what was on my mind. I was going to tell Charles, "I want out. I can't do this anymore, I won't be this person anymore!"

Two days went by before I saw him again. Casually walking in like he had only been gone for a couple of hours. He as usual began making small talk, kissing, and hugging the children, looking around to make sure everything was in order. That was his M.O. He even used to pull white glove inspections as if he was in the military. Gee whiz. I remember that day as clearly as I can see through crystal. I was seething. This was just what had driven me to this point. He had no accountability. Zero! *How dare him. The nerve of him!* Of course I didn't say anything. I didn't want to start anything in front of the kids, I could wait. I did wait.

Late that night, kids in bed, three glasses of wine down, Charles sweet talking me, I decided to tell him how I felt. Just as I had rehearsed in my head, I spilled it all out, randomly stopping to make sure he was hearing me. "Are you getting this, do you understand what I am saying?" He looked like a deer in the headlights. I thought, *I must be drunk*, his expression was confusing me. He said nothing in return. He had tears streaming down his face, he wiped them away with the back of his hand and got up and left the room. He went straight to bed. No shower, no words, nothing, he just went to bed. I stayed up and finished off the bottle of wine. It was a big bottle. I always purchased the big bottle so it would last. On this night there was nothing left to put back in the refrigerator for another day. I didn't care and I sure as hell wasn't going to go in our room and get between the sheets with him. Not after the way he blew me off. I slept on the sofa.

Charles left the house before the sun was up. That was not unusual. When he worked, he worked hard and didn't pay much attention to clocks. In fact he never paid much attention to time. He ran perpetually late. I was upset that he had ignored giving me a response. *Oh well, so it goes.* I need to figure it out, decide what my plan was going to be.

Later that day he came home so excited and happy. *What in the world?* I couldn't believe him. I was so disappointed that he hadn't taken me seriously. I wanted to be taken seriously and it seemed like no one ever did. A little later he said he had some great news to share with me. I really wasn't interested, but agreed to listen. I had done nothing but listen for years, what would one more day hurt. He said the Peninsula had brought us nothing but bad luck and we should move away. "We tried that! Remember Reno?" "How about Arizona, near your parents?" "My parents lived two blocks away from us in Sparks and look how that ended." He just continued rambling on.... "Here is the best news; I talked to Mrs. Farrar today. I told her we had never been on a true family vacation and I'd like to take you and the kids back east. She is going to pay for our trip!" *Really, I mean really?*

You see, Mrs. Farrar was a very, very wealthy woman who owned a house down the coast. It was a beautiful, unusual house built on rocks right by the ocean; built to withstand waves crashing against it. Her home had once been featured in *Look* magazine. She was kind and generous and for years the Sims family had tended to and cleaned her home. Washing her massive windows and cleaning her floors, oven, and bathrooms were all part of it. Her house required muscle to keep it up to its original beauty. The sea spray can be hard on windows, but their cleaning team made hers sparkle. She was so kind she would fix lunch for the crew and sit down with them.

Charles had taken trips up and down the California coast on her behalf to buy a German Shepherd. She had one that was spooked by the sound of the waves. The shepherd was her preferred dog if he had the right demeanor. She and Charles had planned his hunt and he found the perfect dog for her. Regarding the trip, she was very sweet and had known the Sims family for many years. I wasn't surprised that she would do this for him; she loved him, just like everyone did. I was surprised that he would ask her.

Well, within a month all of our belongings were in storage in readiness for the move and we were on our first family flight ever headed to Washington D.C.. Our children were so happy to be going and I was too, with one small detail that could have been different. Remember the secretary who went to happy hour while I was home babysitting her children and mine? We weren't going to stay a week in a hotel; we were going to stay with her and her kids. They had moved to Maryland a few months earlier. Charles assured me the affair was over. I was so happy to see those kids. My kids were so happy to see them. She was friendly, welcoming, and a perfect hostess. Her home was nice and the summer weather was beautiful. I pushed everything out of my mind. We took all the kids to the White House and to the Smithsonian. We went to an amusement park for a day. We barbequed in the evening. It was a great time. I trusted their affair was over.

Charles and I rented a car and drove to New Jersey to see my beloved Grandma. It was the first time as an adult that I had been able to see her. She held and kissed my babies and told them all about me as a little girl. It was a trip of a lifetime. I couldn't have been hap-

She held and kissed my babies and told them all about me as a little girl. It was a trip of a lifetime.

pier or more grateful. The only trips we had taken as a family were to Los Angeles so this was totally fantastic!

We flew home to pick up the car and head to Arizona. It was the last time our family of four would ever board a plane together. Fresh start, one more time, here we come.

Saying good-bye to everyone on the Peninsula was hard but most of all I cried like a baby saying good-bye to my ride or die bestie, Pat. We had become so used to being together constantly and sharing everything. We hugged and kissed and wiped each other's tears, promising to keep in touch. Whew! It was a tough goodbye.

During the first year, we initially stayed with my parents for a very short time in Sierra Vista. Then we stayed with Toni, her husband Karl, and their daughter Dena in Tucson. We lived in an apartment for a few months; our nephew Michael lived with us and attended high school. We both secured jobs, then moved to a gorgeous house complete with a swimming pool. We had truly arrived in Arizona. Everything seemed to be going good until the company Charles had been doing some work for reneged on paying him. It was devastating. He didn't like Tucson despite the kids being in school and our son playing baseball.

Alisa, first day of school, AZ

It all changed with a trip to Tempe. We took one look at the mural painted on the side of the Marcos de Niza high school building, the grounds and the neighborhood and said, "This is where we want Charles to go to high school." We moved to Tempe and Michael moved back to California.

While we were moving in I lifted a box simply marked in Charles' handwriting *Bedroom, Personal.* I wasn't at all curious. I figured it was old papers from the janitorial business or something. I intended to put it on the top shelf in our bedroom closet. As I tried to hurl the box up, it fell open and all its contents scattered over the floor.

I recognized the handwriting. I had seen it on pink telephone message sheets a thousand times.

Envelopes, lots, and lots of envelopes in all shades of paper. They were not bills or business correspondence. Nope, but I recognized the handwriting. I had seen it on pink telephone message sheets a thousand times. Time: 10 am, Name: Mr. Smith, Message: Please call as soon as possible. That kind of message pad. The writing on these assorted envelopes was in the same handwriting that had filled out all those message pads.

I sat on the floor and gathered a few in my lap. My heart beating so fast and hard I thought I would die, I opened one. The words on it stood out like neon lights in Vegas. I read fast, always have, but I was trying to read slowly. I could see what the next sentence said but I sure didn't want to. I should have just closed it up, put it away, and thrown the box of letters in the trash can. Slam it shut and get on with my life. But you see there is something very daunting about a letter addressed to your husband at his old office that says, " Hello Baby," "Baby I miss you so much," "Baby I'm horny thinking of you," "I lay in bed and remember the things we did," "Every day I want to be with you," "Nothing has changed our love." You see, when you read things like that, you go into shock, especially when you were fool enough to think it was long over and fool enough to forgive both parties and fool enough to actually think that the woman who was writing this mess to your husband wanted your friendship and regretted ever hurting you.

When a person goes into shock it is not unusual for the body to tremble, it's not unusual for tears not to fall. I was there. No tears, just trembling hands and weak knees. Curiosity urged me to open another, and another, and another. Each letter said pretty much some-thing along the same lines, "I love hearing your voice," "I loved talking

181

to you." I kept reading. They say if you look for trouble you will find it. I was simply trying to put a box away and trouble still found me. It's true, I didn't have to open and read even one of the many letters, but I did. "Are you sure Norma doesn't suspect anything?" "I hate the idea of you being with her!" There were hundreds of letters in that box. I only read a few. I imagine if I read more, I would have pulled into my shell like a turtle. I know to this day that if I had read more I probably wouldn't have been able to handle it. I knew when to stop. I had to stop. My sanity was at stake, it was far too much to wrap my mind around. So I didn't. I confronted him with the box held out. I wanted to hear what story he would concoct.

He responded with outrage. What was I doing looking at his f---ing letters? They were none of my business! Who the hell did I think I was? If he'd have wanted me to see them, he would have given them to me. Hell yeah, he saved them because they are precious. I have no idea what she is really like he said. "She is the only person who has ever really loved me." *Oh my God, Oh my God,* I still had no tears. I had rage. I guessed that since I had read his precious letters, discovered his secret treasure box, that now he would get physically violent with me. I figured his days of doing that to me were going to be short lived because every day our son was getting taller and stronger.

In my rage, heart beating, legs weak, I stood there and double dared him with an ice cold stare to hit me.

I couldn't take too much of a beat down on his watch. Charles Jr. was always watching me, eyeing the situation, monitoring what went on with me. He had been doing that since he was small, but now that he was ready for high school, he would intervene if he thought I was going to be hurt. That would be ugly. I would never want that, to put my son against his father. I wouldn't be able to handle it. I still didn't cry, not even at the thought of that. Maybe I was cried out. I don't know. In my rage, heart beating, legs weak, I stood there and double dared him with an ice cold stare to hit me. I didn't say it in words. He knew what I meant. *You are such a liar,* I was thinking. *I think I hate you or I wish I could hate you. I am hollow. There is nothing left of me to empty out for you.* I wished he would just pack up his stuff and go to her. I would never speak to her again as long as I lived. That much I knew. That much is still true. She is dead to me.

What he did next was surreal. He took his precious box filled with declarations of undying love, lust, and betrayal, put it in the car, and drove away. That house was settled by me and my kids and when he returned a couple days later he acted like nothing had ever happened. Not wanting to cause turmoil for the kids, I kept silent about it all until they were not around. Apparently, he expected great things from me since he had given up his life to be with me and our kids! Good golly. Well, I wouldn't want anyone to sacrifice the ultimate for me and then let them down. I mean honestly. How the hell can you tell your wife that you could have had a great life with some conniving cheating hussy, but you gave it all up for her and the kids?! I went sullen for months.

I don't think my kids noticed too much. Before school started I sent them to stay with my parents in yet another new city. Daddy had taken another position in Upland, California, he just kept moving up the ladder. I was struggling financially as usual and a break in the grocery budget would be a good thing. I would make large pans of baked tuna casserole and that's what we ate for a week. The next week I might make a huge pot of spaghetti. It would be good for them to not see their mom upset and unusually quiet. This way I wouldn't have to cover it up or explain and my parents could buy as many groceries as needed to keep them well fed.

When it was time for the kids to come home, I lied to my parents. They had done more than enough. I know they would have gladly bought school clothes, but I said I had the money to shop. I did not. Their father did not. We had a big garage sale. We went to the swap meet and sold things. My kids would not be going back to school without at least the basics; new shoes, underwear and socks, and a couple of outfits. They would also need school supplies. They did get what they needed even if our house was minus needed items.

There was a code of silence between Charles and I about the box of letters and how heart felt they were to him. I never wanted to speak on it and I didn't. I also never wanted to hear him say her name again. I could never live up to the expectations he had of me to make his life wonderful. I just knew that I would never be like her. I could never be like her! I also knew that I

I wish I could tell you things got better as time went by. In so many ways life was good. I had so much to thank God for every day.

would never be like so many of the women he had been with. He had a type and I wasn't it. Blonde, blue eyed, wild, working girls, happy hour attending, un-shy, brazen in many ways, and most definitely not "church girls." In other words he liked the ones you don't take home to Mama. I, on the other hand was the façade, the one he took home to Mama and the one he could point to and say, "That's my wife and those are my beautiful children."

I wish I could tell you things got better as time went by. In so many ways life was good. I had so much to thank God for every day. Charles eventually was hired as an assistant coach at our son's high school and greatly enjoyed working with the kids. Just like it was anywhere he went, everybody loved him. I was proud of him for giving his best. He had the creds for the job. He knew kids and he definitely knew football. He poured himself into those young men; the parents loved him for it and the kids loved him even more. I looked forward to our Friday nights—games, booster club and pizza at Minetti's with the gang after the games were over. We were all together. My little family. I loved that part of our life together; it felt like we all fit together like pieces of a puzzle.

We'd often go out to eat with the football team and our kids. As long as we had money, treating Charles and Alisa to an evening out was no problem. It was a joy. Charles was fun for our kids. He was the dad who took a car full of teenage girls to Circle-K late at night and let everyone buy bags full of snacks. He was the dad our son's friends could relate to. Cool, hip, in with them. He was awesome. He still had rules; don't disrespect the curfew, keep things clean, stay out of his way when he was in a bad mood.

Our life seemed to flow much like a long river, taking bends and slowing down in areas long enough to create still waters, but then just when it seemed so peaceful, it would crash over some unseen waterfall onto jagged rocks. Always the unexpected was to be expected.

We had it all, by outward appearances. Charles was large in stature with the biggest charismatic smile. Women always said he was like a big teddy bear, hugging him all the while. He felt compassion for the poor and homeless; we often made sack lunches with our kids and drove under the bridges to pass them out. He was diligent about providing anything his parents wanted or needed. He was the proud father and son. He was always generous and taught our kids about tithing, although he seldom was able. He read his Bible all the time. He was a true contradiction in personality.

One day, many years ago, I told his mother about an epiphany I'd had. It's strange, I know. I was removing a large load of clothes from the dryer. They felt so warm and comforting. I wanted to continue holding them close in my arms, cradled to my chest and tucked up under my chin. For that moment I was transformed to a peaceful place, so warm, soft, cushy. I didn't want to put them down. I began to fold them one by one, making neatly organized piles that brought me a sense of calm even if it was fleeting. I knew that there would be more towels to wash and take straight out of the dryer with dirt and stains gone. I would have another opportunity to embrace their warm comfort. I thought, *How silly it must sound to talk about warm clean towels right of the dryer, as if that could relate to anyone's life but mine. Surely someone must grab the towels and want to cry. Someone must hold them close for comfort.* I tried it with my kids. Urging them to think of the warmth and how good it felt to hold something tangible in their hands, fold those towels and complete one small organizing task. I had gotten to the point where the linen closet didn't have to look like something from *Better Homes and Gardens. Keep the pile neat kids, that's all I ask.*

CHAPTER 23

Contradictory Life

T he number of abused women in the United States is esti-
mated to be one in three. How very pathetic. I could count,
one, two, three, that's me. My husband, who had vowed to
love me, cherish me, and honor me was quick to contradict those
vows. An old song by The Stylistics, who crooned about breaking up
to make up was so applicable to our relationship. First you love me,
then you hate.

The ongoing abuse continued, usually occurring in our home,
often in front of our kids. I was deeply committed to making things
work, especially given the number of years I had invested in our marriage. I was the eternal optimist and I couldn't walk away. Each time
I was slapped, screamed at, or punched, I thought it would be the
last time. I didn't want to destroy the lives of our children and the
relationships I had with the Sims family by leaving. I truly loved them
so much. It's unexplainable. Who can explain love? The heart does
what it wants, but as we mature we should discern between good and
healthy and dysfunctional. I worried that my relationships with all the
other people I loved would be ended somehow too.

We were living a life of contradiction. Webster defines this as "inconsistency, the act of contradicting, discrepancy, something that contains contradicting elements." It also defines the conflict between two forces of an idea. My life was full of contradicting elements and ideas.

Charles and I did certainly have conflicting ideas although we agreed on much. I believe the forces were Satan taking advantage of the contradictions in our convictions. Cartoons illustrate this with an angel on one shoulder and the devil on the other. One urging you to do right and the other telling you to do wrong,

I have concluded that very good people often do things that are hurtful to the others. Good people often do things that surprise us, catch us off guard because we are taught to see things in black and white, good or bad, with an invisible line down the middle. The truth is the lines are blurred. We all cross over from one thing to the other, contradicting ourselves and our own convictions at times. Some just take things to the extreme either because of lack of coping skills, personality disorders, undiagnosed mental illness, and many factors in between. We are all capable of destructive behavior that usually goes unnoticed by the world but is most felt by those we promise to love. We do not commit to those outside our family circle in the same way we commit to our family and especially to our spouse. With marriage we take a vow, we make a covenant, and yet this journey of two lives headed in one direction often becomes anything but divine bliss.

One, two, me. Why couldn't I have what numbers one and two have? I felt ashamed and unworthy. I began to blame myself for the lack of control over my life. The more I felt I had failed, the deeper my conviction to keep forging ahead.

> *I felt ashamed and unworthy. I began to blame myself for the lack of control over my life. The more I felt I had failed, the deeper my conviction to keep forging ahead.*

I believed that just around the bend we would be fine, sailing along in tranquil waters. I was not realistic; I was the everlasting hopeless romantic. One day our day would come....

Every time I'd think about throwing it all up in the air, unable to take one step further, Charles would surprise me with a random act of kindness and love. It always included generosity, affection, and conversation about the future. It was like he had intuition that perhaps I was in a bad place. He'd fix it. Time and again, he'd fix it. I always went back to hopeful belief in our marriage and most of all our family. I thought he loved me by his efforts not to walk away and to try harder to keep the bond between us. So when he tried harder, so did I.

I could forgive and I would ask forgiveness too for anything I had done. But often I was dumfounded, unsure what I was asking to be forgiven for. Charles would often accuse me of motives and actions that were far removed from reality. I definitely never wanted to hurt him.

In my maturity I can look back and see the contradiction clearly. In my youth I looked through those famous rose colored lenses and my perception was skewed. I passed my tinted lenses on to my daughter, I know she's never felt like she is worthy of holding out for the love she deserves. She never has been willing to wait for things to gradually unfold and give her the love she is worthy of. I catapulted her to search for love and approval in all the wrong places. It's been a heartbreaking reality for me. Our story is one of dysfunctional families and how the dysfunction transfers from one generation to the next. The cycle must be intentionally broken but that part is hard work.

I think every relationship has contradictions; the question remains how you handle life in those times. In our marriage, our family life, the contradictions came in ways not clearly visible to others. As I look back, I think this started early in our relationship. The double standard was probably the first thing I noticed. Anything Charles wanted to buy, anyplace he wanted to go, he did; for me it was a different story. The double standard also applied to verbal expression of opinions. His opinion counted, mine did not. He ordered me to shut up and I did.

When it came to possessions, I have never been materialistic. From the time I met Charles, I loved his generosity. He gave me lovely gifts chosen with thought and care. When I did shop I usually had to return the merchandise because my choices didn't meet his approval. He said it was the wrong size, wrong color, just wrong. It was just easier to wear the clothes Mama sewed for me or that he purchased for me.

He bought beautiful, expensive cars. Over the years he had cars that at times we could afford, no doubt, no problem; other times we struggled to keep up bills and pay car notes. Some of the expensive foreign cars cost so much to maintain. But having something so nice made him happy and proud. He always had the identifying key ring to place upon the bar; it helped start small talk with women, "Oh, you a have a Porsche, oh you have a Benz, oh you have a Beamer." "Yeah, I like cars." I was never allowed behind the steering wheel

…having something so nice made him happy and proud. He always had the identifying key ring to place upon the bar; it helped start small talk with women…

of those cars, they were strictly his. I drove a Pinto station wagon, a Sentra or some similar "mom car." I was satisfied and always kept my car clean. I should clarify, my son kept it clean as soon as he was old enough. and washed it weekly. My transportation needs involved taking the kids from here to there, running errands, or going to work. I was fine and didn't complain. But I did think right from the beginning I should have had access to driving one of the pretty cars, if only every now and then. But I, like many young women, didn't speak up and say what was on my mind.

A huge part of living a contradicted life is keeping things from the ones you love the most and those who love you in return. When you live in abuse, whether mental, verbal, or physical, you begin to ask yourself "Why?" "Why am I not enough?" "What does the other person have that I don't?" You say to yourself a hundred times that you are done. But then you have been in it for so long, you don't really know how to get out. Is it even possible to get out? You know from experience that a few bad days usually turn for the better. You think you can overlook once again and forgive, but the pain and hurt keep popping up in your mind, always lurking just around the next bend. Most of all, abuse is a contradiction before God. But He sees all, knows all.

So how do you get through a life of contradictions? I don't think it can be balanced. My life was difficult and stressful, at best. The scales would one day tip and the balance would either become good or bad. Not sixty-forty or thirty-seventy, I was betting on 99.9 percent good, happy, and stable. I prayed a lot and God gave me enough strength for the next thing in front of me. I always remember the lesson Mama taught me—note to my young self, God always knows what's best. I longed for Him to show me the right thing to do and what was best for my children. And He did, He gave me strength in the middle of that abuse. He helped me to persevere, choosing to love even when the easy thing to do would be to act mean. I've asked God to not let my heart be hardened. And He has done that. I believe one of the most important things in life is to be intentionally loving. When we live intentionally, we intentionally love those people God puts in our lives.

In the decade of the 80s things were, incredibly, much better. I thought so anyhow, I guess I wanted to believe things were better so I ignored what was right in front of me.

Back then cell phones were cumbersome electronic bricks. Charles had one and began spending a great deal of time with it pressed to his ear, even at home. I can remember him sitting in the car in the garage talking on the phone. Whenever I opened the door to ask if he was coming in soon, he'd gesture with one finger pointed toward the sky meaning "give me a minute." Before I was out of ear shot his conversation and laughter would resume.

I wondered who he was talking with and what he was so happy about. I didn't ask. I'd figure it out in time. Maybe this was part of his midlife crisis. After all, everything was different. Maybe he was having difficulty accepting that.

With mounting financial troubles *again* and obvious secrets being kept, I felt betrayed and resentful. Although *God help me* was my creed, it seemed like life was never going to level out.

I was hopeful and excited when we planned a much needed date night. Typically, we went out for dinner a couple of times a month but had not recently. Although I love cooking and being in the kitchen, eating out is a relaxing and enjoyable treat. We decided on one of our favorite restaurants near our home and I was looking forward to a nice evening together.

I dressed up; I did my hair and makeup, I felt so happy. I felt good. As we walked from the car to the restaurant we did not hold hands, we didn't talk. As we waited for the hostess to seat us I tried to strike up a conversation, but my words drifted and fell somewhere into thin air. He didn't look at me. I don't think he was aware of the effort I had made to look my best for our date. I don't think he noticed I was wearing his favorite of my dresses, One he had bought for me. We sat across from each other silently looking over the menu. The silence was broken only when the waitress took our order. She brought our drinks to the table and set them carefully on the paper coasters in front of us. Charles gulped his Jack Daniels and Coke and began running his finger along the rim of the glass staring at the ice cubes. I reached across the table to touch his hand and he pulled it away and rested it on his leg under the table.

I had felt this before…I tried to sell myself on the notion that this was somehow new, but I couldn't. I knew this was a pain I had experienced too many times in our history. In the past, I had filled the emotional void with my children. I tried to at least, children can't really fill the space in your heart that belongs to your spouse and vice versa. I had always made the best of it, until I couldn't. I gave my children more love, more attention, and told myself everything would be all right. This time was different. My children were growing up and didn't need me like they used to. The last thing they wanted was more Mama.

As usual, I figured it all out but kept it to myself and just kept taking care of my children. He was having an affair again. There were people in my life circle that I could openly share pain with but I knew they were sick and tired of hearing it year after year. Scenario after scenario was on repeat and I'm sure those around me were tired of it. They never said so, they were always loving, always supportive, but I thought to myself that they were weary of me and all this crap. They probably viewed it as you would a horse with a broken leg. It can't be repaired, its pain is not going to be eased by anything, so just take a gun, and put it out of its misery! It's the kindest thing to do. Why hadn't I done this with my broken marriage years ago? Why hadn't I mustered up enough courage to put it all to an end? I just don't have the words. I loved Charles that much that I kept trying to hang on.

I had always made the best of it, until I couldn't. I gave my children more love, more attention and told myself everything would be all right. This time was different.

Why do people rebuild a house in the same spot after a tornado destroys everything they owned, knowing there is a strong chance it's going to happen again? Why do people choose to live in a flood zone knowing they could be wiped out any day? This was the land their father owned, how could they bring themselves to move on? Why does someone choose to forgive the person who killed their child while driving drunk? What makes a person pick up a bottle after years of sobriety? There are so many variables to this life we live and we are such contradictory people.

I just struggle to find balance. I want to live an intentional life. A life that at the end my family will know more than anything that it was about love. So out of love for the people who have treated me best and been there for me the most, I just let that one ride. I just wanted to focus on getting my kids through school.

CHAPTER 24

Forgive Me Father

Alisa was at her friend Valerie's for the weekend. They were still doing the teenybopper things that teenage girls do. I wanted her to have fun. They were hanging out, listening to music, eating junk food, and talking about things that wouldn't matter next month or next year. I was relieved to have her gone. I had reached bottom. I had nothing more in me. Why at this time, on this day? Oh, I suppose it was a collision of events. I had given so much. I had been through hell and back. It felt like I had made the trip a million times and now I felt exhausted. I reflected on opportunities I passed up that I should have chosen, not for myself, but for my kids. I had failed them more than I had failed myself and that was an unbearable thought. Charles was in the Marines now and I still felt like I had failed him in a million ways.

It was a beautiful Friday afternoon. When I got home I was met at the bottom of my stairwell by two neighbors. These two young men knew my son and my husband. "Hey Mrs. Sims. How's it going today? How's Chuck doing?" I tell them he's okay and I miss him so much, but I'm sure he's going to do great. They go on to tell me more. One says, "You know that woman Chuck's dad is seeing? You are so much prettier than she is. She is kind of a skank. I see them together in Houlihan's all the time. I don't know what he sees in her. Man, I'm telling you, if you came in there you'd have a lot of play." I laugh and say, "Thank you." It was like a knife through my heart. "You guys take care." Then I take myself upstairs to the sanctuary of my apartment. I didn't want a lot of play.

Half an hour previously I had met Charles to give him two hundred dollars in cash he'd asked to borrow. It was my payday. I didn't ask what he wanted it for. I agreed to meet him near his apartment at the corner of 40th St. and Baseline. His Mercedes was just washed, which was no big deal in my mind because he always kept a clean car. Hanging in the back seat was dry cleaning he just picked up, which I also had thought nothing of. Now I was piecing it all together.

I sat at my table for a few minutes mulling it over and then I tried to call Charles. I wanted to ask him what he wanted the money for. No answer. A few more minutes passed and I remembered seeing a number for Kim on something. I have no idea why but I did have her number. With my heart pounding and hands shaking I dialed it. "Hi, this is Kim. Sorry I can't take your call. If you reached this recording I'm at the Red Roof Inn in Flagstaff with my Lover Boy for the weekend. Please don't call me unless it's an emergency. Bye." Her Loverboy! Who the hell calls someone their "lover boy?" Now I knew where he was and who he was with. Most of all I knew why he had borrowed money from me. I was hurt, angry, and sad. I was disgusted with myself. I was such an idiot. I would do anything for him. I would not stoop so low as to call the hotel.

People told me I was pretty. *What a pack of lies. I am not pretty. I am not smart. I am not capable of keeping a life worthy of living intact.* At that moment every thread in my body was unwinding from my

I wanted to pick up something and smash that mirror into a million pieces until it resembled what I felt inside. I was unfixable.

soul. I had lost control. I was a lost soul. I walked to my bathroom mirror and stood staring at myself. I looked empty. They say your eyes are the window to your soul. All I could see were tears forming deep puddles of dark mud, muck, mire. Nothing pretty to behold. No grace, nothing good looking back at me. I didn't see a pretty face in the bathroom mirror, I felt hideous, foolish and so damn ugly, I hated what I saw. I wanted to pick up something and smash that mirror into a million pieces until it resembled what I felt inside. I was unfixable. I could never give my family the dreams I aspired to. I would never be the woman I hoped to be. I would never walk proudly before them and say, "I am…," instead I would forever have to say, "I couldn't…." My heart was too broken for me to even imagine anything positive.

I wanted it all to end. I just wanted to get off the merry go round. There was no point. I had lost hold of hope. I hurt and damaged my kids, who I loved with all my heart. I hurt them deeply by my inabilities and insecurities. It was so unfair to them, they deserved so much more than what they were getting. If I couldn't understand myself and this life, how could they? Why should they be dragged along? Shouldn't they have the chance to stand upright and proud and make the very best of themselves without me? I wanted to do better for my children.

I'm sure as I said many years ago, I probably should have been in therapy. I needed therapy for the eating disorder I'm positive I had as a child. I needed therapy to overcome fears. I think perhaps for the fear of letting go. This would be my day to just let go and give it all over to God. *I'm so tired. I give up. I surrender my children to you and pray that they will know how completely I loved them with every fiber of me Lord. But something is pulling on me, it's unwinding me and I can't find the glue, the strength, the muster to hold myself together any longer. I just want to end it. I want to be in your presence. I want out. Please God just take me.* I looked into those dark puddles of muddy water that were supposed to be my eyes, and saw no bottom, no *joy*, nothing. Feeling nothing but pain, in desperation I knew not to call on any of the handful of the people that love me most. I went to Alisa's bedroom and lay across her bed holding her pillow, it smelled like my baby girl. I looked around at all her girly girl things. She's my spicy sweet girl. She can be in my lap like a toddler one minute and turn back into a feisty teenager the next. She has always been smart as a whip; I know she can become anything she puts her mind to. I couldn't worry for her. She was such a precocious little girl, a handful for sure. She will be better with a stronger, brighter, more determined, more accomplished woman to guide her through her life. I prayed for her to have that, *Please God, I know I always said that over my dead body would someone else raise my kids, just don't let it be a skank as the young men put it. Let it be someone truly incredible.*

I went to my room. It was so peaceful. I found my bottle of pain medication. I sat on the edge of my bed and methodically laid the pills out on the night table one at a time. It was as if I were going to exterminate something horrible. That horrible thing I needed to do away with was me. I went to the kitchen to get a glass of water. When I came back I took off my work clothes and slipped into my favorite soft silk nightgown. I looked in the mirror once more. Like a hunter looking through his scope one more time to make certain his prey was clearly in sight before just pulling the trigger. Yep, there she is, the pitiful, ugly, disgusting failure of a daughter, friend, woman, human being, wife, and most of all mother. How many years had I screwed up? It was all unredeemable. Surely God would forgive me. He knew all. He has seen all. *No time for self-pity* I told myself. The tears I cry are just for the pain I will cause by this because even this, even this, will be counted as one last selfish act. I know that, but I take one pill, then another, then another, and so on until soon the last pill in the line is there for me to take. "Voila." How silly but what else should I

> *That horrible thing I needed to do away with was me. I went to the kitchen to get a glass of water.*

say? I swallow. I lay back and get comfortable under the quilt. Tears soak my pillow.

I wish I had written a note to say how much I love Mama and Daddy and thank them for being the world's most patient, loving, generous, understanding, and incredible parents any girl could ever have hoped for. I wished I had told my son what an amazing companion and friend he was to me when I was all alone; he was never, ever unwanted. He was a great gift to me from God. He was a good, good boy. I wished I had told him my dying wish for him would be to love faithfully and kindly and to try hard to work on that temper. I wish I had told my beautiful baby girl to go give the world all she has to give and never stop being curious and bright. I wish I had told her to love with all her heart because love is beautiful when it's fully given and received. I wish I had taken the time to tell her she was a gift I waited and prayed for and God sent her to me. She was a blessing.

However, I didn't write any notes. If I was found, I guess it would be assumed I had enough of enough of whatever it was. That was it. There I lay on my soft bed, and I slept for a short while and then....

God said..."**NOT TODAY!**" I woke up, pain in my belly and barely made it to the bathroom, projectile vomiting. "Oh my God, Oh my God, Oh my God!" On my knees in front of the toilet the vomiting seemed endless. I thought it would never stop, I couldn't even catch my breath between hurling. I thought *this must be hell because I'm sure not in heaven.* Finally, I stopped and sat with my back against the bathroom wall. "Okay Lord, apparently I can't even do that right, geez." Then I laughed. I laughed at myself. What a sight I must have been. I turned on my shower, jumped in and washed my hair and tried to shift my thinking. Maybe God had intervened. *Maybe, just maybe I am still here for a reason. God, why?*

I actually did my hair, put on some makeup, dressed, and went for a ride in my car. Everything looked different, as if I was seeing it for the first time. I was hungry for sure. I decided I'd cook for myself and have some wine. I didn't want fast food and I didn't want to go to a restaurant alone. My life changed in many ways that fateful day. I wasn't even on my side of town anymore but when I spotted a Fry's grocery store I parked and went in.

He was pushing a cart with a bag of dog food. I noticed him. Who wouldn't at least notice him? He was tall and handsome with a brilliant smile. He saw me and smiled. I went down the next aisle and there he was again. We played a game of hide and seek until we were at the checkout counters. He was at one checkout and I was at another. Our eyes met and he smiled again. I smiled back, blushed, and looked away. When I went to my car, suddenly, there he was standing next to me. "Hello. Couldn't help but notice you. Hope you don't mind me saying you're very pretty." "Thank you." *Liar*, I thought, but he was pleasant. We stood there and chatted for a couple of minutes and established that we were both currently separated from our spouses and he asked if he could call me sometime. We exchanged numbers. His name was Andre.

That day changed me completely. Andre did call me. He did ask me out. He took me to listen to jazz. He took me places I hadn't been. He also took me to bed. It wasn't right. He was still legally married and so was I. It was like the song that talks about loving being wrong but not wanting to be right. He treated me good. He was kind, gentle, and respectful. We sizzled. I don't know if it was part love, part lust. It was just so good to be wanted and treated like, "I'm proud to be with you and I'd be seen anywhere with you." At one point we seemed like we were moving in the direction of commitment although it could have been complicated. We were always extremely discreet and never hung out at either of our homes. Eventually some family members on both sides did find out about us. Ultimately, we broke off the affair and resumed our lives. I asked God over and over to forgive because I knew it was wrong.

Andre had come into my life on the darkest day like a ray of sunshine. He was sweet and built me up when I needed it most. He helped me put things back in perspective and helped me find some self-worth. He gave me strength to realize that even if Charles walked away with a blonde, white woman and never looked back at our family, I would be okay because I have inner strength and I have God. Yes, I have a well of hurts deeper than the ocean but that's where I am going to pull what I need to get by. That's where I will go to teach children and future generations what I learned. Andre helped me see myself differently because he saw me differently.

So although it was sinful and wrong, "Forgive me Father for I have sinned," I learned through those sin filled times with him. I can say, "Thank you, Andre. Thank you for the love and thank you for holding up a different mirror than the dark one I stared into on the day I swallowed a bottle full of pills."

CHAPTER 25

Graduation Day

By the day my son Charles graduated high school, we had moved so many times I had lost count. I sat at the dining room table in a brand new house on Kristen Avenue addressing his announcements. The house was in Mesa, but glory to God, we were able to keep him at the same high school from start to finish albeit that it was a long distance from our home. From some of our homes he had been able to ride his bike to school. He was dedicated to sticking it out at Marcos De Niza and was heavily involved in school life, including the Jr. ROTC program, and playing multiple sports. He got up early, backpack on his back; clean uniform on a hanger, covered by a plastic cleaner's bag and off he would pedal. On rainy days we would drive him, but for the most part he was independent and responsible.

On his graduation day I was a weeping mess. I cried from the time I got up, realizing he was crossing a threshold. He wasn't my little boy anymore. Of course he hadn't been for some time, but I always still saw him as my baby. After graduation he was going on a senior trip to Hawaii. I was afraid to let him go, but knew it would be wonderful for him and my insecurities couldn't hold him back.

I got my hair cut very short as a way to mark the event; it was a whole new chapter in our lives and I decided to go for a new look. Charles Jr. had been through hell and back by my side, he had had some glorious days, and now this was his big day. He had achieved a lot and I was extremely proud of him. I had been ever since the first day of school when I held his little hand. He did it! He graduated. He gave me his high school diploma and told me I had earned it by being such a good mother, always being there for him. I was honored and my heart was touched.

☙ United States Marine ❧

Enlisting in the military was as far from Charles Jr.'s plans after graduation as the moon is from the sun. In our house the rule was you either work or stay in school. So after high school Charles attended Mesa Community College and Scottsdale Community College before transferring north to Northern Arizona University. We spent a lot of money preparing him for the journey to leave home. We bought him a television, warm bedding, micro-wave, food, meal-tickets, books, new winter clothing, just to name a few essentials. Sending him away to college, I wasn't prepared and there was nothing drastic I was going to do to mark the day. I just stood there holding my baby, sobbing.

When he was settled in trouble found him. While at college he majored in partying and he got in fights over silly stuff. "See that girl over there? That guy slapped her!" Upon hearing things like this he would deck the guy no questions asked. Everyone would fall out laughing because no such incident occurred. They knew he would fight a grizzly bear. The Dean called and suggested we bring him home until he was a bit more mature. So we did. At home he hitched himself to a group of friends we didn't approve of, they were clearly using him.

His father always had his finger on the pulse of what was going on in our son's life. Charles Jr. had never really been a part of the street world because he had been sheltered. A dad who used to wear a police uniform knows a thing or two about street activity. So, this young man who was surely on his way to becoming an adult started getting into the clubs, no doubt with a fake id. Before we knew it he was on the fast track. To trouble, that is.

> *His father always had his finger on the pulse of what was going on in our son's life...A dad who used to wear a police uniform knows a thing or two about street activity.*

One evening Charles Sr. walked into a club young people often frequented. And someone gave him a pertinent piece of unsolicited information. "Hey if you see Chuck, tell him the package is under the sink in the bathroom." He played it off like it was just what he expected to hear. "Oh yeah, yeah for sure, I'll tell him." He went straight to the bathroom and retrieved the package. It was marijuana. He was being used as a go between. Deliver, collect the money, and receive a small cut of cash. His father thought, "Oh hell no, not my son!"

That next day, before a serious conversation could be had, someone pulled a gun on our son in a parking lot asking him about drugs. The very next day his father asked him to go for ride. They drove straight to the recruiting office.

"Oh Dad, no, I'm not going in the military, it's not for me." His dad said, "Hey Charles, who is asking you to enlist? Let's just go in and see what they have." Once my son saw a Marine standing tall, sharp, and stylish in his uniform, his face lit up. The Marine looked sharper than the other men there. It was a real possibility. The next thing I knew he was off to MCRD for boot camp. It was a move his dad made to remove him from the dangerous elements he'd gotten himself tangled in. We had no idea that Desert Storm loomed ahead.

৩৩ Boot Camp Graduation ৩৩

Three months later we were in San Diego preparing to watch Charles graduate. We were so excited to see him. He looked like a different person, so thin and tanned. He spoke differently, saying, "Yes ma'am" and "No, ma'am." I just about fell out of my seat when I saw him take a bite of his least favorite candy bar in the world, an Almond Joy. I loved this candy but he and his sister both despised anything with coconut. Under past circumstances he would have never eaten a single bite. The marines had taught him gratefulness even for things he once hated.

Charles Sims II, USMC graduation, San Diego, CA

We laughed, talked, and walked around the base as Charles pointed out his barracks. I already had a clear picture in my mind from his letters. His college sweetheart, Terry was with us, they held hands and looked at each-other googly eyed. I didn't mind sharing his special day with her at all.

Soon our visit was over and we parted ways until the next day—graduation. He was truly a model Marine; young, strong, determined, and teachable. They had stripped him of his past identity and he was now a United States Marine, part of the select Few, The Proud, The Marines.

When we arrived on the base we were directed to the auditorium designated for the ceremony. There they were, all these young soldiers, sitting with their hands on their knees staring straight ahead. I scurried down the aisle, straining to see which one was my son. All of their haircuts were alike; all were suntanned; only the dark-skinned black Marines were easy to pick out from the group.

When I finally spotted him my excitement took over and I waved and grinned, calling his name. "Charles, hi sweetheart, we're here!" No response, just a straight ahead stare, but I noticed a tiny bit of a twitch. I realized then that I was embarrassing my son. He couldn't respond. He wanted to say, "Oh Mom please sit down!" I felt his vibe, so I did.

The graduation ceremony was rather long as it was a big class. Later, his sergeant spoke to us. He told us what a remarkable young man our son was. He had been number one in class but deferred to a young classmate with a wife and children. He told the sergeant to move him ahead of him. It was such an unselfish thing for him to do after he had worked so hard to earn it.

We left the MCRD (Marine Corps Recruit Depot) and headed to Old Town San Diego where we walked and had a celebration dinner. Charles Jr. was friendly and we enjoyed the time together. We were so proud of our son and he was very proud of himself. He looked handsome in his tailored dress uniform, tall, tan, and fit. Everything felt right.

While Charles was in boot camp, his father had told him he would hold his credit cards for safe keeping. He didn't keep them safe; he ran them to the maximum limit as he had done with mine, so we embarrassingly had to share a room with Alisa and Terry during that graduation trip. I had only enough money to travel there, rent the room, and feed us all. Charles, my husband, was once again between jobs.

As his mother I felt compelled to tell our son the truth to the extent I knew it. I didn't know the complete truth and at the time Charles and I were once again separated. When I told him his response was just, "Don't worry about it Mom. I'll take care of it. No stress."

This was reminiscent of the day he graduated from high school and told me he wouldn't have ever made it without my support. He was once again all thanks and gratitude and he said I had earned it as much as he had. I felt like crying again at his graciousness even after he had been used in such an unfair and undeserving way.

I didn't want to tell him what much of the money had been spent on. Yes, there were necessities, gas, dry cleaning, and miscellaneous items. But then there was Kim. I wondered if he knew about her. This wasn't the time or place and under no circumstance could I bring this up. I knew that one day it would *all come out in the wash*, as his Mimi used to say about anything done in the dark.

Charles Sr. was still seeing Kim and seemed to have fallen in love with her. This was the reason that I was once more separated from him. I was sure this separation was final. Like I said before no matter what in life, no matter all the years of up and down and all the crazy turn arounds, we had an agreement about Christmas holidays and anything regarding our kids. They were *our* kids and it was set in stone that neither he nor I would ever bring anyone else to an event for them. Not to a game, a recital, a school function, certainly never a birthday party, and Christmas was strictly families until they were grown and had families of their own. This was non-negotiable. Always!

I was still working at American Express and while I couldn't make any kind of adjustments to my own account, I was able to monitor what was spent and where. I about fell out of my seat, hit the floor, and had a fit when I saw the list of charges on my card. Phoenix Florist for about ten arrangements, even Happy Halloween. What the hell! Ladies Foot Locker, hundreds of dollars' worth of tennis shoes and outfits, dress stores, jewelry stores, fine restaurants for break-fast, lunch, brunch, and dinner. Theatre tickets, Tickets for a concert. Airline tickets to California and to…oh the best of all, tickets to see Barry White! Oh my God. I was never going to be able to pay all of that. It wasn't a revolving card. What you charged on American

Express was due the next month. I had never been to a concert except to see Andy Williams and the Lennon Sisters for my parents' anniversary and that concert was more for them. It was bad enough that this was done to me. I found out that he had also bought two first class airline tickets to go to Chicago for a week during Christmas. Oh no, he must have lost his mind.

Always, always I tried to keep painful things from my kids. I waited until Alisa wasn't home, then took off my wedding rings and threw them in Charles' face. Told him to kiss my ass and go straight to hell. He was a user and a manipulator and worst of all a liar. I said, "Go ahead and go to Chicago, if you do we will never have another family Christmas." I don't know what was wrong with me that even with thousands of my dollars spent on some woman named Kim, I was focused on Christmas. I told him to get out of my house, he made me sick! He did make me sick, I was sick of myself, always trusting him, always believing him. I had no back bone. No self -esteem. I was just an idiot, once again.

I was still working at American Express...I was able to monitor what was spent and where. I about fell out of my seat, hit the floor, and had a fit when I saw the list of charges on my card.

He told me that he wanted to take her to San Diego to our son's graduation. *Are you freaking kidding me? You must have lost your ever loving mind! She better not step one foot near my son. He is MY SON! Not hers, she has had no part in his life, why should she come.* No one could ever know how angry I was with the whole situation. In front of Alisa I tried to play it off, I did not talk about it.

Before Charles' graduation he had sold the airline tickets through an ad in the paper and gave me the cash. I paid it directly to the card but I couldn't get it cleared up by the time graduation rolled around. That's why I only had money enough for one room, with two queen beds. The entire situation was humiliating.

When I found out that my son's card had also been basically ruined, I cried so much and so hard that I cried myself right into a migraine headache. I didn't tell anyone the details, I wanted Charles to enjoy being in the spotlight. He loved his dad and he loved me and it was his special time, so let's not dwell on anything we could deal with later.

I have cried over every milestone my kids have had in our journey together, tears of joy, tears of anticipation, and tears of excitement. The day they started school, the day my son moved out, and every other special event, tears fell. I knew my children were growing up, but now it was evident that my boy had morphed into a man in no time at all. I would have never imagined the fears and demons I would face in life while he was away.

Being a Marine I knew he would be away. I tried to prepare. A little more time together would have been great.

Charles Sims, 29 Palms
military base in CA

CHAPTER 26

Me and Alisa and Baby Makes Three

The rivalry between Alisa and Charles was tiresome. "You love Charles more than me" and "You love Alisa more than me." Ugh, it was ridiculous. I had one a boy, and one girl, it doesn't get any more perfect. I had exactly what I wanted, why couldn't they just get along?

By the time Charles had been away to college, come back, then left again to become a Marine, Alisa was more than ready to be the center of attention *finally*. I'm sure that as a child he felt like her existence robbed him of his rightful place as the center of attention. She felt that if he would just go away she would get all of the attention. Attention, attention, and more attention. It was a war of rivalry. I was trying to achieve balance and didn't want to give too much or not enough to either one. It was enough to drive me crazy. The bottom line was that I absolutely loved both of my kids.

"Deal with it and when in doubt consult Your Heavenly Father, their manufacturer."

When I signed up for motherhood I missed the small print that read, "Warning! These children come with DNA from both sides of the family. It's just the way genetics work. No guarantee of how they will behave or react in any given situation. Deal with it and when in doubt consult your Heavenly Father, their manufacturer."

After Charles Jr. left to embark on his own life, Alisa and I settled into what was a very nice routine. I went to work every day at my job at American Express and she went to school. She was involved in extracurricular activities and continued to be an honor student as always, but I could see her interest in her boyfriend Kevin was trumping studies. It was normal for us to pick up Kevin for a bite to eat and it was not unusual for him to spend countless hours at our apartment. I really liked him so much. He and his family were welcoming people and made us feel like family. They were my kind of people. I thought I was always keeping a watchful eye on the two of them.

Kevin spent the night often and I would insist that Alisa sleep in my bed with me, so there was no hanky panky between the two of them.

Long story short, Alisa began to sleep excessively and I thought I better take her to the doctor. As I sat in the waiting room with her I was speaking to her through clenched teeth in a hushed tone as I snapped each page of the magazine in my lap. "You better not be pregnant Missy!" People around us stared at me. I didn't care but she did. She lowered her head in embarrassment.

Alisa and Kevin, Tempe High School prom

211

The doctor confirmed my worst fear for my baby. She was pregnant. For days I couldn't bring myself to say the right thing so I said nothing at all. I prepared meals and plopped her plate down on the table with an angry, "Alisa, come and eat!" I couldn't do much more. I cried in the bathroom. Standing in the shower my tears felt like they matched the flow of the shower drop for drop.

Finally, I reassured her that things would be all right. We will get through this. All of her classmates were on board with the, "Kevin and you are going to have such a cute baby" comments, and I knew this to be true. However, I was more concerned about her completing school.

The hardest thing for me to come to grips with about my daughter being pregnant was the idea of letting go of the dreams I had for her. She was an exceptional student and had always been so smart and ambitious. Now, I was fearful that she was going to take the same path that I had traveled. I knew that would mean sacrificing herself for the sake of her child. I would have to do more sacrificing in order to let her still be the kid I knew she was.

> *...I was fearful that she was going to take the same path that I had traveled. I knew that would mean sacrificing herself for the sake of her child.*

I was sad for her lost innocence and dreams that would now have to be deferred. I wanted so much more for her life than I had carved out for myself. News travels fast in the family and before long everyone knew about the baby that was coming. Snide remarks aside, I had to protect my child from the world she wasn't ready for.

Charles had moved to Paso Robles in California and was living with his parents by the time Alisa was several months into her pregnancy. I honestly can't explain the how and why of my decision that it was in our best interest to move to California. I had ended things with Andre. Charles was done with Kim. Women were always done with him when his money dried up. Maybe I didn't have to make another idiotic decision that would affect my daughter like it did! Charles didn't even have his own place and I didn't have the economic stability to set us up. So Alisa and I moved in with her dad and his parents in an apartment. My poor daughter with her pregnant belly was sleeping on the floor. That surely wasn't in her best interest. Looking back, I think it was one of the stupidest decisions of my life! I went to work in a small dress boutique and shortly thereafter secured a job with the county welfare department. I worked as hard as I could to get us into a place of our own quickly.

I found a brand new apartment complex in Atascadero, a town between Paso Robles and San Luis Obispo where I worked. I didn't have money for furniture and I am ashamed to say my credit was tapped out and tanked for the most part, so I had to improvise.

I went to the Salvation Army and purchased used beds. Yuck! I thought they were the worst but they would be better than the floor. I bought plastic mattress covers and padded mattress covers to go over the top of those so the cold plastic wasn't so uncomfortable. I sprayed at least a full can of Lysol Disinfectant Spray on each mattress. It was humbling. They were used, but they were clean and we were off the floor. I also purchased a table and chairs and a sofa, end table and a lamp. Just the bare minimum. I had a house full of furniture in storage in Arizona but hadn't moved it to California. I was uncertain about the future so we just moved with the bare necessities.

We did still try to do a few fun things although nothing expensive. We mostly went for rides and stopped for a burger or ice cream. One great laugh that I have with my daughter to this day is about the pizza delivery man. One day I ordered a pizza and paid by check. Unfortunately my check bounced! Who bounces a check for a pizza? Well, I am the one. It was very embarrassing to say the least. He called several times and I told my daughter, "If it's the pizza guy, tell him I'm not here," because I didn't have the money! Of course on payday I made good on it, but when I look back I shake my head. What a way to live!

◟◦◞ Justin Matthew ◟◦◞

Alisa was having an uneventful pregnancy. My son was stationed overseas in Korea and Charles was trying to find work in the Paso Robles area.

By this time my son had learned the full extent of what his father had done to his credit and was way beyond upset. He had basically told his father he was done with him, which broke his heart. The truth is that Charles had violated a trust and used his son in an almost unforgivable way. Eventually, he was able to forgive his father, but it would be something he always remembered, even to this day.

I had to return to Phoenix to a hearing regarding my American Express card as management was working with me on clearing some of the charges and I was paying off the rest. After asking the doctor if Alisa was okay to travel, she and I set out on a road trip to Arizona. Everything was fine; we visited my parents and she spent time with Kevin and his family. After a nice couple of days, we said our good-byes and headed back to California. On the trip Alisa said, "Mama, the next town we come to will you please stop at a hospital?" You can't imagine the panic I felt! Of course I stopped. The next town was Blythe, California. It's a one-horse town but thank goodness they had a doctor. He examined Alisa and told me she was experiencing pre-eclampsia and would need to deliver the baby. We could go back to Phoenix or, his advice because she was so young, continue home and have the doctor who had been car-ing for her deliver the baby. He would be most familiar with her case. So I called Charles and told him what was happening. The doc-tor kept us for a couple of hours to make sure she was stable, then we got back on the road.

I didn't want to make Alisa nervous so I just said, "No worries, everything will be fine." I could see she was swelling more and more by the minute.

This necessary stop put us on the road later than I wanted to be. I worried that we didn't get an earlier start. I worried about darkness falling because I am night blind, I can't see twenty feet in front of me in the dark. I didn't want to make Alisa nervous so I just said, "No worries, everything will be fine." I could see she was swelling more and more by the minute. Her face looked puffy and distorted. Her shoes were off and her feet had become two squishy pads at the end of her legs. She didn't look normal or well. I was having stomach cramps from my nerves. I began second guessing the decision to try to make it home to Atascadero. I think we should have gone back to Phoenix. Now I had no choice, I had to keep going forward and it was getting darker and darker. Soon I would be entering a portion of the highway called *blood alley* because there were so many treacherous accidents there. I was praying silently in the foggy dark.

Out of nowhere a carnival truck appeared directly in front of me traveling in the same direction. The cab had lights on it and the trailer was lit like a Christmas tree! Bright colorful lights enveloped the entire truck and all I had to do was stay in the pocket right behind him. He maintained a nice steady speed that I could keep up with. *Thank you Lord.* I wanted to cry but my tears would surely have blurred my vision. I had very special cargo on board and this was a heavy responsibility. I gripped the steering wheel with both hands and stared straight ahead, just praying that he was going near my home. He was, I turned and he kept driving straight! When we turned into the driveway of our apartment complex Charles was pacing up and down in the dark. He knew that I am night blind and he was so afraid for us.

He took one look at Alisa and got in the driver's seat. Over the pass we went to the hospital. She was immediately admitted. The doctors explained to us how critically ill our daughter was and the Red Cross sent for her brother to come home. She was at risk of seizures, placental abruption, stroke, hemorrhaging, and possibly death.

Who else would I have wanted at our side during this time besides Charles? This was our little girl and she was in trouble—real trouble.

Charles was a praying man and right now prayer and his presence were the only two things that gave me comfort. Honestly, at that time I didn't care about anything from the past. All I could think about was the future. I was hyper focused on wanting Alisa to pull through this healthy and happy with no tragedy in her very young life. The doctors had definitely planted a huge fear in us as her parents, although we knew our role was to reassure her, comfort her, and love her through what was ahead.

Alisa likes to chuckle and tell the story of our one lapse of good judgement as we left her for a run to JC Penney as soon as they told us we were having a grandson. I don't know what came over us. There she was hooked to all kinds of monitors, crash cart at her bedside, her brother enroute, and what do we do? Go shopping! To be honest, we were not gone long, but did return with all things boy. Alisa was not impressed as she was far too ill to care. After that we didn't leave her side.

The plan was that if the baby wasn't doing well upon delivery they would fly Mama and baby to San Francisco. My grandson was delivered by caesarean section after it became evident a normal delivery wasn't possible. Charles and I were sitting nervously in a waiting area but I was listening attentively. When I heard that baby cry, I lost it. I fell to my knees and thanked God for his life. I wept like a baby not yet knowing how he was, but I knew by the cry he had made it. I didn't know how Alisa was. Charles pulled me up to the chair next to him and just held me and cried and told me that his faith had never wavered. I knew he was telling me the truth.

A nurse came to talk to us and escorted us to a different area. We scrubbed our hands and pulled on surgical gowns. Within a few minutes I was holding my grandson; the first to actually hold him and cuddle him. The beaming nurse

He was so funny, like a little puppy he sniffed and snuggled right under my neck. I love the way he still hugs me and snuggles my neck!

who had brought him was dressed in scrubs, hair tucked under the hospital bonnet, shoes covered in operating room slip covers. She held him like a football and gently passed him to my waiting arms. He was very tiny and was the most precious baby I had ever held. He was so funny, like a little puppy he sniffed and snuggled right under my neck. I love the way he still hugs me and snuggles my neck!

Justin was a little preemie baby; both he and his mama would have to stay in the hospital for a while, but at that moment I could only stare at his tiny angel face. He was beautiful. I didn't want my tears to fall on him but I'm sure they did. They were tears of thankful-ness and joy and I was washed in utter humility. God is so great and mighty and wondrous. I had been so afraid and now I felt so blessed to hold him. I opened the swaddling blanket and counted every little perfect finger and toe. I took off his knit cap and ran my fingers over his soft wisps of hair. I kissed his face and felt his soft breath against my face. This was a perfect, tiny gift from God with the most pro-found impact on my life. I was a mother and I loved being a mother, but now I had become a *grandmother*. I was completely overwhelmed with the emotion of it all. For a moment, I didn't know what to say or do. It was too much! I was ready to break into a happy dance but too humbled by the beauty and graciousness of it all to do that. It was more like a moment to fall to my knees in adoration of God Almighty for the miracles he performs. Holding this tiny new life, my grandson, not yet named, was so humbling it was a riveting moment in my life. It was my one great gift of joy after so many dark days and so many ups and downs.

Somehow I knew I was going to be focusing on loving this baby and taking care of Alisa and just letting go of the past. I knew right then as I held him that my life would never again be the same. I knew that God had given me a new purpose and a new meaning. I had a new joy. He was not my baby, I had no illusions about that, because I still had a daughter who was very much still like a baby herself. My baby, then, before, and even to this day, Mama's baby she would be.

My grandson was her son, but he was my new focus. A true gift from God. I would need strength, resolve, determination, a lot of love, and a lot of joy. And most of all I would need my faith in God to help my daughter with raising her baby boy. I was in one hundred percent!

As for Charles, the moment he held Justin Matthew Sims was the moment his life transformed. Matthew means "a gift from God" and that's exactly what he proved to be for all of us. I don't think Charles was ever the same man. He fell instantly in love with his grandson. Period. Full stop. Then the same nurse in bonnet and scrubs gently took him from us with much still to be done.

As for Alisa, they had so medicated my poor baby girl that someone asked us was this an adoption situation. No! No! No! It certainly is not! Can't you see she is very sick and you have drugged her up, she's out of it? They had offered her the baby but she didn't show much enthusiasm. When she was finally more awake of course he was the first thought she had. She wanted to see and hold her baby. She was well on her way to being a good mommy.

The baby shower was scheduled for a date after his birth but Alisa was still in the hospital. The doctor released her to come home for a few hours so she could attend. She was very embarrassed because of course she wanted to do her hair, makeup etc. but there was no time or opportunity. Honestly she looked a hot mess but she had just been through a pretty big ordeal for a young lady! She didn't have a nice outfit to wear or makeup to put on. She doesn't like seeing the pictures of the baby shower. They certainly are not Pinterest worthy. Fortunately this all predated the days of online everything, Pinterest, and Facebook and the comparison game of "my life is so perfect and how is yours?" Gosh even the baby books that we thought were such a nice touch back then are tacky compared to today's standards.

My best friend Pat was wonderful in helping us prepare for the baby. She was able to collect much of what we needed from many of her aerobic students in the classes she taught. They generously brought blankets, onesies, sleepers, and a crib and mattress. Everything was all new or like new. We bought a beautiful crib set and all the other necessary items. Justin had everything a baby needs, we lacked for nothing.

Charles Jr. made it to San Louis Obispo and after seeing Alisa he instantly bonded with his nephew. It was love at first sight. We were so thankful the Red Cross had afforded us the opportunity to have him home with us at this time. More than anything we were relieved for the positive outcome instead of the one the doctors had laid out as a tragic possibility a few days before.

Before long, Alisa and Justin came home from the hospital and Charles returned to Korea. I had to return to work and Alisa was very nervous at being left home with a brand new preemie. Her boyfriend Kevin, Justin's daddy, came to visit and meet his son. It was a really sweet time. The kids were both so young and in love and both trying to be good parents. They were doing a great job! Pumping breast milk, dropping bottles, crying about it, trying again, and laughing about it, we enjoyed watching the two of them bonding and taking very good care of this itty bitty baby boy.

Things went off the rails for me when Kevin asked if Alisa and Justin could travel back to Arizona with him to attend his family reunion. I gave permission against my better judgement. The day they left a sense of emptiness came over me that I couldn't explain. I went to work every day and came home only to have Charles, who had moved in with us, pick fights with me and keep me up all night interrogating me about ridiculous things. "What is Charles (our son) doing?" What is Alisa doing with Kevin?" What about this, and what about that?" "Don't take your ass to sleep when I'm talking to you!" I was so exhausted and upset. He slept during the day when I was at work. I didn't understand what he wanted or expected me to do. I'm not a controlling individual so I

> *I went to work every day and came home only to have Charles, who had moved in with us, pick fights with me and keep me up all night interrogating me about ridiculous things.*

wasn't in favor of calling anyone up and telling them off, which was often what he told me to do. I'd sit on the edge of the bed and think to myself, *Why in the hell am I here? Why do I keep doing this to myself over and over again? I need an escape plan.*

Alisa had manipulated her way back to Arizona. I don't blame her. Kevin and her friends were there. Her dad was suffering from depression and some other form of mental illness. It was hard for a teenage girl to understand his moods. She loved him so much but she was helpless to make anything better for him. I think the distance was healthier for her but he didn't see it that way. I couldn't say a thing in defense of *anyone!* Alisa temporarily stayed between Kevin's family and my parents, eventually moving in with Mama and Daddy.

We lived in Atascadero and I worked over the grade in San Louis Obispo at the County Welfare Department. Did I like my job? I don't think I'm cut out for work within the system such as it is. Having been at the other end of things for as many years as I had been, perhaps I had too much empathy to do my job well. I know what it's like to have no money for food, no way to get the shut off utilities restored, no way to get the prescription you must have. I know what it is like to be working every day and still not have enough money to make ends meet. I understand what it feels like to be proud and not want help, but desperately need just a little hand up, not a hand out. I understand not wanting to be in the system when you would much rather work and earn your own way. I fully grasp it all. Even now, I still feel badly about the woman whose husband beat her but she didn't qualify for assistance. She missed the mark by just a few dollars. I asked her to wait for me until I got off work; I drove her and her children to a McDonalds, bought them a meal, and then dropped them off at a family shelter. She was barefoot, she had no jacket. She just grabbed her children and ran. Someone had dropped them off at the county office. I cried wishing I could do more. I hugged her. She was a stranger, but I knew her pain. A coworker was watching and listening when I told her to wait for me and reported me to my supervisor. I was written up and a formal reprimand placed in my employee file. This was the first of a few similar incidents. It clearly wasn't a good fit. Honestly, people come there looking for help and resources. They usually have children in tow, especially very young children.

So one day, I left that job and on the same day decided that I was also leaving Charles and going back to Arizona. There was nothing to be said that could convince me to stay and he didn't try. I packed a few things, gassed up my car, and headed to my parents' house. I didn't care about any of the furniture, dishes, or household stuff. Throw it all away for all I care. I had a house full of things in storage in Arizona.

One thing I discovered when I arrived at Mama and Daddy's house, home is truly where your heart is and right then my heart was wherever Alisa and Justin were. I felt peace! Charles was very angry with me. He told me I must have really wanted to leave because I had left panties in the dresser drawer and my toothbrush in the bath-

> *...I discovered when I arrived at Mama and Daddy's house, home is truly where your heart is and right then my heart was wherever Alisa and Justin were.*

room. "Throw them away." "Wow, when did you become so mean?" I felt like telling him, "Since I got so tired of your crap." A little sleep now and then would have been helpful to his cause if he wanted me to stay with him. I was showing some early signs of failing health. Stress was not a good thing for me.

Before long I bounced back as I always have. I found a job, then another. I saved a few paychecks and got us moved into an apartment and the furniture out of storage. We could breathe. It wasn't great; it wasn't like any of the nice homes we had lived in before, but I could afford the rent. I had Alisa, Justin, and myself and my niece Kelle stayed with us for a time. Life was good. The baby was perfect and healthy except that Alisa wasn't nursing him anymore and he was allergic to most formula. He cried a lot at night so we'd walk the floor in perpetual motion or I'd walk outside with him. Looking up at the open skies, the moon and the stars seemed to calm him.

Our home was a haven to many extended family members. We loved children and all the kids in our large family knew that they were welcome to stay with us at any time. Over the years many took us up on it, Michael, Adrian, Kelle, and Kim to name a few.

I didn't file for a divorce. I didn't quit talking to Charles. I didn't quit caring about Charles. I didn't quit loving him. This was another time that perhaps I should have, but I didn't. He wanted to leave California and come back to Arizona. "Oh my God Charles! This is insanity! I can't live my life like this. This is just way too much. This is idiotic. It isn't going to happen. I'm done. I'm concentrating on making life livable for Alisa and the baby." But then it did happen. He was back and in our home. He was there and he said he would do any-

It was truly remarkable. Charles was humbled by a baby. The airs he was used to putting on were stripped away and there he stood, vulnerable to the world.

thing and he did. The formula that Justin needed cost a lot of money and the man who had always been too proud to be seen in anything he deemed below his standard, took a job as a pizza delivery man, and used his money to buy baby formula, diapers, wipes, and whatever else was needed.

It was truly remarkable. Charles was humbled by a baby. The airs he was used to putting on were stripped away and there he stood, vulnerable to the world. Everyone could now see openly the failures of the business dealings that had left him broke, the lost jobs and hopes and dreams, and the complete lack of logical planning to prepare for the future. Our life thus far had been one haphazard scenario after another with no forethought given to maintaining stability for ourselves and most assuredly not for our children. There was no way I wanted to continue down that course for my grandson.

I knew I was as much to blame as Charles for the nomadic life style and the shameful and outrageous situations we had drug our kids through. I was adept at regaining my momentum and could usually ricochet or bounce back, but I was exhausted. I didn't really want this reconciliation but I was in a covenant with Charles. I was still legally his wife and he my husband. We worked at it and he began to morph into a different person. Just as I was primarily focused on Alisa and Justin it seemed he was too. Hallelujah! I wanted my grandson to experience the best of what our family life had been and I wanted to shield him from the worst of all that we had been through.

It was vitally important to me for Justin to be surrounded by both sides of his family without drama. There wasn't much to speak of. His daddy's family was great, so warm, loving, and inclusive and lots of fun to be around. I cooked nutritious meals for my children and dinner time was family time, even when their daddy wasn't home to eat with us. As helter skelter as my relationship with Charles had been over the years I had never spent a birthday without him, nor had we ever not celebrated our anniversary. Our children always had a birthday celebration with family and friends. Justin would have the good times that bond family together, I would make sure of that. I just knew I didn't want stress and instability attached to his little life if I could help it. That was my determination and my prayer.

CHAPTER 27

Money Pit to Homeless
to Joyful Song

While all of these changes were taking place with my kids and grandkids there were also changes occurring in my own life. I had lived in so many locations and each was more of the same. I was always trying to get a foothold, reaching for something to grab onto. Try to hold tight, smile, don't let on that I'm worried sick about anything, don't let on that I'm embarrassed, ashamed, anxious, or feeling inadequate in any way.

I had more talks with myself than I can begin to recall. Wiping the steam away from yet another foggy bathroom mirror to stare into my own bloodshot, swollen eyes had become a regular occurrence. How could I tell myself the truth about that? How was I trapped in my own life, loving parts of it so much that I gave thanks every day and hating parts of it so much that all I could do was beg God to show me the way out? I couldn't see a way out without hurting someone, so many people depended on me. I was breaking under the weight of the uncertainty of my life. The pieces of the puzzle didn't fit together. I always knew there was something missing just as I always knew there was something there that I didn't want. What was I to do?

I had brought us through one dilemma after another hadn't I? There was the time we'd been homeless. We didn't have to be. My parents always had my back. They would always give shelter to me, my kids, and my grandson Justin. When I brought Charles back into my life after moving back from California my parents weren't happy about it. After we moved into the house with the great potential and they saw my excitement they tried to get on board but they doubted whether my trust in Charles was wise. They didn't have much confidence it would work out. I can't say I blame them.

What I saw was a house that had a lot of room and a big yard with a pool in a nice neighborhood. We moved in and I dove in. I spent a lot of time thinking about the endless possibilities of the improvements I could make to our home. I was enthusiastic, we drained the pool and painted walls. We pulled up worn out dirty carpeting that was beyond cleaning. I tore down old, ragged window coverings and the sunlight seemed to make everything new again. I worked hard and gave my pay checks to my husband with full trust. I should have known better, but all I could focus on was the potential of a beautiful home for my family, especially my daughter and her baby boy. I didn't realize I was wishing in the dark.

Months passed before I knew anything was wrong. The foreclosure notices had been served. They went unanswered because Charles had hidden them from me, the way a child hides a bad report card from their parents. When it was down to the wire and we were going to be locked out by the sheriff, that's when he confessed to me that he hadn't been making the mortgage payments. He also hadn't saved a dime of the money and we had three days to be out! With nowhere to go and no money it was all I

> *Months passed before I knew anything was wrong. The foreclosure notices had been served. They went unanswered...*

could do to keep myself from flying apart like a house in a tornado. I was panicked but knew we had to do something. I was furious with Charles but I think my disappointment was even greater than my anger. And my fear trumped all. I was just trying to put down roots and anchor my life.

The little money we did have was enough to rent a U-Haul and put our belongings in storage. I was grateful that my parents let us stay with them until we could get on our feet. They were always there for me and never let me down. My tears continued falling uncontrollably, my soul was crying out. *How much more Norma Jean? How much more? Why Norma Jean? Why do you do this to yourself and your family? Why?* I didn't want to present myself as this weak woman who weeps over the pain caused by the pitifully poor decisions she makes over and over. No, no I wanted to put on a mask and pretend to be okay. I swore to myself that I could handle what was in front of me and come out stronger.

One night at my parents' house and it was clear that it wasn't going to work with Charles living there with us. I wasn't going to ask him to leave. My mama was very vocal and very outspoken about how she felt. She couldn't believe it and was outraged with him. As far as she was concerned it should have been the last straw for me and she told him that! Her innuendoes implying me, Alisa, and the baby were still welcome were just too much. Instead of staying, I got a motel room with a kitchenette. The room had two double beds, a small table, a refrigerator, and a microwave. The only place there was privacy was in the bathroom. I was going to make it work come hell or high water. I wasn't going to let this be my hell.

I got up each morning and went to work at my day job. After work I darted into the bathroom like superwoman to change into my uniform for Hertz Rent a Car at the airport, where I worked until eleven thirty five nights a week. On the weekends I picked up extra hours at Hertz if I could. I paid for our room one week at a time. I never mentioned to anyone that we were homeless, not even my best friends knew the shame I felt. I told myself that many people are just one paycheck away from being homeless. I'm an optimist and kept thinking I was one paycheck away from being back in a place of our own. I saved every penny I could, planning for the day I could find a place we could call home. I didn't spend money on anything extra for myself no matter how much I might have craved a sweet treat or wanted a new pair of shoes. I had a goal. This certainly gave me a new understanding of how the truly homeless feel. I felt blessed in my humiliation. I thought about all the times I would pass a homeless person on the street and say, "But for the grace of God that could be me." By God's grace I did have a job, a place to sleep, and a place to bathe.

Kevin came to visit many times while we stayed there. He and Alisa would take Justin to play in the pool. He didn't judge our circumstances. He had grown up in a family where he learned that life happens. Good and bad. This was just such a hard time but I was determined to make things better for my family.

Finally all my hours of work, saving, and doing without paid off. I had enough money for us to move to a two bedroom condo. I was so excited that I overlooked or ignored the fact that the neighborhood was filled with rowdy college students who partied day and night. I thought it would be quieter during the week but it was nonstop. The walls of my condo vibrated with the bass music. They were a friendly bunch, often greeting me, "Hey, how are you doing?" From time to time I could smell marijuana and it quickly became apparent that this was no place for a baby boy.

༺⊙༻ Not Your Ordinary White Girl ༺⊙༻

"I'm *not* your ordinary white girl!" Ferol told me one day, radiating confidence with a snap of her fingers. That was, and still is, a true statement. When we met her she had wavy, luxurious hair below her shoulders. Her hair could have starred in a shampoo commercial. She cut it short soon after we met and has kept it that way in keeping with the no nonsense kind of woman she has become. Maybe she always was.

It was a sunny Sunday afternoon when my son brought Ferol to the house. It was probably the most hideous of all the houses we ever lived in and it was a money pit. She stepped down into the sunken living room, looked around as if to size it up, and faced the infant carrier she toted toward the corner. "Please don't bother him; I'm trying to teach him to be independent." "Excuse me, did you say, you're teaching your baby to be independent?" "Yes, yes I am." "Oh, okay." As soon as she stepped into the other room I turned the seat around, unstrapped her baby boy, and picked him up. He grinned at me and I grinned back at him with delight.

As I got to know Ferol, I realized her unusual name fit her when every now and then I'd glimpse a flash of wildness in her hazel eyes. It was a little disconcerting at first but I got used to it. I had never been so close to a girl that was in the stage of her life where she'd fight anyone. I do mean anyone. Her name fit her to a tee. Alisa once made a smart alec statement and Ferol got the best of her in a physical knock down.

Just as Ferol could fight she could also be gentle, kind, compassionate. I realized that she and Charles had been brought up by vastly different mothers. Although she had learned to fend for herself early, she did have people in her life she really loved, respected, and spoke highly of.

She and Charles Jr. had met during a Friday night happy hour at a local bar called Houlihan's. He was stationed in Twenty Nine Palms, California and could make the drive home for the weekend and easily return for duty. His dad spoke to her first, "See that young man over there? He's my son." That was it. Next thing I knew I'm blindsided and falling in love with a baby boy named Chawn.

Charles and Ferol didn't have a long courtship and like everything about their relationship even the wedding was unconventional. They announced that they were going to Las Vegas to get married and we could come if we wanted to. My feelings were hurt and I opted not to go since it's not quite the same as "we are getting married and we'd really like you to be there." So they went alone and as soon as they came back the trouble seemed to start. They were both so strong headed and had been raised in completely different environments.

Ferol and Charles, Christmas

Ferol was pregnant the day Charles was called for deployment to Saudi Arabia for Desert Storm. It was a tense time for the whole family. He knew we would indeed look after his little family with love and care and never neglect them in any way. Chawn was an integral part of the family. He and Justin were growing fast and I enjoyed dressing them in matching outfits. If I bought one it was easy to buy two. The boys were fast buddies; we went everywhere together and they were inseparable when they were with us. Ferol and Chawn's home was now at the Marine base in Twenty Nine Palms.

Every day we watched the news in nervous anticipation of what was to come. My son's name was on each of my friends' prayer lists if they didn't attend my church. We prayed daily for the troops at large and of course for the safe return of Charles. Many mornings I would walk into my bedroom to find Charles Sr. sitting with his face in his hands, back slumped and body wracked with sobs, defeated. I would kneel in front of him and try

Every day we watched the news in nervous anticipation of what was to come.

to console him although fear ran around inside my own head and my anxiety was off the wall. I would close the bedroom door for privacy's sake but sometimes little hands would push open and enter, "Papa don't cry. Uncle Charles is going to be okay, Jesus is watching over him." Well, we'd have to scoop him up and give him the biggest hugs and kisses for bringing words of comfort. Sort of like, "A little child shall lead them."

We stayed close to Ferol and Chawn in the absence of Charles. On Sunday mornings we all attended church together. It wasn't our home church but the church where my sister-in-law and her family went, Prayer Assembly Church of God in Christ. During one service Ferol went into labor and before we left the pastor prayed over her and the coming baby.

Labor was long and hard and it was difficult for Ferol not to have Charles there; she seemed angry about it. Her language was pretty foul and she directed some choice names and words at him. I was able to see my beautiful granddaughter, Shanay Airnet Sims, make her entrance into the world. Her middle name is in honor of her Auntie Alisa. My emotions overflowed with tears of joy. As soon as Ferol's

pain subsided, so did the mean and angry things she had been saying. Those eyes sparkled again with great delight, love, and happiness. It was a beautiful sight. I was try-ing to take it all in and remember every detail because I knew I'd be asked to tell the story of the day Shanay was born.

We were so in love with Shanay and she really

Shanay and Papa

bonded with her Papa. When she could hold her head up and look around, she'd fix her eyes on him and watch where he was going. When he came closer to her she would break into a huge grin. He often sat and held her for hours.

The local news team came to our home to interview Ferol, Charles, and me. They mainly wanted to do a story about Shanay being born out at Williams Air Force Base while her father was deployed. It was very special.

When Charles came home from Desert Storm Shanay was five months old and it took a bit of getting used to. She somehow preferred her papa over her daddy. She wasn't used to this new face *We didn't know it then, but he had PTSD. Hell had etched horrific memories in his mind and soul that weren't going to vanish.* and complexion and size. Everything about him was different. She adjusted though and they did bond; she loved her daddy. Charles was very proud of his family. His little baby girl, his little boy, and his wife Ferol.

Charles sensed that something had changed while he was gone but couldn't identify what it was. He knew he had been through hell and back, but he was relieved and happy to be home. Yet, there was something he couldn't identify. He would ask me, and he'd ask his father, "What is different? What's changed?" We tried to encourage him and let him know we were just happy to have him back home safely. We didn't know it then, but he had PTSD. Hell had etched horrific memories in his mind and soul that weren't going to vanish.

I have a lot of great memories from the time that Charles and Ferol were married. We did lots of things together; family time, picnics, and barbeques, or just hanging out. Justin, Chawn, and Shanay were like the three amigos and spent a lot of time together. I dressed Justin and Chawn alike and doted over Shanay, buying them the cutest little outfits. We played for hours on end. Chawn called my son Charles, "Daddy." I have pictures and memories of all of us together.

Happy faces on happy days. When Charles wasn't deployed, he taught Justin how to ride a two wheeler and he taught the boys all sorts of boy things. They stood on chairs in the kitchen helping me cook or bake cookies. But Charles and Ferol's relationship was full of turmoil. When it was good it was very, very good and when it was bad, well it was like Armageddon!

Ferol didn't like military life. Charles would surely be deployed again if he stayed in and made a career of it. He chose to get out but he and Ferol divorced anyway. It was a difficult time for everyone. We were pulling for them, praying that their marriage would work. Although they came from such totally different backgrounds, I felt they loved each other and I didn't want their family torn apart. Things got really ugly and I cried a lot. I tried to keep my grace and dignity and always remember that Ferol is the mother of my grandchildren. I tried not to take sides and be a safe place to talk. Twenty five years later, I still hate to hear negative things in these situations. I think we can show other people what we expect, or what we will accept. I want to show my kids and grandkids by my own behavior that it's important to talk respectfully about others.

L—R - Shanay, Chawn, Justin

I grieved when Chawn was no longer going to call Charles "Daddy" and when he made it clear that he also didn't have to obey because Charles was not in fact his "real" daddy. In my book that day should never have come. Chawn was a child and I would not have let him call the shots but would have let him talk about it. It was just far too easy for him to write off Daddy. After that day, the visits became fewer and fewer until Shanay spent her court appointed visitation schedule with her father by herself. Slowly over the years, Chawn leaned more towards other relatives and people in his mother's life. I have always remained Grandma and my heart and home always have a place that belongs to Chawn. Now that he is an adult, I think he knows that Charles did indeed truly love him and always will. They talk occasionally and that's good. My grandson and I are good and I count our talks from time to time as a blessing. I miss Chawn a lot.

Windsong

Charles and I went to look at the house on a sunny Sunday afternoon. The listing agent was also the owner of the house, was eager to sell it, and said he was willing to be flexible with the terms. As soon as he unlocked the door, I stepped in and felt at home. What an amazing feeling! I wanted our family to be in this house. I guess all things aligned because the realtor immediately said, "Let's see what we can do to get you in this home."

We nearly gave him our last dime but we didn't care. We were ecstatic. I think the defining moment for us came when our grandson Justin saw the house. He was excited, running from room to room saying, "Oh look at this" and "Oh, would you look at this." When

When he opened the door to the backyard his eyes lit up. "It's Justin's park!" he squealed! "I have my very own park!"

he opened the door to the backyard his eyes lit up. "It's Justin's park!" he squealed. "I have my very own park!" "Thank you Grandma, thank you Papa!" To this day this is one of my sweetest memories.

We moved in and life seemed wonderful. We had room to stretch out. I had a place and space for everything. Justin had his own room, our daughter had her own room, and we had a lovely room with lots of natural light. Charles Jr. was in Saudi Arabia and I took snap shots and video tapes to send him. I was so proud of our new home and loved everything about it, including the address; Windsong had such a sweet sound to it.

Charles was a different man than he had been all the previous years of our marriage. He was now a grandfather. It seemed from the moment he had first held Justin his life was on a different trajectory. He had a new purpose and a new dedication. He definitely had a new found *joy*. When Chawn and Shanay came into his life they added even more joy to his role of grandfather.

By the time we moved into that beautiful house on Windsong Drive we had lived in more houses than I can remember. We had more addresses than I want to remember. We had lived like nomads, but I never saw Charles as content as he was in that place, at the time, with the life he was living.

We had a big party for our twenty-fifth anniversary. It was December and the house was decorated beautifully. Poinsettias filled the entry way, a tall Christmas tree reigned over a corner of the living room. Friends and family came to wish us well and celebrate with us. It felt like we had been in a gratified, blissful marriage forever. I sadly knew the steadiness was unique to our relationship; it was not the reality I was accustomed to. But on that day, in our home on Windsong, I was truly celebrating. I had my family around me and I had Charles and he genuinely seemed happy. It was an exquisite holiday season.

I gave up my day and evening job and did home day care, feeling privileged to take care of some of the sweetest little children. I was fortunate enough by word of mouth to be referred to the families of some NFL players. The Cardinals kept me busy and the work paid me very well.

It was also in that house that I watched as Desert Storm unfolded. Having our son deployed was a virtual nightmare of anxiety. That house was marked by big yellow ribbons on the front door and tied around the trees. Neighbors stopped by often to wish our son God's speed. They cared. *America* cared for goodness sakes. It was a hard time. It was in that same house of joy that I would also stand in the bedroom door-

Norma-Jean and Justin

way as my husband sobbed because he felt he had put our son in harm's way encouraging him to sign up for military service. I remember kneeling before him, comforting him as my own heart broke. He was *our* son.

Life went on in a daily rhythm. Our home was filled with love, lots of laughter, some tears, and some problems. We were just like any family. We loved to be together, even if it was only to cook a pot of spaghetti or grill something. We laughed, talked, teased, made lots of jokes, and made others feel welcome in our home. The door was always open to visitors and we were happy to have them. Everyone who visited said they loved the house and more than that, they loved being in our home. It was in this house that we hosted Kelle's rehearsal dinner the night before her wedding. I knew we'd be there to see our grandkids grow up and bring their children to our backyard park. "Justin's Park." He called dibs!

CHAPTER 28

I Can See Clearly Now

I can't tell this story without telling you some of the amazing things that Charles Sr. accomplished. Charles was an inventor, the wheels in his mind never stopped turning. He was an entrepreneur at heart and worked hard at *everything* he did. I believe that if he had the education, and been cautious and wise in his business relationships, he could have achieved success with his ideas and dreams. I know he could have. I saw people around him like sharks in the water when there is blood. It was his blood but he didn't believe me and repeatedly took their word over mine. He couldn't listen to me because he was internally tormented. I know that now.

Over his lifetime Charles was written up in the newspaper and honored at banquets many times. He had trophies, plaques, and awards for numerous activities and accomplishments. He was featured in the newspaper in Phoenix for his invention of the Toyla Tab, a device that allowed a person to raise or lower the toilet seat without touching the seat. He had a U.S. patent on it. I've seen it on toilets in airports and other places as I have traveled. In California he received many awards for outstanding community citizenship and his dedication to serving youth. He was especially lauded for his years coaching the *Monterey Forty Niners* Pop Warner Football and raising money for children. He made a difference in many wayward kids' lives as well as contributing to many happy and well-adjusted kids. He gave a lot of himself and there were so many grateful families.

Charles coaching Pop Warner football

There were so many sides to Charles, it's difficult to give a fair, clear picture of him. He was big and jolly, sweet, and loving, affectionate, kind, and generous. He was also sad, depressed, and volatile, somewhere in a place I couldn't reach.

I'm sure that over his lifetime he volunteered thousands of hours for various charities and organizations. He had a big heart and as a family we always gave of our time if we couldn't give financially. We devoted time to church, school, clubs, and helping those in need including the homeless, the sick, and the elderly.

Charles was the kind of guy that would make friends with unlikely sorts of people. For example, he had a friend who called himself *Lobster Bob* and carried around a ridiculous big plastic lobster everywhere he went. People laughed and rolled their eyes, but Charles liked him and was his friend. He trusted Bob and was left stunned when Bob took a twenty five thousand dollar investment in a seafood business and went south with it. Another friend was a true gun slinger type, traveling the country going to gun shows. By his own admission Charles was his only black friend. On a Saturday afternoon he could be found in his starched Wranglers and cowboy boots, gun slinging and whiskey drinking with Charles.

Charles made friends with people whose basic desire was to convert our family to their religion. There were the Mormons and the Church of God in Christ. He was also good friends with the local Imam of the Muslim Mosque. I met a lot of really nice people along the way but I wasn't going to change for anything or anyone. He was good friends with Ron from St. Thomas, with a loud voice and boisterous laugh. He was fun to be with and we spent a lot of time with him and his girlfriend Anette. Ron was always there to help if you needed it. Some of Charles' friends became lasting family friends, others I barely remember.

When Charles met George he was instantly like a part of our family. Justin called him Uncle George. I met his mother Maxine when she came to our home to play a game of bid whist with Charles and his parents and George. They all had a great evening. I discovered that Maxine and I both have a love of writing and poetry. It's been one of those lasting friendships for all of us.

Maxine is family to us. When Justin was four she came over with the movie ET thinking it would be great fun to share it with him for the afternoon. He sat in her lap, her arms wrapped around him, watching intently. He seemed to really be enjoying the movie, until… he saw ET! He took off running as fast as his little legs would carry him! Maxine ran down the hall after him only to find him in my room on the other side of the bed looking scared and wide eyed. "Auntie Maxine ET scared me!" "Oh, Justin, ET is nice honey, come back and see, he's nice, he's nothing to be scared of." She coaxed him back to the family room but he watched through anxious fingers. To this day

I don't think he has actually watched *ET,* nor is he interested in doing so, but he does love Auntie Maxine.

George was Charles' best friend, he supported him through any and everything. They worked countless hours together on develop-ing and marketing Toyla Tab. They worked together on various other projects as well. George was there when we were up and he was there when we were sinking. He was there any time one of us was hospi-talized, sitting by our bedside for hours. He was also one of the only people who actually witnessed Charles during his violent episodes toward me. He wasn't having it and stood up to him toe to toe and told him so. If it meant he would sit on the sofa in our family room all night, so be it. He sat right there more than a few times and Charles did indeed take himself to bed and let whatever he was ranting about blow over. I was so thankful to have an advocate that I hadn't even asked for.

George was the kind of friend Charles needed. He was loyal and he genuinely loved and cared about him. He saw in him a great guy who suffered from, here it is, and this is the crux of the problem, **mental illness.**

So that's it. That is why our life had been a roller coaster ride. That's why this man whom I loved so much could be so funny, sunny, bright, loving, giving, caring, witty, affectionate, driven and every-thing in the world I could ever want; only to morph into a state of manic behavior that was always a surprise. It could manifest in a spending spree of money he didn't have, or sexual promiscuity, or uncontrolled anger, or drinking or self-medicating. As I matured and as the mental health community has shed light on conditions such as bi-polar, and manic-depression, border line personality disorder and other conditions, I now know the signs and I know that Charles

> *It's better to raise your arm and say, "Throw me a life line." There are so many sources of help for depression...**National Alliance for Mental Illness Helpline 1-800-950-6264***

had a mental illness. I know he knew it. He had to feel it even if he couldn't identify it. There was such a stigma in years past. Our life could have been so much better. We could have been so much happier. He could have had a peaceful, quiet mind. It must have been so hard to always be in turmoil within his own mind. I can't diagnose Charles, I am not a mental health care professional. I hope that anyone who reads my story and Charles' story, the story of us together… will understand that you can change your life. You have the power.

That's the one big take away. You have power! If you are depressed, don't drown in it. Don't bring down the people around you. How many people have died trying to save a drowning person who is fighting so hard they drag them right under in the rip tide? It's better to raise your arm and say, "Throw me a life line." There are so many sources of help for depression. Doctors may prescribe an anti-depressant. There are non-prescription options like talking therapy. Many resources are available online, look for free agencies, or those that offer services on a sliding scale.

Here is the website and phone number for the National Alliance for Mental Illness (NAMI) Helpline: 1-800-950-6264, www.nami.org.

Don't let anything stop you from getting help! If you attend church you might ask your pastor if there are resources available that he or she can recommend. And lastly, if you are employed, most large companies have employee assistance programs (EAPs) for employees and their families. Please consider using these resources.

If you feel like you might be experiencing more severe mental issues please don't sweep what is going on under the rug. Deal with it head on. If you don't, I guarantee you, one day it will cause a situation that will force you to deal with it. When that day comes you will have regret. Perhaps you have poor coping skills, abandonment, or anger issues, or maybe you use drugs or alcohol to calm anxiety, insomnia, or fears. Perhaps you have a cornucopia of issues you can't even think about. Maybe your mental difficulties are of a sexual nature or perhaps you have hatred towards others, whether it's based on race, politics, or class and you obsess and can't shut it down. The world can be so complicated and we are complicated beings. You never want to find yourself in a situation where the law is involved. Be proactive rather than finding yourself reacting to a bad situation.

It took me years and years of living with Charles and not understanding the origin of his behaviors to gain insight. The saying is "you can't see the forest for the trees." I just couldn't see that Charles had a mental illness of some sort. I know now that his father Emanuel Sr. suffered from depression. He was prone to weeping out of nowhere. I used to try understanding and he couldn't explain to me why he was sad and crying. I think it's a hereditary thing; depression does run in our family.

Recognizing the need for help, seeking it out, and finding the right combination of treatment might take some time. You might go through more than one or two counselors before you find one with whom you click. I don't much go for a counselor who just sits while you talk and then says, "Time is up, see you next week." Try to find a purpose driven counselor. Find someone who can try to get to the issues at hand, map out a goal and a timeline with you, and help you see how you are doing. For instance, if

He would have been free of being held hostage to a dark and scary part of his brain. A part of his brain needed help and was crying out...

you struggle with anger issues, you should be given methods of coping so that things don't escalate to a full blow up. You need to be held accountable for making progress. If you are prescribed medication you must take it and be held accountable to do so, or you won't know if it helps or not. Sometimes it might take several tries before you find the right one.

Charles wasn't in therapy. I wasn't either. In hindsight I wish we both had sought more help with this. His distrust kept me from extended periods of counseling. From time to time, I was on anti-depressant meds; in retrospect I grieve to realize what could have been. Yes, yes, yes I loved Charles unconditionally, but I could have loved him better because he would have been better. He would have been free of being held hostage to a dark and scary part of his brain. A part of his brain needed help and was crying out, but nobody was doing a dang thing. When he was sick with anything physical he got medical care, but not for his mental and emotional struggles. He just ignored it and that part of his brain just kept doing whatever it pleased and whatever it pleased was not good. It raised havoc in our life for decades. It took him over the edge time and again. He would throw things, pound tables, hurt a baby kitten, drive a car over one hundred miles an hour on a switch back road, have sex with a stranger, drink a full bottle of Nyquil, throw me against a wall in a rage and then fall to his knees in remorse and sink into depression for a week. It wasn't what he wanted to do. It was that part of his brain that needed help, crying out "help me, please help me." This behavior is not normal. It is not right, it is not good. When it is a repetitive pattern some would argue that he was just a bad man. I stand and hold firm that Charles Sims was by no means a bad man! He was a man who was tormented, conflicted, and in many ways held back from a life of **JOY** he should have had.

Don't let that happen to you if you know that you are having mental health issues. Live your best life. Claim your *joy!* No excuses.

CHAPTER 29

The Day Lupus Moved In

Sunlight streamed thru the vertical blinds in our bedroom and I thought *I'd better be getting up. Justin will be bouncing in here any minute ready to play. Maybe I have time for one quick cup of coffee before he gets up.* I no more than had the thoughts than I felt the pain and heaviness in my body.

Something was terribly wrong. I closed my eyes as if shutting out the light would take me back to night, I could start the day over again, and it would miraculously be different. I opened my eyes again and allowed my brain to take inventory. *Yep. Something was definitely wrong. Okay. Somebody working on the night crew inside my body did something wrong. But, what?* I hadn't figured it out yet. I laid there trying to think it out. I'm pretty smart. I've been to a lot of doctors and I listen well. I could practically be a doctor. Okay, that's an exaggeration, but I do watch a lot of documentaries, care for sick people, read a lot of books and just talk to lots of people about their health issues. *What the hell is wrong with me?* I wondered.

I lifted one hand after much effort. It had somehow gained two hundred pounds during the few hours I had slept. I managed to move it to the edge of the cover. I flicked the cover like it was a speck of lint on a fine dark suit. It barely moved. I flicked again. It was fruitless. I wiggled my right hand back and forth against my body for extra leverage. I stared up at the ceiling fan thinking it resembled a torpedo headed straight for me and I was pinned to my own bed. *Why did I feel like I couldn't move?* It must be a new form of a panic attack. *Where was Charles? Was he in the bathroom?* I was always up first. I took a deep breath and with the back of my hand flung the heavy sheet and comforter combo off my body. I tried to swing my legs over the side of the bed. I just wanted to get up but my legs weren't cooperating. My body wasn't in sync with the memory of what it was supposed to do automatically. My hands and arms felt so heavy and uncoordinated. My legs were weird huge tree stumps attached to my body, too heavy, too awkward for me to push, pull, or move. I thought for a second they might have fallen asleep, like when you lay on your arm the wrong way and it feels like sand running through. I just knew once movement resumed on my part so would normalcy. I thought *If I can get up and on my feet, I can shake this off.* I couldn't do it. I couldn't move off the bed.

> *I stared up at the ceiling fan thinking it resembled a torpedo headed straight for me and I was pinned to my own bed. Why did I feel like I couldn't move?*

I pinched my soft silk gown between my fingers and held tightly although the motion was extremely painful. I pulled it up towards me so I could see my legs. I stared in disbelief. I was shocked at the sight of my knees in contrast to my soft pink gown. They were swollen and fire engine red. I called out to my husband. No Charles. My voice wasn't carrying through the house. It wasn't reaching him down the hall, around the corner, in the kitchen and family room. I called out again. I felt so helpless. The tears began to fall. I'm rather independent and if I could have gotten up, I sure would have.

Finally, he walked in the room asking, "Did you just call me?" "Yes, there is something wrong, will you please help me?" This time I was the one with a plea. He was immediately on my side of the bed. He looked at my legs in confusion and shock. He lifted my hand, exclaiming, "Oh!" as he turned it ever so slightly to reveal a matching fire engine red elbow. He gently laid my hand down and felt my joints. Not only were they burning red, but they were hot to the touch. "I need to stand up, I have to. Please help me get up." "Norma, there is something seriously wrong, let me call 911." "No, no, no. please don't do that. Please, I'll be fine. Help me. I just want to get up." "You're burning up." "Okay, we'll take my temperature and call the doctor but no emergency people....please just...," and the tears overflowed. I couldn't contain them and I couldn't escape to the bathroom to cry in solitude. I was trapped. I hated for him to see how vulnerable I was.

He took both my feet and like forcing a pendulum to swing he pushed them towards the floor and with his big teddy bear frame scooped me up to a sitting position. That was better. My gown was disheveled but at least I was part way there. He grabbed me around the waist and pulled me to my feet. Pain jolted in a zig zag thru my body and I couldn't read the road map. *Was it going top to bottom, side to side, or bottom to top?* I couldn't sense the direction or the origin of the pain, only the reality. I

Charles propped me up, scared because he too knows this is not a normal way to begin a day. "Help me take a few steps."

was used to feeling pain. I had suffered debilitating migraines for years. I had had multiple surgeries and been diagnosed with arthritis at a young age, so I had some issues. I knew pain...so I thought. This was not like ANYTHING I'd ever felt in my life. So what next? There I stood in my soft silk nightie in my sundrenched bedroom on a morning I had looked forward to spending playing with my grandson.

Charles propped me up, scared because he too knew this is not a normal way to begin a day. "Help me take a few steps." He didn't say anything and held my waist like helping a baby take her first steps. I made it to his side of the bed with slow, heavy, shuffling steps, each stoking the fire in my joints. The pain was a 15 on a scale of one to ten. He backed me to the edge of the bed and eased me back to a sitting position. Then, he disappeared into the bathroom and I heard him fumbling in the medicine cabinet. Returning with alcohol wipes and the thermometer, and like a loving, caring husband he took care of me. "You have a temp of almost 103. We need to take you to the hospital."

"Justin is still asleep and Alisa isn't here. I hate hospital emergency rooms. We'll be there all day. They are awful." He agreed that I was right but he was going to call my primary care doctor himself. Somehow he convinced the receptionist to let him speak with my doctor! He could have so much influence. I heard him describing my symptoms, relating that I have a 103 fever, hot swollen joints, can barely walk, and am terribly weak. Then I hear a series of short answers, "I don't know, I don't know, I don't know, maybe," then a long silence, then "Okay. Thank you doctor." He hung up the phone and I waited anxiously to hear what the doctor had to say. "He said to come in to the office and they will fit us in." The wait seemed like an eternity.

I was confident that the doctor would be able to give me a prescription to help cure this bug and have me on my way. Charles laid me back on the bed and left me there staring at the torpedo in the ceiling with a knot in my stomach. I wanted to grab hold of my usual optimism. I always saw the glass half full, always knew there was a better day ahead, but as I lay there looking up, I felt like I was sinking. Even after hearing the cheerful little voice of my grandson, "Hi Papa." "Hi Mr. J." "You ready to eat some breakfast and go bye-bye?" I still felt forlorn. This certainly wasn't the kind of outing I had planned for today. I had planned for us to go to the park with the big railroad car or the park where we could walk around the lake and feed the ducks.

Alisa wasn't scheduled to be home until evening so I knew I couldn't reach her. Justin would have to go with us. Like I said, no worries, in and out with a cure in hand, that was my plan.

Once Charles had Justin fed, dressed, and ready he brought a warm wash cloth and wiped my face like I was a child. "I need to go brush my teeth." "You can skip your teeth one time. It won't kill you." "That's just plain nasty." But I was glad, I honestly didn't want to grasp the toothbrush and move it up and down. "I have to pee." He helped me to the master bathroom and held me as I eased down to the seat. "You can leave." "Oh for goodness sakes Norma. We've been married for 25 years. Just pee so I can help you get your clothes on!" I just stared at him. He laughed and closed the door. When I was finished he helped me up and gingerly dressed me. I felt helpless. I hated the feeling.

We entered the doctor's office like a very odd trio. A toddler, a not so middle aged man, and a very old lady in a not so middle aged woman's body. We took small steps that were painful for me. Painful and humiliating. As I shuffled along Justin looked at me with tender, wide eyes. He would have carried me if he could have. His super heroes would certainly be a great help at a time like this. The other patients stared at us with rude, long "Wonder what's wrong with her?" stares. When my eyes met theirs their expressions changed to "Excuse my curiosity, I can't help myself. You look so pitiful." Under normal circumstances I would have picked up a magazine and flipped through the pages, pretending to be interested, and ignored the rudeness. I wanted to yell, "What the hell are you looking at?" *Maybe I could stick my tongue out at them!* Instead I lowered my eyes and just sat and waited. We didn't wait long.

The doctor played with Justin for a minute. "Can you blow out the light?" He tells us what a great looking kid he is. "I couldn't agree more," I smiled. I'm always happy

I try to forget why I'm here. I came to show off my beautiful grandson. But I know that's a lie.

247

to talk about Justin and anywhere we take him, he steals the show. I try to forget why I'm here. *I came to show off my beautiful grandson.* But I know that's a lie. I'm very sick on this particular morning. Too sick to play with my favorite little boy in the world. I have a problem and all I need is a prescription from my doctor so we can get home.

That was the beginning of my journey down the rabbit hole. Just like Alice in Wonderland went tumbling head over heels into a land of everything odd and new, so I was now experiencing everything odd and new. After that morning at my doctor's office life became a battery of tests after tests, until finally we had a diagnosis. The oddest word I had ever heard. Lupus. I had been seeing doctors for several years for various things. I had debilitating migraines, aches, pains, stomach problems, female problems, fevers, chills, infections, and rashes. I had been told I had chronic fatigue syndrome, I had been tested for Epstein Barr Virus, and many other diseases but there was no specific test for Lupus. My doctors had never even considered it as a possible culprit for my poor health.

Normally the immune system protects our bodies from invaders that make us sick. With Lupus, the immune system can't tell the difference between invaders that cause harm and our body's own healthy organs and tissues. I won't bore anyone with the scientific details but the bottom line is the autoantibody term in medical lingo means "against itself." These cause pain, inflammation, and damage in many and various parts of the body. It can affect your skin and your organs. Lupus is hard to diagnose because its symptoms can mimic so many other diseases. It's actually known as "the great imitator." This explains why I had previously had so many varied symptoms and diagnoses over the years. The fact that the symptoms may come and go also make it unclear at times. The main blood marker which looks at the antibodies is the primary key, along with eleven criteria doctors look for to make the diagnosis. At the time I was diagnosed I met them all. I was in the midst of my first major flare up. Lupus was not and is not my friend. But Lupus and most autoimmune diseases travel with a friend; my Lupus travels with fibromyalgia whom I am also not fond of but I live with them both inside my body. They are unwelcome tenants but I try my best to manage.

CHAPTER 30

Cindy

T he day my son brought Cindy by to meet me, I understood that he had moved on from his marriage, it was behind him. From the start she was very kind. I was experiencing a lot of medical problems and Cindy, although she barely knew me, stepped in to escort me to various procedures when others couldn't. On one occasion she blessed me with essentials I had not been buying for myself because I had been off work and was struggling to cover living expenses. She purchased bath products, hair color, nail polish, teas, and chocolates, just things to make me feel pampered. It was a kind, generous, and loving gesture never forgotten all these years later.

Cindy was different in many ways than any of Charles' past interests. She was quieter, more mysterious, not an open book at all. It was a bit harder to really feel like I "knew" her well, but I easily felt love for her. She was more mature and settled in her demeanor, a truly responsible, focused woman. She was single, with no children. The day Cindy fell in love with our little Shanay was the day I think Charles let himself see a future with her. I knew that would mean marriage because he is the marrying type. No one could fit into his life without loving his children. That was an absolute must! At first the two of them took both Chawn and Shanay for scheduled weekends, but then just Shanay as Chawn's focus changed.

Charles and Cindy

We accepted the marriage and loved Cindy with our whole hearts. It hurt me as a mother to see my son give his love and heart to someone whose family didn't want him for their daughter. They didn't attend the wedding. I swallowed my tears on that day. I felt for her because every bride wants to have the blessing of her parents. I felt she deserved more, but it wasn't for me to judge them either. Her brother was there, unjudging and loving, that's what she needed and what she deserved. I felt that in her maturity she had waited and saved marriage until now, she knew what she

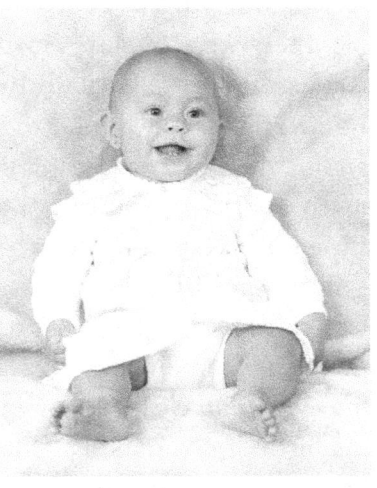

Alexandra Rae Sims,
Allie, six months

wanted and felt she had found it in Charles despite her parents and sisters' views.

They settled into a life, making a comfortable home, taking nice trips together, and obtaining the great things that yuppies go after. One new car after another, even trading a car after Shanay threw up in it on a trip to Disneyland! They were able to do almost anything they set out to do. Then came Allie. Alexandra Rae Sims. I was in the room for her delivery, holding the video camera. And what did I do? I got so caught up in my emotions I began to cry for joy and missed her grand entrance! But I was there. I was so happy. At the time of Allie's birth Charles and Cindy had temporarily moved in with my parents while waiting for a home they were purchasing to close. This was right up my daddy's alley. Each day he walked several miles with Allie, stopping only to show off his great granddaughter to anyone they met along the way. When they moved out to their house my parents were so sad to see them leave; they loved having the baby under their roof.

Charles and Cindy had a beautiful home. She was a good wife and a good mother. They were great hosts for any function—Christmas dinner, birthday parties, etc. They usually traveled out of the country for Thanksgiving.

There were fractures in the marriage, I could see them but of course, now the dynamics were more complicated and we really wanted things to work for the best. I never felt the best decision was ending their marriage but it did end. It became a mess, far from the lovely start. It was very hard to stay uninvolved no matter how hard I tried. But once again things got rocky and I was sucked into drama I didn't want. I tried to make it clear to both that I was not the problem, nor a part of the solution. I would not stop loving Cindy because they weren't in love anymore. I had gone through five years of bonding closer and closer to her, including being in the delivery room for the birth of my granddaughter. We had experienced family celebrations and family vacations and she affectionately called me "Mom."

Our family loved her. It was the worst of situations. I fully supported Charles and I tried to rise above it all.

While I had great admiration for Cindy's parents on one hand, I was deeply hurt by them on the other. I think my hurt was masked in a sort of indignation that I would never express. What I admired was the way her family was able to provide that stable childhood, beautifully documented in professional portraits taken by the same photographer from year one until high school graduation. They did this for every child. Family recipes were meticulously documented and family traditions carried out. All these things I had dreamed of doing; my son had met a woman who also understood and valued tradition. Cindy's parents never formed the same kind of bond with my son that she and I shared. I always found it ironic that a family with racial bias or prejudice could raise a daughter who could fall in love with a black man. Allie was born on Cindy's father's birthday. Happy birthday Grandpa! At any rate, after everything Cindy meant to my son and to our family how could I just wipe the slate clean? It couldn't happen. It would never happen.

CHAPTER 31

Brian

In the meantime, we thought Alisa and Kevin would surely straighten out the ups and downs and back and forth of their relationship. I loved Kevin. He spent a lot of time around our family and we spent a fair amount of time with his family. They were a warm, welcoming, big family. He and his younger brother Johann lived in a small house with their grandmother, grandfather, and their mother at the time I met them. I think everyone hoped that although they were young it would work. The problem was that they were young and they made silly mistakes that hurt each other deeply and eventually undid the hopes for their future.

Alisa dated a couple of other people and we knew something was different about her friend Brian. The laughter coming from the living room during his visits was contagious. He would just show up. "He's here again, from Texas?" I would ask. I thought he must really like her a lot to make the trip so often. Brian was thoughtful, well-mannered, and very generous with Alisa. She seemed quite happy when he came around.

She and Justin moved to Texas and lived with Brian for a time. We traveled to bring Justin back to Arizona to stay with us for a while and she came soon after. Brian proposed to Alisa after he asked her father's permission and approval of the ring he had chosen for her. We were quite impressed with how traditional he was, we liked that about him. We were impressed that he promised to take care of Justin as well as her for the rest of their lives. They started talking about wedding plans and life after Brian graduated from college. Weddings take time to plan and money to pull off so this would give us ample time. They both wanted a big wedding and that's what we planned for. We just had no idea what was ahead.

Alisa and Justin

Alisa and Brian did have a beautiful beginning to their relationship but it didn't stay so beautiful. It became tainted, fraught with dysfunction and fights over things that couldn't be controlled by the other. At one point I felt it would be best to end it. They didn't. I thought Alisa and Kevin would take their child and move forward. They didn't. All I wanted was what was best for everyone, especially my little grandson.

One evening Alisa was experiencing stomach pain and her father took her to the emergency room while I stayed at home with Justin. Charles called me with an update. "The doctor says she's pregnant, and it looks like more than one." "Wait, what? Did you say pregnant? Oh my God! More than one. Like twins! Oh My God!" When they came home Alisa swore the doctors had made some kind of mistake and didn't know what they were talking about. The doctor suggested seeing her OBGYN ASAP.

Alisa was lying on her back in the dimly lit ultrasound room and I was with her. "Okay, let's take a look." The technician squirted the warm jelly over her belly and began rolling the head of scanner around while staring at the screen in front of her. "Let's label these babies Baby A and Baby B, no, no on second thought let's label them Baby A, Baby B, and Baby C!" I was immediately ecstatic. I was grinning and all but jumping for joy. "Mama it's not funny." My baby girl had turned ashen and tears gently ran from her cheeks to the pillow cradling her head. "Oh Sweetie…." I didn't have

> *"Let's label these babies Baby A and Baby B, no, no on second thought let's label them Baby A, Baby B and Baby C!"*

the words to glue her world back together as quickly as the ultrasound in front of us had thrown a boomerang. Three babies. Oh my God!

When she came to herself, the main thing on her mind was she wasn't having three babies with Brian before they were married. The Cinderella wedding would not happen now but they were going to be married before they had these babies. Brian was in shock too. Everyone was. This wasn't a case of using fertility drugs. All natural, one, two, three and they were surely on the way. So Brian and Alisa had a lovely wedding on a spring day in April with family and friends to wish them well. Brian's mother chose not to attend, which was extremely hurtful for them

Brian and Alisa

both. They needed love and support. His other relatives were there; his father, his grandmother, and aunts all came. Alisa looked very pregnant although she was just in the beginning stage.

Her pregnancy was difficult and high risk. She was young, which was a good thing on one hand and not so good on the other. As the pregnancy progressed she was on bed rest and closely monitored. We went for regular ultrasounds and case study by the University Hospital. The goal was to carry the babies as close to term as possible, all while trying to get as much nourishment in them as she could. She had difficulty eating and keeping her food down. She slept in a recliner. She swam in the pool every day for buoyancy relief of the weight she was carrying.

Justin was looking forward to being a big brother. It was going to be a huge change for him. Not one sibling, but three. He had always been the center of attention. He spent a lot of time with us. He was already an old soul and spent hours listening to his papa tell him Bible stories; his favorite was Job, of all things. This little boy had a thirst for knowledge, but he was also a young prayer warrior. He was believing and trusting that his baby brothers and his mama were going to be fine because he asked God to take care of them. Our friend Uncle George took him to the class for siblings at the hospital. He came back excited to tell us all about it. "I'm going to be a really good big brother!" And he has been.

In July Emanuel Sims Sr. became ill and although we're a praying family, God called him home. He passed away on July 11, 1994. Alisa was expecting three little babies within a week, but was distraught at not being able to attend the funeral of her beloved Gramps in California.

⟡ The Three Amigos ⟡

The babies were delivered via C section. The medical teams for each baby were set up and the babies' names were written on the white board in anticipation of their arrival. Brian videotaped the birth and every year on their birthday for years the triplets sat together with their parents and watched it. It was amazing to see.

Baby A—Anthony, Baby B—Brandon, Baby C—Christopher; the delivery didn't go in order. Christopher was first out, then Anthony, and then Brandon. All the babies were beautiful, perfect, and healthy. Brandon had a hard time transitioning but after being in his little bubble for a few hours, he was fine. It had certainly been a stressful pregnancy for Alisa. God blessed them and blessed our family.

The most amazing gift was that her tiny little Brandon looked like he had been kissed by Gramps before he went to heaven because that little baby boy looked just like him! Talk about *joy*, to look at him and say, "He looks just like Gramps!"; our hearts overflowed with joy!

Brian, Alisa, and Justin were all very excited with their new family. I was just so thankful to God for bringing them here safely and in good health. I knew that my baby girl was tired. This had taken a considerable amount out of her and she wouldn't have much time for recovery. Her little family was going to need her.

They lived in a two bedroom apartment in the beginning. Brian had just graduated from college at UTEP in El Paso, TX and was starting a career in the world of finance. We brought the babies home from the hospital in Uncle George's car because it was the only one big enough to hold three car seats. The babies were so small they all slept in one cradle. Within seven to eight weeks they moved from the cradle to a shared crib and eventually to three separate cribs. Brian and Alisa purchased a minivan and moved from the two bedroom apartment to a three bedroom house. They were on their way.

The Three Amigos, L-R Anthony, Brandon, Christopher

CHAPTER 32

Devon Troy and the Rainbow Baby

On November 10, 1995, my baby girl lay in her bed in the maternity ward at Chandler Regional Hospital. Things were not going well for her and the baby. It was far too early; they tried everything but couldn't stop her labor. Tragically Devon was stillborn, he was not yet ready for this world. We were all broken hearted, stunned, and bewildered. We hadn't been through anything like this before and the hospital staff were neither helpful nor compassionate. They didn't even offer Alisa or Brian the opportunity to hold Devon. I was allowed to watch as the nurse bathed and dressed him in the tiniest of preemie clothes. Oh how my heart was aching, I wanted to just pick him up and hold him. I didn't say a word as I gazed at him, memorizing every tiny detail while my heart broke. Alisa was inconsolable, her heart in agony as her world stopped. My world stopped with her. I held her and cried with her. How could it possibly have happened? We were all in disbelief. The staff just gave us instructions with little empathy attached. "Call the mortuary," they told Brian, "the sooner the better." However, someone compassionate taped a piece of paper with a picture of a butterfly on Alisa's door, the signal to other staff not to come bouncing in asking, "How is our little mommy doing today?"

My baby girl was sorrowful and lost. She was barely hanging on. When she was discharged from the hospital we all rallied around to help with the children at home and to plan something to honor Devon. Justin actually chose his baby brother's name.

Devon was cremated and we had a private service with our family at Brian and Alisa's' home. My friend, minister Francine Sample, officiated. It helped to have this ceremony to acknowledge him and celebrate his short life. We all longed to know him. Tiny as he was, it was clear that he was going to look exactly like his brother Brandon.

In memory of Devon, Alisa has a tattoo of a butterfly on her ankle and on top of her foot she has his tiny foot prints...

In memory of Devon, Alisa has a tattoo of a butterfly on her ankle and on top of her foot she has his tiny foot prints, the exact duplicate of his footprints they took in the hospital. So symbolically he always walks with her. The butterfly is beautiful...sometimes we only see a very special butterfly for one moment, but we remember it for a lifetime. She carried her baby for months and then saw him for only a few minutes, but his memory is with her forever. Alisa and Brian have a grief that will never heal and binds them in a secret place no one can enter because of the great loss of their child. The rest of the family grieves for Devon also. Siblings, grandparents, uncles, aunties, and cousins, we miss the opportunity to share our love and our joy with him. My grandson is with me forever. This beautiful baby boy is a part of our family. We wanted him to be with us but God called him home before we could have the opportunity. He is loved. He is remembered.

❧ Rainbow Baby Girl ❧

More than anything in the world Alisa longed for a baby girl. Some people surely thought she was crazy with a house full of toddler boys but it was her heart's desire. The boys had everything blue and all the boy toys as well as sweet stuffed bears and bunnies too.

Their daddy was already daily sitting Justin and the three amigos in their infant seats in front of the television tuned to ESPN. This longed-for little girl was going to eventually be lost in a sea of sports talk, smelly boys, and testosterone. Alisa wanted pink bows and frilly, dainty, girly things to match her own girly girl style. She hoped for a baby girl to one day grow up and be close to her like she is to me. I clearly understood. But after carrying the triplets and tragically losing Devon, I wasn't sure another baby was in her future.

However, God heard her prayer and although her pregnancy was just as wrought with difficulties as the others and required a surgery and bed rest, on March 7, 1997, Bria Nicole Shaw was born. As with her siblings, she was also delivered by cesarean. She was a magnificent, little pink bundle of love. She didn't have a single wrinkle anywhere and had a lavish head of dark hair and full rosy cheeks. Her parents were elated and overcome with joy. Her name is a compilation of Brian and Alisa…Bria, Nicole catches the "n"

Bria Nicole, age one

from Brian. She even has a dimple in her chin just like her daddy.

They call a baby born after a loss or a miscarriage a rainbow baby. Bria came to show Alisa and Brian, as well as the rest of us, that joy can come after the storm and there are rainbows. She has colored our world with happiness and smiles.

CHAPTER 33

Pierced Sparrow · Angel Visit

A s with everything that I had ever hung my hopes on for twenty-five plus years, the house on Windsong was a dream that ended. It was truly a heartbreaker and required me shoring myself up, pulling on my big girl panties, telling a few well thought out and calculated lies, and putting on another deceitful but pleasant smile for the world. It was so hard to do when inside I was screaming out loud, *Nooooo!* and *Why, God?* I was tormented by what this did not only to me but to my family, but we had no choice. I was also secretly enraged with Charles because I had placed my faith in him, again. I saw such change in him. He wasn't the man he used to be. He was much more focused on family, but obviously financial matters were still a problem.

Through the years, although we lived like nomads, Charles and his brothers tried so hard to keep their parents in the home they loved so much. Nobody ever wanted to let Mom down. After the family scattered it was no longer possible to say, "the proceeds from this job are for Mom." Everyone now had a different way of earning income.

As things unraveled, Mom and Dad lost the beloved "Sims House" on the hill and we all grieved.

Mom and Dad moved to Arizona to be closer to us and put stakes down for a new start. They lived in a new, rented house on our street but it was nothing like the home they left. They were living on Social Security and times were lean.

We could also walk five minutes to my parents' house on Stottler Avenue in Chandler. It was great! It felt like the best part of the old days when we had all lived in Seaside. Before long LoVera and her family moved to town. They stayed with Mom and Dad for a couple of months before getting a place of their own.

Charles' health was failing. Our car was gone. Income gone, and now I was on disability due to lupus complications. Since leaving the house on Windsong I had returned to work to try my hand at leveling out financial things. Charles was on the fast track with his inventions. He was marketing, had an office and employees, and was being written up in the Phoenix newspapers. He had promises of big money from big investors but it was all grossly mishandled. He was dealing with some very corrupt people but wouldn't see it as he was anxious for things to work in his favor. It all hit the bottom.

The stress was getting to me. This is one of the triggers for Lupus flare ups. Before our move to the condo we lived in another house and his mother moved in with us. This was also promised to be our forever home. One day Alisa came to visit and in the large, beautiful mesquite tree shading the front yard was a sparrow, my favorite bird, pierced through the heart and stuck on a branch. She came in the house distraught because to her the sparrow symbolized me. Alisa occasionally had uncanny dreams and visions of things to come. The next day, as I was pulling some weeds in the yard I began to feel pain and sensation in my chest that I knew wasn't normal. I went in and told my mother-in-law who lived with us at the time and Charles I needed to go to the emergency room. Charles immediately took me, but by the time I got there my blood pressure was bottoming out. They put me on a gurney in a room with curtains all around. Before I knew what was happening they had pulled the other beds from around me. I threw up a bucket of black gunk and passed out. My heart stopped and they hit me with the paddles. More than once! They didn't know what was wrong. I went into complete organ failure and although they had gotten my heart started again it wasn't keeping up. The cardiologist came and I was given a temporary pacemaker. Family was gathered and told I probably wasn't going to make it. My sister-in-law LoVera, the prayer warrior of the family, asked the doctor if she could come to pray over me. Of course she did. I wasn't aware of anyone around me. But I know without a doubt that God gave me a vison and a choice.

So, my vision and my choice came while I was in the hospital. I could feel myself slipping. Some would say this was a near death experience. I just call it miraculous. I was in darkness but only the kind of darkness that consumes you when asleep, it wasn't a dark room kind of thing. Just eyes closed and seeing nothing and then…well, then I saw the faces of each of my grandchildren. Like I was being shown them would best describe it. Then I saw my sweet baby grandson Devon and he had a glow about him, glorious and beautiful. I wanted to go to

> *I saw the faces of each of my grandchildren. Like I was being shown them would best describe it. Then I saw my sweet baby grandson Devon and he had a glow about him.*

him and cradle him, hold him, and caress him. Although just a baby, he looked at me knowingly. His eyes were like windows to his soul saying it is all okay. "Come, love me, hold me, and be with me, there is peace here, there is *joy* here, and there is sanctuary here." Then I saw Justin! Behind him the others, but Justin! It was as if God said, "I know you are tired, I know you are sick, and if you want to come, Devon is here. But if you will fight, I will give you strength and I will give you the way back to be there for a life with your *joy*. Your grandbabies need you. And most of all you will not break Justin's heart. He is the one who will glean much from you to pass on to the others and to future generations." It was all unspoken but understood in an instant. There was no time, no way to measure, no separation of space and time, of light and darkness. No words to speak. God granted me rest and restoration.

My own baby girl was there with me on that first night. Everyone else left me, I don't know why. She told the staff there was no way she was going to leave her mama. She had fallen asleep and told me later that at one point a nurse woke her to tell her they had lost me again for a minute. They later inserted a pacemaker. Alisa stayed with me and I'm so thankful that she loves me so much. She advocated for me when I couldn't speak for myself. I needed her. Her father tried to be there but tired easily. He had health issues of his own.

When I came around I opened my eyes to realize I was in a hospital bed with many, various bottles hanging from IV poles. I lifted my hand as high as I could; I'm not sure if I really did or if I thought it. I wanted to speak up and show my "Hallelujah Jesus here's my praise to you." I wanted to give Him my best "Thank you for saving me." I already know I'm saved by His blood, saved by His dying on the cross for me and my sins, but this was in real time, saving my real, physical life. I knew then and I know now that I will be with Devon, but I have a lot of living to do and a lot I need to give to my family. In an instant I understood that I was still there lying in that bed, with all the poles, the medicine, the machines beeping and whirling, because in a split fraction of immeasurable time in a vison from God, I chose Justin. I couldn't break his heart. I understood that God was telling me I had much to teach him that would be passed to the others. Justin was a light in the darkness. He was an old soul who understood more than I knew he did. He is a warrior who will valiantly fight and win many battles because the Lord is on his side. He is chosen. His parents may not even realize it, but it's in his name; in the middle between first and last Matthew; a gift from God. He will not fail and I will not fail him. I wanted to shout "Thank you God for saving me. Thank you for my vision. Thank you Lord for my family. Thank you for Justin as he truly is a gift from you!"

Further proof to me of things that can knit one closer to God Almighty are many other small incidents that do not make sense but I know that I know they happened. Others may doubt, but I know it was only by God's good grace and mighty love that I was able to pull through.

I was in and out of sleep, aware of people doing things to me but too sleepy to see what and why. One day I could barely open my eyes but I felt someone very close to me and I could feel the love in the room. I opened my eyes then and there was this beautiful woman wearing a nurse's uniform. Dark hair, dark eyes, and I'd say perhaps of Hispanic descent. Her nationality is not important; I merely mention it to describe her in more detail. She carried a bouquet and told me she wanted me to have these flowers from her garden. They were lovely, aromatic fresh cut roses in a

> *One day I could barely open my eyes but I felt someone very close to me and I could feel the love in the room. I opened my eyes then...*

variety of glowing colors. She held them under my nose and I sniffed. Then she placed them on the bedside table, stroked my hair, and gently touched my face. Her touch was so comforting, I cried. She told me to have no fear I was going to be all right and to rest. I thanked her and watched her leave the room before drifting back to sleep.

In ICU they discourage fresh plants and flowers. Yet, those flowers sat there. A day or so must have passed and I wanted to see her again. I wanted to tell her I hoped she knew what her kindness and tenderness and the gesture of flowers meant. When I asked about her nobody knew of her. Not one single person had seen anyone like her. "No, she doesn't work here." "No, no one like that I've ever seen." Over and over I got the same answer. Yet the proof was sitting right there. Perhaps she was a pink lady and I had mistaken her for a nurse. That also was not the case. The smell of roses filled the air and gave me a comforting sense. I know now that she was an angel who came to me to give me a message of comfort and hope. She left evidence that she was there so I would have no doubt. I can't blame it on the drugs they were giving me. I can't blame it on the fact that no one else saw her. The beautiful, fragrant flowers were tangible evidence.

One day sometime during my stay, I opened my eyes because I felt a familiar touch. The oddest thing in the world, eyes closed and many, many people touching and caring for me but this was different than the rest. I could feel the love and concern. I opened my eyes and there stood Pat! Oh my God! She was there with me. She had come. She always comes. She has always found a way. What a tear-filled visit. I was overcome with *joy* to have my very best friend there with me. I don't remember how long she stayed in town or any other details, just feeling utmost happiness at that moment. Her being there confirmed for me just how sick I really was. But I also knew that I was on my way to recovery. I couldn't have been more grateful.

Before I left the hospital my body and blood values returned to near normal function. The temporary pacemaker was removed, my own heart was working fine and keeping up with every beat. I was so happy to exit the doors and breathe in the fresh air and sunshine. I felt like I had just been given a new lease on life. There was much to do and I had plans to make.

Of course no one leaves the hospital and jumps right into the drill of everyday life. It takes a few days to regain steam and get things in motion. Once I had momentum there was no stopping me.

༄ Chrissy ༄

When I first met Chrissy I have to admit I was torn. I was fiercely loyal to Charles' previous wife, Cindy. I was also loyal to my son. I absolutely wanted him to be happy. If he had found happiness with someone else I of course wanted to support him. I just told myself to be a little guarded. I didn't want to fall into a pattern of getting close and loving his loves and then if things unraveled being expected to put my feelings aside. I don't operate like that emotionally. If I love you, I pretty much am probably always going to love you, unless you personally hurt me. I had been through his break up with Ferol and I still loved her and would always have her in my life because of Shanay. I knew the same was true of Cindy because of my granddaughter Allie.

When I met Chrissy, I couldn't help but really like her even though I tried to keep my guard up. She was funny, bright, and spirited. She is ten years younger than Charles and made him laugh. Before I knew it they were getting married. I was sincerely worried that his divorce wasn't going to happen in time but just in the nick of time it did. They had a beautiful wedding and began their life together. Chrissy was a wonderful stepmother to Allie, who adored her, and to Shanay as well. Shanay was a bit more reluctant but in time also developed a relationship with Chrissy.

As with all of my grandchildren born naturally, I was in the delivery room to experience the birth of Zachary Ryan Sims, Charles' and Chrissy's son. He is the youngest of my eight grandchildren and oh the joy! He is the very best thing to ever happen to me on Friday the 13th!

Charles and Chrissy

CHAPTER 34

Hope

The house of the sparrow held promise of finally being our forever home. We planted trees and made improvements, thinking we would benefit in the years to come. It was not the case. Charles had made a bargain with someone who may as well have been named Lucifer. It was an awful, painful experience that led to profound disappointment when the funding for the house did not materialize. He was lied to and let down by shady businessmen conducting shady business deals. A shady businessman up to his eyeballs in shady business deals bargained with Charles on the future of Toyla Tab, hoping to steal the patent. Charles trusted him. As a result we lost and once again were forced to move.

The afternoon when we went to see the condo in Ahwatukee it was unusually dreary and overcast, my least favorite kind of day. The owner/agent had every light on and the space appeared cheery and clean. It was affordable and we took it. The day we moved in, I felt like we had been tricked. It was a beautiful sunny day, my favorite kind of day. The condo was dark. Darkness oozed into every corner and the walls seemed to intentionally block the sunlight. *Oh no!* I thought. *I'm going to hate this!* I didn't hate it though. I adjusted and adapted. And coped by keeping the lights on at all times.

I fixed up the two bedroom place we now called home. One bedroom was for the grandchildren, full of toys, books, and things for the kids to enjoy. The other room was ours. We enjoyed summer afternoons in the pool with the family. There was a long period of time we didn't have a car and shopping was conveniently just across the street. During this time Charles began dialysis. The clinic sent a little medical transport bus by for him in the morning and after five and a half hours they brought him home. I used to walk him out to the bus the same way I did with my children when they were young. Sometimes I could feel the lump in my throat and the tears welling up before I could turn and head back to our condo. I was dejected that his health had come to this.

I tried so hard to be a good wife, a good life partner, taking care of him through sickness and in health. Over the years we had been together he had gone from being an athlete in perfect health to a man in serious, declining health. It was a hard struggle. I was often silently angry with Charles for not participating more in taking care of his own health. I was sad that he hadn't heeded the warnings of not just one or two doctors but multiple doctors over the years. This was preventable! That was the thing that was so infuriating. It didn't ever have to come to this, a life bound by being plugged to a machine, having his blood cleansed of all the toxins and returned so he could be ready to perform as near to normal as they could get him. This was my hero. He was the college jock, the tennis player, the guy who could run the dunes with a child piggy back. Now, he could barely walk twelve feet without difficulty. At first he kept making efforts to try to push the envelope and see if he could regain some of what he had lost.

> *He was the college jock, the tennis player, the guy who could run the dunes with a child piggy back. Now, he could barely walk twelve feet without difficulty.*

When Justin was playing Pop Warner football Charles longed to be there to guide and coach him. He knew him better than any coach on the field. Justin inspired him. This grandson was a natural athlete from the time he took his first steps. The coaches were always open to pointers from someone with so many years of experience. Many days he made it to the field by way of a cane, a walker, or the assistance of me or a family member. There were a few times when he pushed him-self terribly hard to be there. He loved his grandson so much that he would do anything.

Papa's Kickback Time

He wanted to be there for all of his grandkids as they participated in the Saturday games or cheered from the sidelines like our cute little cheerleader granddaughters. I loved the way this big guy wholeheart-edly loved and cared for our grandkids. There were no restrictions on what he would do for any of them. On some days he would pick up Bria and take her to the Dollar Store. He'd let her buy bags of candy to share with her brothers and cousins, teaching them all how to be generous. Charles would also have the kids do what he called "Kickback Time." This involved having them lay on their backs with their hands behind their heads and one leg crossed over the other. This taught them all when it was time to be quiet and settle down, something their parents really appreciated! One of his favorite things was inviting everyone to impromptu barbeques at Kiwanis Park, just to have fun being together as a family.

One frightening day the rescue unit had to be called to the football field when he collapsed. That really scared the kids and was a symptom of his further declining health.

During the years we lived in the condo, I had my own bouts with Lupus and Fibromyalgia. There were days of debilitating migraines but I knew I had to keep moving forward. I babysat for a time because it didn't require me to go anywhere. I made handcrafted little dolls that I called "Angel Babies." I would do just as much as I could and tried to stay productive and busy.

At this same time in my life I began to see my mother's health failing. With arthritis and severe cellulitis in her legs, she was becoming less mobile. Mama also had cardiomyopathy which made her fatigue easily. She had Daddy bring her for a visit as often as she was able to get out. I have pictures of us all in that tiny condo having dinner around the small dining table. It was home for the time being and we were trying to enjoy it like it was exactly what we wanted. It was not! Sometimes what you want and what you need are vastly different. We needed to be there because it let us live within our means and control what we could.

While on dialysis Charles found hope for brighter days in lighthouses. Along with his strong faith in God Almighty, he said he could suddenly relate to what the shining beam meant. He bought sketch pads and colored pencils and watercolors, becoming quite the artist during his long dialysis treatments. He also drew old barns, his mother's favorite, and began earning money off his artwork. People were fascinated that he was self- taught and full of passion. They bought his work because they liked it and he was relatable.

༺☙ Vows Renewed ❧༻

Charles had been on dialysis for a couple years when he asked me to forgive him for all the past hurts and renew our vows. I had forgiven him long before he ever asked for it. He sold enough artwork to pay for a lovely ceremony and reception at a local golf course. He replaced my ring with one that made everyone say "wow" when they saw it. He really stretched himself out there to try to make me happy and give me the best possible anniversary gift ever! He exceeded every expectation. Pat was there, my kids and their families were there, my parents and his mother and youngest brother Donald were there as well as a few very close friends. It was a beautiful day, sunny and warm. He looked handsome in his dark suit. I wore a wedding gown I found on an outlet store clearance rack. I loved the tea length gown with a chiffon layered skirt and long lace sleeves. Toni sent me pretty gold earrings for the occasion, their clear gems glistened and sparkled in the sun.

We stood outside in front of my minister friend Francine. She wore her minister's robe and a grin bright enough to match the sunny day. She had put so much into what she wanted to say to us. She hoped for a bright future filled with many more years of love. She spoke eloquently about love and hope and chided us to remain prayerful. Charles had asked her to publicly state that he was doing this because he wanted a new start and wanted forgiveness for all past hurts. He wanted me by his side to walk into a happier life. He wanted to be secure that he had my love. He had always had my love. There was no question. He had always had my forgiveness as well. It was heart touching and special. He looked very healthy on that day and we both beamed with joy.

Our anniversary falls in December. Unlike our original wedding, which was beautiful but had no hint of Christmas in sight, this time Christmas was on full display. The reception area was decked with gorgeous trees and festive centerpieces. He didn't hire a DJ but did have music. He took me by the hand and slow danced to Luther Van Dross singing *Here and Now*. He danced with his mother, the sweetest sight, and I danced with my son and grandson. We ate delicious food with our friends and family and cut the cake like newlyweds do. I was overjoyed. This was the kind of moment I had waited for, for more years than I can count. It was our 32nd anniversary. People usually do such events for their 25th or their 50th. We did celebrate our 25th with a great big party at our house on Windsong, but I felt in my soul it wasn't genuine. At that party the best of it was seeing how excited

> *I was overjoyed. This was the kind of moment I had waited for, for more years than I can count.*

Justin was to be there. In nearly every picture he was standing right next to me. For this day we included Justin and Shanay, beautiful in their holiday best. I just kept thinking *Wow, he did all this for me!* I felt so blessed and grateful. My parents were particularly happy. They had also waited a long time to see that I was Charles' one true love. He made it clear that the old ways, old habits were gone and this was a new beginning. It was a time to celebrate!

That evening Pat and her then boyfriend Doug took us to The Phoenician resort for a special dinner. We were floored by the service and the food. The plates were set before each of us in unison by waiters with tea towels draped across their arms. The Phoenician is known for impeccable service of every kind. Doug generously said, "Don't look at the prices of anything, order anything you'd like." I think dinner probably cost the equivalent of our entire day. He and

Pat also booked us a casita for the night at another lovely resort, the Camelback Inn. They drove us and picked us up the next day. Our friends contributed in a huge way to making it a day with memories to last a lifetime.

CHAPTER 35

I Never Could Have Done
It Without Jesus

Eventually Mama developed such severe infection in her legs that she had to be hospitalized for a lengthy period of time. The doctors wouldn't release her to go home so Daddy and I arranged for her to be admitted to a skilled nursing facility. She was resistant and didn't want to be there. I didn't want her there either but the situation was untenable. She and Daddy had a house full of pets, two dogs and two cats, and the house needed sterilization and a thorough cleaning to reduce the shedding pet hair. They opposed it. They didn't want anyone coming in to do anything! I wanted to clean, their grandkids wanted to clean, but they fought all of us on it. Their answer was a hard no! Neither would they consider giving up their beloved pets. Perhaps with the pets and carpets gone and new flooring Mama could live at home and have a visiting nurse. It was not to be.

Mama was signed into Mi Casa Nursing Facility. I cried like a baby the first time I walked in there and down the hall to her room.

An ambulance had brought her the short distance from the hospital to the facility. I just knew Mama was going to hate it there. She did have rough days but for the most part she perked up. It was like she suddenly had a new lease on life. She got to know all the nurses on the floor and they loved her. They were kind and attentive. I could call the nurses' station on her wing at any time day or night and they always gave me concise and honest updates.

We had a private telephone line installed in her room so that even though we weren't in close proximity I could talk to her multiple times each day. My children and their families visited her often. Daddy gave up the pets and moved out of their house and into a small patio home within walking distance of Mi Casa and visited her every day. They still fussed and fought; he'd leave and come back later. Some things never change. Mi Casa offered Mama the opportunity to socialize, albeit in the controlled environment, and she adapted like a trooper. She often talked about going home but it seemed a huge hill to climb. I wanted her safe and well cared for and as happy as one could expect. However, I struggled with great guilt. This was my beloved mama. I wanted with all my heart to be able to care for her but I felt drained from both Charles' and my own health issues. The two of us were in and out of the hospital repeatedly, one after the other.

Guilt made me question everything I was doing. It seemed I could never do enough. How could I have bathed her at home? The facility had a chair on a winch that was used at bath or shower time. Special medicated dressings had to be changed twice each day.

Norma-Jean and Mama

At Mi Casa it was consistent and scheduled. She received infusion therapy for the ongoing infection. I didn't need to worry about her being in pain, it was controlled.

As time went by I observed Mama's new sense of purpose. She was teaching other patients to crochet or knit. She took on the task of starting a patient advocacy group with the other patients. They would meet and discuss anything from the meals they desired to have served, to the way the nurses handled their individual cases. She would then bring these concerns to the staff. They liked having her there. She was definitely unique. She enjoyed participating in group activities and attended Sunday morning worship held in the big communal

> *I observed Mama's new sense of purpose. She was teaching other patients to crochet or knit. She took on the task of starting a patient advocacy group with the other patients.*

living room. Every single holiday was celebrated with fanfare, complete with decorations, food, and entertainment. Mama had her own television with cable. She loved watching basketball, football, gymnastics, and figure skating. She had a weekly appointment at the on-site beauty parlor and looked better. She was clearly doing better in all aspects of her life. I was there with her as often as I could be, at least two or three times a week, and chatted by phone on the days I couldn't make it. When I called to let her know I was on my way, she often asked me to bring her something from a nearby restaurant. She favored chalupas from Taco Bell and fish and french fries from Long John Silvers. I would often sign her out and we'd go to the local shopping center. I'd throw her wheelchair in the trunk and off we'd go. I loved to see her with her big sunglasses and a smile on her face, and basked in her joy. We'd shop for little things she wanted and have lunch. Sometimes the kids would take her out. All in all, when I look back, I'm grateful for the three extra years I had with her. Surely she wouldn't have lasted as long if it were not for their care.

❧ Trilogy ❧

One day before we were due to sign a renewal on our lease, our son took Charles and me for a ride. He knew it was time for a change for us as well. Although I wasn't saying anything he knew my heart. I mainly wanted more space and natural sunlight. We drove around different neighborhoods and then he took us to Trilogy. It felt like the gates of heaven had opened. Actually, it was the gate to a gorgeous community. There was a golf course, a full service restaurant for residents, walking trails, and more. He parked in front of the house he wanted to show us. It was brand new and yes; it was very light and bright. It was perfect.

With the help of family we moved. I was now closer to Mama. Charles had to change dialysis centers, which was difficult after being with the same staff for years. He adapted just like Mama did. Soon he had friends there. I wondered how we could maintain everything and applied for multiple jobs. I was hired by America West Airlines.

Charles always talked about wanting to travel, but even with my free flight benefits we only flew twice. It was too physically difficult. There's much to be said for living your dreams when you are able. It's sad to feel defeated when you're trying to do something you always dreamed of but postponed. Try to make it happen, nothing is promised.

Oh how we loved that house in Trilogy, it was truly a great place. We ate lunch or dinner in the delicious, affordable restaurant once or twice a week. My mother-in-law could come to stay for a few days as well as LoVera. Our kids and grandkids visited often and daily life was okay. I worked in the afternoon until eleven at night. The airport was a pretty far drive for me. I'm not a comfortable driver and am always anxious, driving at night is the worst. I knew I had to keep my job so I did all I could day to day. Daddy was of course, my buddy; he was always there for me even though his life had been upended.

Charles was getting weaker and weaker. He tried to do exercises like flexing his legs in his dialysis chair to strengthen his muscles and encouraged the other patients to join him. He was losing weight but he was still a large man. He often fell and I had no choice but to call the paramedics as I was simply unable to help him up. Right outside one of the gates was a fire and rescue department. The greatest guys worked there and often helped us. Just as Charles was in such failing health I too was struggling and was in and out of the hospital.

Oh how I loved being there in Trilogy, in spite of the health challenges I was happy.

⧼⦿⧽ Good-Bye Mom ⧼⦿⧽

My mother-in-law had come for a visit at our home in Trilogy. We often drove an hour or more all the way to the other side of the valley to the senior apartment she moved to when we lost the house on Kelly Lane in Tempe. Charles had always been good to her and would give her the world if he could. However, on what would be her last visit, his language and behavior to her were mean and aggressive. I do not know why. Yes, I do. It's back to the mental illness. She was never one to cry easily but that day she cried. I felt awful and defended her against his harshness. A few weeks later we would take Mom to the emergency room for back and stomach pain and she was diagnosed with pancreatic cancer. As soon as she heard the diagnosis, she gave up any desire to live and requested that her medications be stopped. She was resigned and wanted her journey to end. Although she would never hurt herself in an attempt to end her life, she also was not willing to do anything to save it. The matriarch of the family, the one whom everyone had loved spending time with, was running out of time.

She was transferred to a hospice facility known to be one of the best near her daughter Linda. The staff was empathetic, warm, friendly, and helpful. Our large family gathered from everywhere. When we started our married life, we all lived in close proximity to one another, but now we were scattered. Some of the family had stayed in California and we were in Arizona. Her grandchildren came to her bedside from wherever they lived. Her room at hospice seemed so full of life for someone who would soon be leaving us. We all knew how strong she was and like everything I had known her to do, she was doing this on her own terms as well. The lack of insulin to regulate her diabetes and lack of medication to control her high blood pressure only took a couple of days to impact her. I wanted to make them give her medications. They did give her medicine, but it was morphine for pain. That's what hospice does is provide palliative care.

Mom's children, grandchildren, and church folk surrounded her, keeping vigil. Her granddaughter Alicia has the voice of an angel and sang songs. We all listened, sometimes even joining in, but we were not blessed to have her voice. There were giggles from time to time when a story was shared. Little kids played nearby and we were once again together like we had all been in the big house on Mescal St. back in Seaside, California.

Mom's children, grandchildren, and church folk surrounded her, keeping vigil. Her granddaughter Alicia has the voice of an angel and sang songs.

Over the years I had become more Sims than Jackson, although I was born Jackson I knew very little about them. I knew Sims family history, family stories, and family birthdates. I would miss Mom Sims with all my heart.

My baby girl, Alisa didn't want to leave her grandma. When, weary from the day, everyone had left to go home and rest to be able to return the next day, she stayed at her Mimi's bedside. As she nodded off the nurse urged her to lie on a nearby couch and catch a little nap. She reluctantly agreed. She had barely fallen asleep when the nurse gently woke her up and told her that she was gone. Just like that.

It was only a few minutes. The nurse explained that so often the dying person will wait until their loved one leaves the room to take their last breath. It's like they want to spare them the pain. Alisa called her cousin Alicia first and asked her to notify everyone else.

It was such a difficult and truly sad time for the family. However, I had to smile to myself and say Mom died on her own terms. No fighting the disease. She just said "Come on. I'm ready to go and there is nothing anyone can do to change my mind." So, good for you Airnet Sims!

There were two services for her. The first one was in Arizona and I wasn't able to attend because I had to have emergency gallbladder surgery. The second was a service in Paso Robles followed by her burial which was attended by people from far and wide. At that time I shared a few words that described our long friendship:

Of all that I am, I hope in the end that my children will love me as yours have loved you and they will be proud to have called me their mother. Your children are so proud of you. Now I'm a grandma with my own clan and just as we started I'm Mrs. Sims too. I've learned so many lessons, too many to count....One thing I know is that no matter by what name they call you, Mrs. Sims, Airnet, or Mimi, I've called you my mother, my friend. And for that I'm so grateful because you've taught me so much. You gave me a family of brothers and sisters to call my own. We've experienced friendships and laughter, hardships and tears and countless talks through the years. One thing I can tell you, you raised all your children and your work was well done....

That is the main thing I learned from our past. Love is the answer in all that we do. I'll think of you often as I always do. I'll have many questions as my life goes on and for some of those answers I'll look up to you.

CHAPTER 36

Please Don't Go

After we had buried Mom, Charles became very depressed. We started having weekly home counseling sessions with Hospice of the Valley. This grief counseling was a wonderful service they provided and seemed to help Charles some. However, it was not enough and it seemed like he was losing his desire to live. When his mother left the world she took the largest piece of his heart with her. I don't think anything or anyone could have truly helped him. I tried and others tried. His mood could swing from sunny and positive to dark and dreary in an instant. Every time the counselor came to talk with us I needed to grab a handful of tissues. Charles would start off in a soft, low, monotone voice telling the counselor how much he missed his mom. He described how he felt like his heart had been ripped right out of his chest and he had such sorrow in his eyes. I would look at him, listen, and weep.

Charles needed a strong desire to live if he was going to overcome his health problems. Throwing in the towel was not an option! But oh God, it sure felt like that was what he chose.

He now had a pacemaker to keep his heart rhythm stable after experiencing several bouts of losing consciousness after dialysis. The doctor had first approached his loss of consciousness as a result of perhaps removing too much fluid during the treatment. Finally they diagnosed him with a heart problem that could be handled with a pacemaker.

Charles continued to draw and paint during his dialysis treatments. He was selling drawings and notecards of his lighthouse artwork. Most of our days in Trilogy were truly enjoyable. We had the grandkids over often and they filled the house with lots of reasons to laugh.

I remember one sunny afternoon, Charles took my hand and pulled me to the center of the kitchen. The radio was playing our song *Always and Forever* ...... It was really sweet. He had enough energy to lead me around all the while singing along to the radio. I had no idea that would be the last time I ever danced with him. If I had only known what the future held I would have danced longer. I would have held him closer. I did tell him I thought it was sweet to dance in the kitchen for no special reason. That's what made it so special.

Within a few days Charles was admitted back to the hospital. He had been on dialysis for five and a half years and was very sick but I felt for sure he was going to get well and come home. Thanksgiving was just around the corner and he told me that more than anything he wanted; to be at home for Thanksgiving. I don't know how he mustered enough strength but he was able to come home. Our family came for dinner and as weak as Charles was he wanted to sit at the head of the table with his family. He wasn't able to stay up for very long, but he enjoyed each moment.

...more than anything he wanted; to be at home for Thanksgiving. I don't know how he mustered enough strength...

We helped him back to bed where he promptly fell asleep. That was the last time Charles would sit at the table with us. I think he knew.

That's why he pushed so hard for it. It's a memory that will always be with me.

Within a few days he was readmitted to the hospital. The stay there ended when the doctors informed me that he needed a skilled nursing facility with capability for rehabilitation. The hospital arranged for his transfer and I met him there with our kids.

I was an emotional wreck, full of a fear that I couldn't express. I had to be strong. Charles needed me to be his advocate. He was barely speaking now, his body weak and frail. He had a decubitus ulcer, in lay terms, a bed sore. Now there were wound care specialists and doctors talking to me about inserting a feeding tube. Although he would take an occasional bite of food if he was coaxed, a bite every now and then certainly was not enough to sustain him. Family was coming and going at all hours of the day and evening. The physical therapy department sent staff to make sure he was being turned regularly. They used every tool at their disposal to help Charles. During some of his lucid moments they tried to sit him up in what they called the "Cadillac of Chairs." He hollered out in agony and hung his head in exhaustion. I cried at the sight of him in such a weak condition. I understood what their goal was, but mine was vastly different. I just prayed for him to survive and not to suffer. Each day he was getting sicker.

On December 17th, I dressed up, put on makeup, and went to the hospital with our wedding photo album tucked under my arm. It was our 35th anniversary. Charles opened his eyes long enough to glance at me. He gave me a sideways twitch of a smile. I kissed his cheek and forehead and rubbed his hands. Then, I pulled up a chair right next to his bed and leaned in as close as I could. He was conscious but seemed very drowsy and his ability to tune in and focus would come and go. I placed the album in my lap and turned each page slowly, narrating page by page as if I were taking a blind person on a tour of our wedding day. "Oh here's a picture of me and Linda. She was my maid of honor, I know you remember that." I could write a book about Linda, she's classy, funny, and sweet. "Remember that time she and I burned out the transmission on the golf cart running it up and down the hills?" "You remember, of course you do." One page at a time, I tried to describe every detail of the photos. Linda and her husband Ray were the epitome of an officer and a lady and Charles was so proud of Ray. "You remember how close you and Ray are. I love that you asked him if he could look after Charles Jr." I was wishing and hoping and praying for him to perk up. He could hear me, I know that. He could respond when he was touched. Here and there we shared in his moments of total lucidness. I just wanted more than anything for him to get well and come home.

I began spending nearly every waking moment at the hospital. I would sleep in the big reclining chair the staff brought in his room.

Things were not getting better. The bed sore was getting progres-sively worse despite their best efforts to heal it and Charles was now in excruciating pain. The pain medication was increased daily. We talked to him even when his eyes were closed. We weren't sure if he was hearing us but we kept trying because we felt that he knew we were there. The grandkids made pictures that we taped on the wall at eye level. Alisa and I decorated his room for Christmas. Although we weren't sure how much he was aware of us, we made the best efforts day in and day out to bring him some joy and our expressions of love. The decorations reminded us all of how much Charles loved Christmas! It was pretty clear that he was not going to be home for this Christmas.

ᙉᙍᙎ My Heart Shattered ᙎᙍᙉ

Charles was transferred to the I.C.U. ward on December 23rd. He had developed sepsis. On Christmas Eve Alisa dressed Bria in a little holi-day plaid jumper with tights and Mary Jane shoes. Bria looked so pre-cious, dressed to visit her Papa, and give him lots of hugs and kisses. I planned to leave Charles long enough to attend Christmas Eve service at our church in Tempe. Before time to leave the nurses asked me to please have a seat out in the family waiting area. They needed to work on Charles for a few minutes. So, I waited with family. A storm raged inside my body and mind; I felt my stomach drop and felt like I had swallowed raw fear. It swelled up from the bottom of my stomach to my racing heart. Ka-thump, ka-thump, ka-thump, I heard my pulse in rhythm with my heart. Louder and louder and faster and faster. I wanted to cry but I had to be brave. *What are they doing to him?* As I wondered a nurse came towards us swiftly beckoning me, "He's dying!" That's all I heard her say sandwiched in between some other comments. Then I heard her ask me who I wanted to come into the room with us.

I didn't want to deprive any of the people who loved him of the chance for one more moment. I didn't want to deprive him of the chance to leave this world surrounded by his family and the love we all had for him. I wanted to orchestrate this moment but I couldn't. I was sadder than I had ever been. I should have known this time would come. We had been at the brink so many times before but God always brought us through. I was thinking of everyone else at the same time I was thinking, *Please dear God, just give us a little bit longer.*

My son didn't know when he arrived at the hospital that his father's time had come. He simply pushed the room door open and our eyes met. He knew then. He couldn't handle what was to come. He had discussed this with his dad long before that day. He was frank and honest when he told his dad he wouldn't be able to watch him die and furthermore he never wanted to view him after he was dead. I think Charles tried to leave when our son was not there. I think he wanted to die without Charles II being present. When he pushed that door open the grief overwhelmed him

I was so proud of my family. They were loving, strong, and brave.

and he retreated. He couldn't stay. I understood. I already knew.

I told the nurse everyone could come in. I was so proud of my family. They were loving, strong, and brave. After they were in the room with me for a few minutes the nurse asked me if I wanted a moment alone with my husband. I selfishly took it. I knew if I didn't I would never be able to reclaim the moment. I knew I had something to say and I wanted to try to voice it.

The nurse had cleaned Charles up. He was wearing a fresh hospital gown and his face was freshly washed. The tube in his nose had just been adjusted and other bottles hung on the IV pole. He was connected to machines that dripped and beeped. The nurse reached up to turn down any volume on the cardiac monitoring screen. A little blood ran out of his nostril. She joked with him. It was kind of odd but also so endearing. She said, "I just cleaned you up and look." She took a wet wash cloth and gently patted the blood away. I appreciated how gentle she was with him and the way she spoke to him as if he heard every word and was engaged in the conversation. Time was slipping away from us very rapidly but I just wanted to stay in that single moment for as long as I could. My heart ached like it never had before, each beat so painful, I thought it would explode.

Alone in the room with Charles, I looked at him. I studied his face and held his hand. I rested my head against his chest like I had done thousands of times in our life together. But I knew this was goodbye. I held my head up and wanted to speak to him. He always had the last word. Never in our relationship had I ever had the last word. Today I would. What could I say? How in the world could I have any command of language suitable to say goodbye to my husband, my lover, my friend, the person I shared my entire life with? I put my hand over his heart. I wanted to convey this was from my heart to his. I said, "Charles I love you with all my heart. I will always love you. But God made you. You are his and he loves you more. I know you're tired. It's okay for you to go. You can let go and go to God. He is waiting for you. It's okay Charles. I have always loved you. I always will. I will see you in heaven."

The rest is swirly and jumbled in my head. I remember the nurse reaching to turn off the monitor. I don't remember the moment I left that room. I've tried to go back there in my mind. I've tried to walk backwards from the lobby to his room and see who was walking with me, who said what. I can't because God let me experience as much as I could and then protected me with some sort of grief induced amnesia.

Christmas Eve has always been a day of joy and celebration in our family. It has always been a day of preparation for Christmas day. For several years my son and I had a tradition of spending the day together. I would ride with him as he made last minute deliveries to major corporations and we would stop for a nice lunch before fitting in some shopping for last minute gifts. We would be mindful to return home in time for family Christmas Eve activities.

How could Charles die on Christmas Eve? He wasn't just kind of into Christmas, he was Mr. Christmas! My head was pounding and I suppose I must have been in shock. I remember my friend Anette hugging me in the hospital lobby.

I couldn't go home. I couldn't be alone. My home was where we lived together. I woke up Christmas morning in my son's house. I heard him talking with his girls in a very soft voice "You girls try to be quiet. Don't bother Grandma. She is very sad because of Papa." I thought *Please, please just come and snuggle with Grandma. I need to be hugged.* I couldn't manage to say anything. *He died. He died.... He.....died.....He will not be coming home ever again!* I wondered where he was. I wished I had stayed with him in that room until they made me leave. *Why did I leave willingly? Why am I always so accepting of situations? I should have pitched a fit! I could have just climbed up in the bed and spread myself prone next to him.* I could have been there by his side until he was safe and sound on the other side.

I felt secure being there with Charles and Chrissy and the kids. Lord, I really didn't want to bring sadness to them or their children. I couldn't be selfish. Charles had just lost his dad, the most important man in his life. His children had just lost their grandpa and Chrissy had just lost her father-in-law.

On what would be his death bed, before he lost the capacity to communicate, Charles asked our son to always look after me. He also asked Ray to always look after our son. He never asked me in point blank terms but he had always talked with me about being strong to help Alisa with her kids. We talked about continuing traditions, but it was always just affirmations of us being on the same page. We wanted the same things for our children and grandchildren. We had talked about spending more time with our

> *On what would be his death bed, before he lost capacity to communicate, Charles asked our son to always look after me.*

grandkids. With all the hurts of the past behind us, we agreed to spend more quality time together. Charles had always been a teaser. He would tease me saying, "If I die and you remarry, I will be standing in your bedroom watching if you think you're ever going to make love with someone else." We'd laugh but he planted a seed in my mind. Now, here I was. One of us wasn't supposed to be gone for good. I couldn't think this was final. He was just going to be in the hospital for an extended stay. *No, Norma you can't lie to yourself. He is not coming home again. Never!* I wondered where he was.

I remember a little bit about how the family came to help me. Charles had no life insurance and we had no money in the bank. He died on December 24th and rent would be due on January 1st. Our landlord would not extend any grace. Family helped pack the house and my son filled his big box truck and stored it all in his garage. Our church was very caring, loving, and benevolent and paid for his cremation as well as a celebration of life service.

The service was really beautiful and I remember parts of it clearly. There were lots of people there and my best friend Pat was by my side. I can't remember the details of when she came in from California. I know she took care of some of the flowers and food and talking to people as we gathered after the service. My family and the church staff were walking me through everything else. My brother-in-law Ray dealt directly with the mortuary as I was literally a basket case. I would lie in bed at night steeped in morbid thoughts. The associate pastor delivered a beautiful eulogy and they recorded everything for me. Beautiful songs were sung and people who knew and loved Charles spoke words of tribute. Some of those who spoke were young men he had coached and some were friends. But probably the most touching was to see his grandson Justin walk up to the podium and give a full throated, heart wrenching tribute to the man he called Papa. He talked about how he was like a father to him. His Papa would have been incredibly proud of him. I was and I know our entire family was. He exhibited tremendous strength. His heart was broken just like ours but he knew he had to do well by his Papa while he had the opportunity. I don't think there was a dry eye because everyone knew that there stood Papa's joy. Yes, he had his own children, but any grandparent knows the magic that happens once you become a Papa or Grandma. Justin had been the first. He was the one who pulled Charles out of the life he had been living and gave him a new purpose. Everyone close to us knew this unspoken truth.

So here we were together in unity and in love to mourn the death of Charles Sims who was gone too soon. Charles, the life of the party, would party no more, but many party glasses would be raised in his memory. Charles Sims would not be forgotten. Not by the people in the church that day, not by the people in the social hall eating plates of sandwiches, fruit, and cheese, and making polite talk. I would overhear the questions, "How's the family doing?" or people would say to me, "How are you doing?" I had no idea. As I said I remember parts of it clearly but other parts are a blur. I met friends of his sisters and brothers who had come to support them. The Sims family is big and well loved. It was evident on that day. People had travelled from out of town and I was grateful. I tried to be kind and hospitable and make sure that everyone knew how much it meant. His brothers and their families came in their motor home and parked in front of my son's home.

I can't even remember when it all ended. I don't know when our loved ones left. Verda stayed in Arizona to be with me because she said the hardest part is once everyone leaves. She was right. I remember the day she drove me to the mortuary to pick up his ashes. My legs were trembling, my hands were shaking. I didn't want to go in there. All I had to do was walk in and sign a release form but I couldn't do it alone. That's love. She gave me support and love that day. My son and I purchased a beautiful wooden case to put the urn in.

> *Verda stayed in Arizona to be with me because she said the hardest part is once everyone leaves. She was right.*

When Verda finally decided to return home, I began to try to slowly live life day by day with a new purpose. I had Charles and his family and Alisa and her family. I found lots of joy with the kids and visiting my parents.

At night I would wake up and feel very alone and often very frightened. I wouldn't want to wake up the rest of the household and yet I was so very afraid of the dark. I started reciting, "Yea though I walk through the valley of the shadow of death I will fear no evil" and I would begin to feel as if I was pro-

Zachary and friends

tected. I knew I could flip on the light switch at any time. My son and Chrissy weren't ogres. They wouldn't have had a problem with me turning on a light but I wanted to be respectful of moving in and taking over their space. My youngest grandson Zachary was a toddler and decided that he would rather sleep with me than in his own bed anyhow and it worked out great for both of us. His mama would put him to bed and he would climb out, come downstairs and sneak into my room. I didn't mind at all.

I had a yellow, athletic bomber style jacket that Charles used to wear all the time before he died. It still smelled like him. I started wearing it all the time. I would fall asleep holding that jacket. The pillow that had been on our bed at home still smelled like him. It smelled like his cologne and his hair grooming product, TCB, a sweet, clean, almond scent. I couldn't bring myself to wash it or change it. I just cuddled that pillow, holding it just so I could hang onto the scent of him. It was fading as time went by.

CHAPTER 37

The Visit

Months later I went on a trip to San Diego with Alisa and her children. I took that yellow jacket with me but I didn't wear it everywhere because I was afraid it would get dirty and I'd ultimately need to wash it. We went to the famed San Diego Zoo and to the beach. I told Alisa I missed her daddy so much I couldn't stand it. I felt like he had just left abruptly. She said, "Mama, pray for a dream about him. Pray for a visit from him." We went to sleep one night, Alisa and me and all five kids split between two queen beds. I prayed. Somewhere in the midst of my foggy sleep I had a dream. I was sitting in church on a pew with my face in my hands. I felt someone sit next to me and put their arm around me. I thought it was a fellow church member but I got a hint of the cologne and opened my eyes. There he was. Charles was sitting right next to me. "Hi. Oh my gosh. You look great!" He looked awesome. He did not look at all

Somewhere in the midst of my foggy sleep I had a dream. I was sitting in church on a pew with my face in my hands. I felt someone sit next to me...

sick. Wearing a button-down dress shirt and a nice v-neck sweater, his face looked clear and bright. He looked content. "You came back!" He just smiled. "You're going to stay aren't you?" "No, I can't stay." "Ohhhh." And then I knew. He had come to let me know he was fine. It was as if I had seen him from the other side. I was relieved. I understood. I woke up and looked around the room. It was very early in the morning. The children were still sleeping. I wiggled myself free from the arms and legs spread over me and slipped on some clothes. I quietly opened the door and stood on the balcony. I wanted to say thank you to God for the wonder of answered prayers. I knew Charles was at peace and out of pain and suffering. I wanted to shout "Hallelujah!" Although I enjoyed the trip with Alisa and the kids, this was the stand out moment.

༄༅ Dream Vacation ༄༅

A couple of months later Charles and Chrissy took me on a trip to the east coast. It was quite an extraordinary journey. I know it was their idea of easing grief. I'd been working hard at it. The counselor from Hospice of the Valley was still coming and I was armed with an arsenal of books and articles on grieving and self-care after the loss of a spouse The entire family had been through group grief counseling. We went once a week at a local catholic church. The facilitators were wonderful, sincere, comforting, and full of empathy. The children made memory boxes. It was all super hard. Those in the group would all share the stories of our grief and talk about our loved ones. I was drowning in the sorrow of other people's loss. It was becoming too much. My granddaughter Allie was very emotional and struggling. After losing her papa she really was clinging to her daddy. I worried about how she would be with him so far away. But this was going to be an adult trip. No children, just the three of us. I was excited to go.

We planned to visit the lighthouses up and down the New England Coast. Charles had been painting them during his dialysis sessions and therefore they had deep meaning for us. On the flight I wore Charles' yellow jacket and felt as if he were coming along with us in some way. I couldn't wait to actually stand in front of some of the lighthouses he had brought to life in his drawings.

Charles was self taught and took up art as a form of therapy and relaxation. He loved to portray lighthouses as a symbol of hope.

My scrapbook from the trip is filled with incredible pictures. We went to Boston, Montreal, Toronto, New York City, and all sorts of lovely cities in between. We put lots of miles on the rental car and logged many miles in our walking shoes. We took ferry rides across various bays; New York Harbor, Martha's Vineyard, and Niagara Falls are a few of the sights we visited. Sometimes as we walked I was in awe as I looked around, and then it seemed my mind would drift off somewhere and suddenly there I was following Charles and Chrissy again.

Every morning I woke up happy to be with them but sad that I was now a widow. I missed my husband more than anything in the world. A hundred times a day I twirled my wedding ring around my finger, stretched my hand out to admire the sparkling diamond and was so grateful knowing the sacrifice he had made to get it for me. Although the weather was hot and I couldn't wear his jacket during our daily outings, every night I snuggled with it scrunched up on my pillow. If I wasn't speaking out loud to him,

Chrissy, Norma-Jean, and Charles

I was speaking deep from my soul to him. I looked up to the bright blue skies and thought, *I miss you so much, but you are free.* Then, as if to suddenly wake up or sober up I thought to myself, *What if it was all just a dream and he is not dead? Of course he is dead! I'd never be on a trip like this without him if he was alive.* The weather was perfect nearly every day of the trip except for the day we visited Niagara Falls; it poured rain but it wasn't cold. I had always wanted to see the falls and it was striking how beautiful the Canadian side is compared to the American side.

To this day I am ever grateful for the trip although when I look at the photos there are some things I still don't recall doing. I am inter-

I looked up to the bright blue skies and thought, I miss you so much, but you are free.

ested in visiting some of the places again. Charles Sr. would have been thrilled that we saw his beloved lighthouses. Our family has embraced his love of lighthouses and the special meaning they had for him. We, his family, own his message. The message is one of hope and light. It's a message that will carry on and endure for future generations.

The corners of my broken, achy heart were being cushioned with the soft, squishy loving hugs of my grandchildren. Oh how I looked forward to seeing their smiles and feeling their love. I think it was better that I did live with someone although I silently resented that Charles had not prepared in any way to take care of me in his absence. Well, actually I shouldn't say that. About a year prior to his death he started trying to buy collector coins. He was able to collect only about thirty dollars worth. I still have them.

I was angry with myself, I had nothing, no retirement, no savings, I felt like a monumental failure. I was under a tremendous amount of self-imposed pressure to fix it. But this was just wasted energy. I internalized my feelings and let the inner battle rage. I would have liked to stay in the house in Trilogy for a while but that was not to be. Instead, here I was with my son and his family and I was quite content. Given the reality of my situation there wasn't anywhere else I wanted to be. Although I was angry at myself, I was still joyful.

I am eternally grateful that Chrissy was not only open to having me move in with them, but she lovingly accepted me and welcomed me without complaint.

Over the next months I felt curiously free. I was able to go where I wanted and do things with my kids and grandkids that would have been problematic at one time. It was the strangest dichotomy. On

> *The strange thing about grief is while you are so shrouded in it you just wear it. It is what you do and you become accustomed to it.*

one hand I was drowning in my grief, coming up for air every now and then, only to plunge deeper the next day. On the days I was up for air I felt like I was free to just be myself on my own schedule. I trained myself not to look at my watch.

The strange thing about grief is while you are so shrouded in it you just wear it. It is what you do and you become accustomed to it. The cloud is over you, around you, it's a part of you. It's sort of like dark, heavy winter clothing that you slowly shed as the weather improves. The sun comes out, the bitter cold leaves and so you begin to peel off layers; so it is with the grief. The sun comes out again one day, and you find that you are smiling and maybe even laughing and wearing something brightly colored. You can say your loved one's name without weeping. Happy memories actually provoke happy reactions and not tears. It means you are moving forward. I was moving forward one day at a time.

I began to work parttime at Auto Mart helping Ferol in the office. It was a mid-sized car dealership in Chandler where she was the controller. It was perfect for me, I was able to come in for a few hours a day, answering phones, doing some filing, and running some errands for the office staff. If I didn't feel well there was no pressure to come. When I was there it was a good outlet. I made a bit of spending money and I met people. I kept busy and made friends both male and female. I wasn't looking for anything more than friendship and I made it clear. I met a new friend Gerri who I instantly became pretty close with. She worked in the local post office and when I would take trays of bulk mail for the dealership she always helped me. We would sometimes meet for lunch on Saturday.

I also met Don. He was filming a commercial for the dealership and we just struck up a conversation. We were both interested in politics and he invited me to hear Howard Dean speak at a local coffee shop one evening. He registered us for the Susan G Komen walk. We went to unusual lunch spots. In addition to politics, we talked family, love of cats, and travel. He knew how to get free tickets to every premier movie showing so we sometimes had fun doing that. There was no romance, it was just great to go where I wanted to go when I wanted to go. Working was a very good outlet and I met customers too.

Cliff was a car buyer for the dealership. He was always around and seemed nice. We were about the same age. He would stop by my desk and chat. One day he said he was going to grab lunch at Perkins and asked if I would like to join him. I did. I was going to pay for my own lunch when he insisted on paying. I thanked him. After that he continued to stop by every time he came to the dealership and was always very polite. He seemed pleasant and I thought of him as my friend. I really liked him. I think when I look back I surely gave him the wrong message. I went with him a few times to places I shouldn't have, I know now that I sent the wrong message.

One night he invited me to go to a place called Rocking Rodeo, a country and western bar. That's not exactly my scene but I was spreading my wings and trying new things so I tried to two step around the floor. I mostly laughed at myself a lot! I was home by ten. It was wonderful to meet some of his friends whom I thought were nice but I didn't see my life and their lives intersecting at all. I'm not a beer and peanut shells on the floor kind of girl. I'm more like crystal wine glasses, candlelight, and roses. He didn't know that. I didn't care. The other place I went with him which was a big mistake was my grandson Justin's football game. Man oh man, I couldn't breathe! He sat so close to me on the bleacher and wrapped me up so tight I was embarrassed. I gave my daughter the "help me" look and she gave me the "What in the hell is going on?" look. I knew it was a huge misstep.

Cliff asked me to invite my father to breakfast and I saw it as a great opportunity to maybe say in front of my daddy that I am still very much stuck in my grief and not at all ready to date anyone. I figured it would be very safe and he'd get the message loud and clear so I asked Daddy to join us and he did. I sat next to Daddy and as long as we weren't eating he held my hand and backed me up as I spoke. I was over fifty and needed my Daddy to sit there with me just as if I weren't even eighteen yet. I said it all. But what did Cliff say? "Olden, you have the most beautiful daughter. I think she is wonderful. I love her." Daddy squeezed my hand. That was a signal to be quiet. Daddy explained that he loved me too. He went on to say that I am his baby girl and have been through a tremendous loss and you know I am just getting my feet under me and he's very protective of me and nobody can rush me to come out of my grief and feel anything that I don't feel. Cliff's face turned red. He hadn't heard what he hoped for. He wanted some sort of a blessing but I was ever so relieved. I liked him as a friend. That's all I wanted from anyone! I didn't want to complicate my life or my heart with emotional baggage when I had many, many years of unpacked baggage yet to open.

When you're a widow people feel a sense of obligation to spend time with you. I think some of them feel like they are doing what Charles would want them to do. George, Charles' best friend, took me to brunch and to baseball spring training, and would sometimes come by and just sit with me. My son-in-law Brian took me for lunch and movie dates. Friends from church called, sent cards, and invited me for lunch or dinner. Everyone in my family kept close tabs as did my friends Toni , Pat, Rhonda, and Anette.

CHAPTER 38

Newly Single

WhEN you are newly single with a lot of life ahead of you, people love to play match maker. I had met a couple when I was at a doctor appointment and it so happened their last name was Sims. What a coincidence. They were very nice. They asked if they could have my phone number so we could get together someday soon. Imagine how surprised I was when I was invited to have dinner at their home the next week. First of all it was quite far. I was surprised because I had met them at my doctor in my part of town. But I went. They lived in a beautiful, gated golf course community. I brought a cheesecake for dessert from a local grocery store.

I was very surprised when I arrived to find they had invited one of their friends for dinner too. The hair on the back of my neck stood up, the same reaction I get when I see a scorpion crawling across the floor. It's just creepy. I was immediately irritated and wanted to leave although that would have been very rude. I was thinking of how rude it was of them to set me up. If I wanted to date I would put myself out there. But I was not ready to date! *Good Lord I am really not interested in anyone like this guy.* I am five feet eight inches tall and at best this man was about five feet three. That was something that maybe I would overlook if I met a really nice person. I wouldn't judge on height, looks, etc. However, this man was just not my type based solely on appearance. It got worse. Painfully, hilariously worse.

I tried to be polite and at least stay long enough to eat dinner. I made small talk and every question I asked verified that he was defi- nitely not someone I would even be friends with. "Do you like to read?" "Read?" "Yes, you know, as in books." "No. No, I do not enjoy reading at all." "Do you like to travel?" "No, no I don't like to travel." "Do you like children?" "No, no I never had any. I don't like kids very much. No patience. I guess that's why I never

"Do you like to read"? "Read?" "Yes, you know, as in books."

had any." Finally, my ace in the hole. "Do you go to church?" "Church?" *Was there an echo in the room?* "Yes, as in to worship." "Oh, hahahaha. No never! I don't believe in ...." I was hanging on the edge of my chair...was he going to say he didn't believe in God? "Yes?" "Well, it's not that I don't really believe in God, but well, maybe I guess I don't. I know I don't believe in organized religion. I haven't been in a church since I was a kid and I damn sure don't intend to go now!" He seemed proud and I knew it was past time for me to go. I graciously thanked the Sims for having me and escaped with the true excuse that I don't drive well at night. They promised to keep in touch and invite me next time they were having a get together. They did. They invited me and I declined kindly.

In my quest to try new things I wouldn't have done before, I had been going places with my dear friend Maxine. We went to mixers or networking events. Once we attended an event where the author Terry McMillan was a guest. We laughed about how rude she was to us. But on another day Maxine asked me to go with her to a different event. She belonged to a golf club that hosted a tournament once a year with black golfers from all over the United States. This was going to be a really nice evening with food, drinks, music, dancing, and socializing. That night I danced with a gentleman from Ohio. He was interesting and talked to me as we slow danced. He walked me back to the table and asked if he could sit and speak with me for a while. I instantly liked him. Obviously he was here because of golf but he told me he loved to travel and he loved to read. I gave him two points right off the bat, one for loving travel and one for loving books! He told me about his daughters. I thought he seemed interesting and when he asked if he could have my number I gave it to him. I didn't even second guess my decision and felt good about it.

The next day was Saturday and he called in the morning to invite me to meet him for lunch in Scottsdale. I accepted. I had not been on any outings that I would categorize as a date prior to this. Jim was my first date with anyone since I had lost Charles and I was certainly nervous. I agreed to meet him as I didn't want him coming to the house and meeting Charles and Chrissy. That seemed just too much. I had no idea if I would ever see him again after that day.

We had a very nice time, enjoying lunch at a high end Scottsdale restaurant followed by walking and shopping. I enjoyed the fact that he was transparent as I learned about his life at home and heard stories of his family and friends. He told me that he was a dentist in Youngstown, Ohio. Oh boy, that's a long way from Chandler, Arizona. After our date he asked if we could stay in touch. I said I would really like that. We started talking nearly every day by phone and before long we had embarked on a long distance relationship. He flew me to meet him in Cleveland and he flew to Arizona several times.

I discovered later that Cliff was stalking me! He had photographed me with Jim from across the street.

On one of his visits we had dinner at a Scottsdale restaurant called Banderas. I discovered later that Cliff was stalking me! He had photographed me with Jim from across the street. There I was just having a nice romantic dinner, not doing anything wrong at all. Just me with the man I was dating having a nice dinner. What on earth was going on? Cliff confronted me later, throwing an envelope of photos in my face as if I had cheated on my husband. Along with the photos he delivered a proposal which I couldn't accept. Of course to marry someone I believe you must be fully in love with no doubts. If I was ever to get married again he was going to have to be "some kind of wonderful." This was not the case.

Cliff had bought the most gorgeous engagement ring, it was outrageously beautiful! Any woman would die for a ring like that from a man she loves. He claimed to have spent more than $10,000 on it. I said I couldn't and wouldn't accept it. He refused to take it back, as if he could force the situation, and I had no choice but to leave it for him with the manager of the automotive repair department. Cliff proceeded to call me every name in the book, I mean every name! No more Mr. Nice Guy! He was showing his true colors now and became very threatening. At this point my family got involved. Ferol told him in no uncertain terms to back off and leave Mama-Jean, that's what she called me, alone, quit stalking and if he didn't he would have hell to pay. In fact, don't come back to Auto Mart! My son sent the same message along with letting him know he wasn't afraid to kick his ass! I was kind of shell shocked by the whole thing. He had been stalking me long after I was dating Jim. Not only did he have pictures from Banderas he also had pictures taken of me working in Auto Mart, driving my car, and running errands. It was scary!

I was taken with Jim, swept away by his cultured, well-read manner. He was intriguing. He was a graduate of a historically black university and had asked me if I would like to go to see the university drum lines compete. I would have loved to but we never got there. Golf was what brought us together. I could have cared less about golf but he lived for it and by proxy I reaped the benefits. What I mean is, golf courses are beautiful places and he only played at the nicest

One thing I greatly appreciated about Jim was that he is a planner. That was a new experience for me.

ones. I rode along and kept score for him. Our evenings would be spent going to four and five star restaurants. One thing I greatly appreciated about Jim was that he is a planner. That was a new experience for me. He would get various travel magazines, articles, AAA, etc., and research hotels, places to see, things to do, great food, and music. He put a lot of effort and thought into planning every trip he invited me to take with him. It was awesome and I loved it. Once he invited me to join him I only needed to worry about packing my bags and getting to the airport. In the past I had always had so much responsibility for everything. It felt good to be spoiled in that way.

At first I thought I was capable of falling in love with Jim. I think it was the mystique of it all. Being alone with an intriguing man far away from everything, I felt love for him. I was happy. I thought he was happy. We were sharing new experiences together and I was seeing beautiful places that I could never afford. I just knew he was special and I had fallen in love with him.

Once I became intimate with Jim, I felt my feelings escaping like helium from a balloon as it slowly settled back to earth. He wasn't sweet and tender, he never said sweet things or called me anything but Norma. I didn't feel the love anymore. I also noticed that he was impatient with waiters and waitresses and hotel staff. I didn't like that and don't do well with condescending. How you treat others says a lot about your character.

I visited his beautiful home. It was tastefully decorated and he was very accommodating and made me feel welcome. But I knew that I would never live there. I had the feeling that it was not to be, our relationship was unraveling.

One bright afternoon we were out on the golf course and Jim hit one of his very expensive "special balls" into the tall grass area. He was searching for it and I thought it would be helpful if I helped him. When I stepped off the cart I didn't

Mud squished through my fingers and my knees bore the weight of my humiliation.

realize I was on the edge of a marsh like area and I sank down to my ankles in muddy grass. I lost my balance and fell forward, bracing my fall by putting my hands out. Mud squished through my fingers and my knees bore the weight of my humiliation. Somehow I pulled myself up to a standing position and back on the cart, my face burning red with embarrassment and tears streaming. You would think a bit of compassion was in order but Jim was annoyed that I had even tried to help find his damn precious ball! The sun would be setting soon and all he could think of was completing his game. There I sat in tears, humiliated, wet feet, muddy, and he's annoyed and impatient! I think I knew I was done. This was not love. Love would have shown some concern for me. Love would have scratched the rest of the game and put my comfort and welfare first before finishing up the score card. The very least he could have done was send me to the pro shop to get some dry clothes. If the money was a problem, that's a problem, because I'm worth it.

The next month he flew me out to Cleveland to go to an Earth Wind and Fire concert with him. We had done many things in Cleveland before. Including games and the Rock and Roll Hall of Fame. I was excited, the concert venue was on the water at night and promised to be fun. Over dinner Jim commented that once you put a ring on a woman's finger she becomes "a b...." That day was the final turning point for me. I am never going to become a b....! Ring or no ring, I am who I am. I thought it was an ugly thing to say and I felt it reflected something in his heart. Maybe he had been hurt in the past but I am not the one. I'm sorry that happened to him. I was ready to leave and didn't really care anymore. He had damaged my soul. No, no I guess I don't love you. I was thinking so hard I was sure my thoughts were resonating through the air around me. *Hush Norma.* I wanted to quiet my mind so the people wouldn't see my angry face and hear my angry, disappointed thoughts. *He's not who I thought he was.*

In all the time I spent with him, Jim never introduced me to his daughters even though he talked to me about them; they were his world. I knew that was not normal. If I was as important to him as he was to me, he would have made sure they met me. My sweet mama told me, "Norma-Jean I don't like how he treats you. You are like a high class call girl to him. He calls you and you go." This was a painful truth I hadn't realized earlier.

I knew I had to end our relationship. As much as I really liked him I couldn't try to continue to be friends with him after having been intimate. Friends with benefits wasn't something I was searching for. I had enjoyed knowing him and I have no regrets. I wish him all the best. I realize that there is someone for everyone and I am not the person for Jim.

That experience was a jolt. I had been sleepwalking and ran smackdab into the wall. It hurt badly. *Why is it that things turn out like this for me?* I wondered. I had been careful. I had not chosen the time to date, it had happened organically. I became internally torn. Maybe it had all been far too soon. Maybe it was a betrayal of Charles. I still felt married in so many ways. I was still wearing my wedding ring. I never took it off. I never stopped loving Charles. After all, I had no idea how to just quit being his wife after thirty five years. My identity was tied to Charles Sims from the time I was a teenager until the day he died. I never really let go even when we were separated so of course, even when he died I was still hanging on! This situation was going to take some serious prayer to settle me down. I had made several giant steps forward and just as many giant steps backwards. What a mess I was.

Not long after that whole situation I was on a trip to California and my sister-in-law Jackie and her husband Ben and LoVera and I were talking. Jackie told me that she had a dream about me and she saw my future husband! "What? Jackie, oh no honey, no husband in my future." Ben said, "Norma, I'm

Jackie told me that she had a dream about me and she saw my future husband! "What? Jackie oh no honey, no husband in my future."

310

telling you Jackie is telling you the truth. She told me she saw him. She knows exactly what he looks like and that you are going to meet a really great guy." "Jackie, you can't be having these dreams and visions!" She and LoVera laughed and they both told me I deserve to be loved and deserve to be happy. My sisters were always supportive and loving. "Jackie, is he going to be handsome at least?" I asked. "Yes, he's tall and dark and slender and looks like Reverend Nance." *Oh my God* I thought.

LoVera told me, "Norma-Jean if you are not careful when you get into another relationship you will duplicate the relationship you had with Charles. That's what you know. That's where you are comfort-able. Be careful honey. Remember what I'm telling you." It was sage, heartfelt advice from my big sister.

I still struggled internally with anxiety and depression. The thought of Christmas music, lights and decorations just brought me back to the many happy family Christmas times we had together and then like being flung from a sling shot back to reality I knew he was dead and gone forever. I would panic, the wheels in my head spin-ning round and round while I tried to hide it from my family. I spoke to a limited few people about how I felt about any of it. My mama knew me well and could see my anxiousness whenever I visited her. Sometimes I would just begin to cry and would wipe my tears and say, "I am fine Mama. I am just emotional. You know life is just different." She would always pat my hand, call me "Sveetie," and tell me things would be okay.

Don't get me wrong. I wasn't always sappy and sad. I wasn't always crying or anxious. There were days that I was more or less defiant in my new found freedom to be who I was free to be. There were no chains on me. I could wear capris with no criticisms. Charles had never liked them. I bought as many pairs as I wanted. I went on trips with my kids whenever I had the opportunity and savored every moment. And yet there were moments when I slipped back to sadly recall how I wouldn't have been able to be there if Charles were still alive. I'd trade ten thousand trips for one more day with him. I'd accept lunch invitations, breakfast, or coffee but I was lonely for Charles. I wanted him to be there to do the traditional things with the family. What about outings in the park, church on Sunday followed by family dinner? What about football games and chili in the fall? Nothing was ever going to be the same again and I knew it. I was outwardly coping just fine but there was still an undercurrent of grief. I just needed to get a grip. I knew I would. I was positive of it. It was paramount.

I was swirling from so many mixed emotions but decided I would dismiss the events of the last few months with Jim out of my mind with gratitude and move forward. I took to my knees and

Lord guide my steps. Lord if you see another man in my life, let him be a man who puts you first in all things...

prayed a simple and earnest prayer. I decided to focus my love and attention fully on my son and his wife, my daughter and her husband, my wonderful grandchildren, and my parents and friends. My prayer went something like this, "Dear Father in Heaven, please bless me and my family. Give me strength Lord to do the things you would have me to do, Lord guide my steps. Lord if you see another man in my life, let him be a man who puts you first in all things because then everything else will fall into place. I will trust you with my life. Amen."

If I thought turning everything over to God was going to miraculously turn the page I was wrong. My anxiety didn't leave overnight. I still struggled.

I realized that in my heart of hearts I was indeed still very much married to Charles. I thought about him first thing every morning and he was still my last thought every night. I had moved past the gushing tears although they could still come unexpectedly. I often thought about him in the solace of the hot steam of my shower or bath where my tears mingled with the water falling over the top of my head and down my face. I wished I could still see the hospice counselor, but the time had run out. I didn't want to do the group thing because I knew I would just get consumed with everyone else again. I needed to move forward.

So, I kept busy with family dinners, and church and friends. I was emotionally schizophrenic. One day I was panicked that I was facing a tsunami of emotions and should take to higher ground for safety. I knew I could outrun my feelings but other days I thought to hell with it all, just stand flat footed and face the black darkness that will overtake me. Can a brain get whiplash? Sometimes I was masquerading for those around me, sometimes I was just trying to survive, and yet other days I truly was just fine. I continued working at Auto Mart as my health allowed. It was the best fit considering I wanted to work but a regular nine to five gig was certainly not on my radar. I wouldn't be able to handle it. I was ever so grateful for Pat. She was the one person who probably knew the real truth about how I was struggling emotionally and she was a great source of strength.

ᘰᙥ Dale ᙤᘬ

My friend Gerri started talking to me about a friend she wanted me to meet. "No. Thank you Gerri!" Day in and day out she was beating the same drum. "He's awesome, you'll love him, He's a Godly man, I know his family, and he's tall." My daily answer was, "No, No, No! I am not interested. I am good. He's probably a dog." One day I walked in to the post office and Gerri really embarrassed me, "Hello Mrs. Coachman."

"Gerri, please don't call me that. I don't even know that man!" "Yes, but I do, and God told me you are going to be his wife." Hahaha! "God told you more than he has told me! No, Gerri, the answer is no!"

When Dale first called me I was stopped in my tracks at the sound of his voice. "Hello, can I speak to Norma-Jean please?"

313

I finally told Gerri that if it would get her off my case she could give my number to her friend Dale Coachman and I would agree to a five minute conversation. I had no idea that on the other end of things she was working on Dale also. He had no interest in meeting me. He was happily single. She was beating the same relentless drum. "She's so nice, she's a Godly woman, she's tall, and she has a nice family." Hahaha. He finally agreed just as I had, I think more or less just to get Gerri to stop nagging. He said he was just committing to a phone call.

When Dale first called me I was stopped in my tracks at the sound of his voice. "Hello, can I speak to Norma-Jean please?" I put my hand over the receiver so he wouldn't hear my gasp, "Oh my God!" His voice was deep and sexy. I was immediately drawn to him. "This is Norma-Jean." "This is Dale." That first conversation was about forty five minutes. He called again and again over the next few days and each time we spoke longer than the time before. We clicked. We talked about anything and everything and sometimes it seemed like nothing at all but yet it all seemed important.

Dale seemed to be genuinely interested in anything I had to say. He asked a lot of questions, more questions than any man I had ever talked to before. I was so relieved that there was none of the "Hey baby, let me tell you something" kind of jive. I absolutely wouldn't have given him any time. If I asked him questions he answered straight forth. In my life, my faith, family, and friends were vitally important and that's how his values lined up too. Our political views also aligned. He was empathetic about Charles and never made me feel like I couldn't discuss him. In fact he asked questions about my life with Charles. He didn't realize it but he was helping me see that I could move forward in life and still honor the family that Charles and I had created. Over time it will grow and change, the grandkids will one day marry and have their own families, but the foundation will remain.

Dale and I talked every day, sometimes several times a day, for a couple months. I looked forward to his calls, they became the bright spot of each day. We laughed out loud together and I loved that. One day I began to wonder if perhaps there was something more to this than I was seeing. Maybe I felt more for him than I should. Maybe I was on a one-way street. Maybe I was just plain silly but I felt like I was in love with someone I had never even met face to face. I mailed him a photograph of me and he emailed a picture to me. I knew of people who met online and fell in love through texting. I always thought it was bazaar but anything is possible with love. So maybe, just maybe I wasn't crazy. I knew I had to find out what this was. I didn't want to be toyed with. When I was alone with my thoughts about Dale, I wondered about the cliché phrase "He had me from hello." *Did Dale have me from hello?* When I saw his photograph I thought he was handsome but I was already drawn to his heart. He told Gerri he thought I was pretty but she didn't mention that I was a white woman. She told me that was a laugh for her. When we first met she also thought I was white, but I told her I identify as black. I wondered if perhaps he didn't find me attractive or if something else was keeping us long distance, so I just went for it and decided to ask him.

"Do you want to meet in person or do you just want to keep talking on the phone?" "Oh," he said, "I was just giving you time. How about getting together tomorrow?" I was shocked! We decided to meet at a very public place for the first time and chose the food court at Arizona Mills Mall. The evenings were just beginning to have a chill so I opted to wear a pair of simple black jeans and a white shirt with a black leather jacket. I didn't want to look like I'd gone over the top, so I kept it casual and comfortable. I was early and ever so anxious. I decided to try to look busy so I pulled out my checkbook and pretended I was trying to balance it or something. But I had another issue. I was so nervous that my body was trembling in a spastic fashion. I couldn't control it! I was so mad at myself. When he walked toward me I stood up to give him a hug. I thought he looked much more handsome in person and he smelled heavenly. I couldn't help but observe he was wearing something similar to me, black jeans, white shirt, and black leather jacket. I looked at his feet, no dirty, icky shoes which is my big turn off, just a nice pair of black loafers. *Thank you Jesus.* When we sat down he was smiling so big. He noticed my shaky hands and later told me he was thinking that I didn't mention any type of affliction like palsy. But when he laid his hand on top of mine I quit shaking. Go figure, he calmed me down with his touch! *Oh geez. This can't be good!* Yes, that was my first thought. This can't be good, but it was. Actually it was incredible that he had a calming effect. I relaxed and was genuinely happy to finally meet Dale face to face.

I had seen the movie *Waiting to Exhale* years ago. I think meeting Dale was not waiting to exhale. I think I had been waiting to breathe on my own again. I was so hurt from the previous years, losing Charles, and trying to survive that I think I was walking around in a daze. I had been getting a lot of assistance from others but wanted more than anything in the world to be in a good place for my family. I wanted to show them I am brave and strong. I believe in rainbows after storms and starry skies after dark cloudy nights. But I am human and I stumbled because I married when I was still a child and lived my life wrapped up intricately for thirty five years with that of another person whom I will always love.

> *I stumbled because I married when I was still a child and lived my life wrapped up intricately for thirty five years with that of another person whom I will always love.*

After Dale and I met in person it seemed our relationship was on a forward trajectory. One afternoon his father called me and spoke to me in German. To my surprise I was able to follow the conversation. I hadn't lived in Germany since I was a teenager but I managed a few simple words and we laughed. His father had a deep, hearty, contagious laugh. He was instantly loving and friendly. He asked if I had a current passport and told me if I didn't I'd best get one because we're going to be traveling together, the four of us. He sounded sweet and welcoming. I could tell he was a pastor but he certainly wasn't stuffy.

On another day, another call. "Can I speak to Norma-Jean please?" "This is Norma-Jean." "Do you know Dale Coachman?" "Yes." I could feel my heart begin to race. She sounded very young. *Oh dear God.* I prayed that this would not be too good to be true. I was trying to fully place my trust in Dale up to this point. Yes, yes of course in the teeny, tiny crevices of my mind the old doubts creep in and I wonder if there's something he's hiding. I wonder if he's telling me lies. But then I don't want to have the doubts and they are so small that I can just think *poof* and away the thoughts go. But now, here's this phone call out of the blue with this sweet sounding voice asking me if I know Dale. My heart beat so fast and loud I heard it in my ears nearly drowning out her soft voice. "Yes, I know him." I wait. One full second of silence, two seconds, "Hi, Norma-Jean. I'm his mother! He gave me your number." I could almost see her smile through the phone. *Whew. Breathe.* I had to tell myself to breathe. I was certainly not expecting that. "Wow you sound so young," I told her. It turns out that Dale's parents were great phone conversationalists just like him. We chatted comfortably for a long time, just like when I talked with Dale, laughter was always part of the conversation and it felt like she was someone I'd known forever.

When Dale and I started dating he was just plain sweet, courteous, and kind. He was also a lot of fun. Gerri suggested I begin a journal to document this new chapter of my life. I have always journaled. Sometimes out of *joy*, sometimes from despair, this time it was a safe place to express questions, new found joy, and feelings I didn't necessarily want to share with family or friends. I would sit with my journal in my lap recounting our date like a sixteen year old writing "Dear Diary..." blushing, wondering if I should put it in words. I felt like I was waltzing through a scene of the *Twilight Zone*. I knew everyone in my family, as well as my closest friends, was watching me

I was the one who had stayed with Charles through a million ups and downs and break ups only to always come back.

closely. Their eyes were always on me trying to analyze my behavior. I was, after all, a widow. I was, after all, a middle-aged woman. I was, after all, grieving the love of my life. I was, after all, a girl that married the love of her life when I was just a child. I was the one who had stayed with Charles through a million ups and downs and break ups only to always come back. And now here I was alone again in life and not by choice. What I would do with my heart was being rightfully scrutinized. Who I would give my heart to was on the line. That was my secret. That was mine and mine alone to hold. Yes, Charles had been the love of my life. That life, my past life, was over as I knew it. I had gone down to the edge of the river of pain and drowned myself deep in the sorrow of my loss.

However, I had saved the best parts of myself somehow. Somewhere inside of me was the young, playful, sexy, trusting, loving, longing young woman who wanted to be a lover and a friend to a man who would love only me. I locked my heart behind a door. I had made a decision. I knew if I ever was going to totally give myself to another man, I wanted to be able to look him in the eye and tell him how truly special he is. I didn't want to spend myself emotionally and physically with all sorts of partners before landing on one that was a good fit. I decided to stop and wait. I didn't expect Dale to come into my life when he did but I knew enough to proceed with caution. I didn't know how to explain to them how deeply I was connecting to Dale. They would just have to see it. They would just have to see me. I wanted my family and friends to observe a dependable, caring, loving, affectionate, self -sacrificing mother and daughter, friend, and confidant.

It was as if Dale had knocked on the door that I had so carefully and meticulously locked and for some reason I wanted him to unlock it. No one else had the key. I never gave it freely to anyone but Charles, but even with him I often felt unseen and unheard. I have said, "I love you" and I meant it. Men have said it to me. I realize that sometimes the words *I love you* are used to manipulate…that's why I said I was in the twilight zone. There were people all around me but it was Dale who realized the true depth of my pain. He was the one to sit with me and let me do the hard work of finding my way through my pain to my healing and to be able to fully give myself and love again. He was willing to kick that door down to let me see his love for me. He did it with patience, understanding, and a lot of time. It all unfolded gradually over the span of our relationship. He gave me space and time to search my heart and find my boundaries. Did I know where my boundaries were? I'm still discovering some boundaries.

Of course all of our conversations weren't serious. We laughed out loud about nothing and everything! We were physically hands-on anytime we were near each other. I've always been fairly shy and somewhat reserved but not with Dale, PDAs (Public Displays of Affection) are not unusual with us at all. One of our first dates was dinner at Ztejas on Mill Avenue in Tempe Arizona. It was on a Monday

She told me in her thick Latvian accent, "Norma-Jean, Sveetie, I think this Dale is the one for you! Yes?"

night and the restaurant was crowded because people were watching football on the bar televisions. We were watching each other. Our waitress commented on our chemistry! Every time she came back to our table she mused about us. It was fun. We were obviously very much physically attracted to one another. It was like static electricity, you could feel it in the air. After dinner we walked hand in hand down Mill Ave. The street was filled with college students young enough to be our kids but we were more playful than any of them. Our kids were older than most of the people around us but we were the ones full of visible life and romance. There were the usual tourists and downtown regulars up and down both sides of the street. We laughed and teased around when out of the blue he picked me up in his arms as if I was as light as a feather. I was all giggles. I didn't want our date to end, it was just so much fun. What a memorable night.

I talked to Mama about Dale. She was all ears. She was also all smiles. She wanted to meet him. Gerri told her how absolutely wonderful with a capital "W" Dale was and of course that was all she needed to hear. She heard it from me and from Gerri. She told me in her thick Latvian accent, "Norma-Jean, Sveetie, I think this Dale is the one for you! Yes?" "Oh, Mama. I don't know. Maybe. We will see. But I'm definitely going to bring him to meet you!"

Mama did have questions about how Dale ranked as far as my list of things I tick off as a big NO when it comes to men. We laughed about my list as we talked about it. Mama called me picky, picky, and picky and she asked me which one of the things if any would I compromise over. "Umm, I don't think any of them Mama. I just don't know." My list was pretty specific; I can't stand the sight of long, nasty, dirty fingernails on a man. Short, groomed nails are a must. I can't stand the sight of nasty, long, untrimmed nose or ear hairs. Beards must be well trimmed and brushed, not kinky, wiry, or full of lint or the potential to catch their dinner. I can't stand the sight of a mature man trying to rock unkempt hair like they could get away with in their twenties or thirties. I think it's hideous. I've already told you that I am a lifelong shoe junkie, I love nice shoes. I look at how people take care of their feet and their shoes and ingrained this habit into my son. He keeps his collection of sneakers clean and lined up fastidiously. It says a lot. I can't stand to see a nicely dressed man wearing a pair of dirty, worn over tennis shoes. I taught him when he was little that shoes cost a lot of money and when they get dirty we clean them up. We don't wear them like that. It's a bad look. It turns me off! My list continued, in this day and time it's a shame to even have to mention it, but a man must wear his pants pulled up. I have seen men past twenty sagging their pants and it's an extremely distasteful look. I like a clean and well-kept car. A car is an expensive investment, why wouldn't you take care of it? It's a statement too about what is valued.

Let's talk manners. They're important. I wouldn't want a man who was a burping and farting machine and thought it was funny. Those are natural functions but being amused by them is for grade school and an occasional comedy movie. No thank you to constant rude behavior. I wouldn't tolerate a man who uses a barrage of profanity. It's not necessary to communicate and I think it diminishes the man and makes him look small. I feel the same way about women using lots of profanity. Of course, I definitely would not ever consider a man who didn't know the Lord. A lot of things on my list might seem petty to someone else but I had discussed these things with my mama for years and she knew they would get on my nerves! Why would I enter a relationship with someone whom I would be judging or saying they are getting on my nerves? It should be a mutual attraction.

I told Mama that my first impressions were all good...but I hadn't seen his closet yet so I had no idea about his shoes.

With regards to Dale, I told Mama that my first impressions were all good and he had not given me any turn offs as of yet. So far he was a meticulously groomed gentleman but I hadn't seen his closet yet so I had no idea about his shoes. We laughed. She said, "You can always buy shoes Norma-Jean, you can always buy shoes!"

Although things between Dale and me were beautiful, I kept talking to myself. I wanted to be prepared if our growing relationship unraveled. My self conversations were clear. *Read the signs daily. They must be saying in big bold letters* **Slow Down, Be Careful, Trust God, and Things Aren't Always What They Seem**. Then I would relive the moment when he first took my hand in his at the mall and how calming he was. I would stop and think about how special he treats me. That's when I had a different conversation with myself. I asked, *What if the signs are telling me 'Go Ahead, Jump, It's real.'* I'm not much of a gambler but I was unwittingly placing all bets on Dale.

In all my life no one had ever kissed my hand until I met Dale. I don't know why not. I can't answer that question. It's such a sweet, innocent gesture and yet so sensual. I can't believe that I was fifty five and had never experienced something so lovely, so tender. I will never forget the first time he gently held my hand in his and turned it over to kiss my palm and then the back of my hand while giving me a soul connecting stare deep in my eyes. "Damn girl, where have you been?" There are many things I feel as if I am experiencing for the first time when I'm with Dale. Neither of us have ever felt this kind of love before.

It was important to me for my family to get to know Dale and for them to like him and approve. It would be difficult enough to be in a relationship with *anyone* after Charles but most difficult if I tried to be with someone they didn't like. It might seem unfair to Dale and I realize it, but Charles left a huge, permanent footprint within the family. His name will always be spoken and his picture will always be displayed. He's not some random ex-boyfriend who has been cast away. He is father to my children and grandfather to eight, plus our grandchildren adopted through our son's marriage. There will be stories repeated and inside jokes told repeatedly over the years. I didn't know if Dale was going to be able to handle that or if he would want to walk away thinking the roots just run too deep. He observed, listened, and understood. And he didn't run. He just stood and showed me how much he cared.

> *Charles left a huge, permanent footprint within the family. His name will always be spoken and his picture will always be displayed.*

When Alisa met him she said, "Oh boy, so you are a PK? You know what they say about PK's!" And she giggled. He looked at her with a puzzled face, "What is a PK?" "Wait, you don't know what a PK is?" "No." 'It's a Pastor's Kid and they say pastors' kids are always the worst, because they're bad on the down low!" She laughed and he did too. He told her this was news to him. Charles had already told me he knew several people who all spoke highly of Dale and so when he met him in person it wasn't like he had nothing to go on other than what I told him.

In our family kids aren't allowed to address adults by their first names so when Dale first met Alisa's children she introduced him as Mr. Dale. In the beginning it was very appropriate. "Hello, Mr. Dale." They really liked him and thought he was very funny. Dale called me Baby Doll and the triplets had a great time trying to lower their voices and mimic him, "Hello Baby Doll." Then they would burst into laughter. When he met me Dale didn't have a clue that Mama called me her Baby Doll. I even had a picture of me wearing a banner she made when I was little just to prove it. Justin was older and he didn't call him Mr. Dale, or Mr. Coachman, he just called him Dale. Dale was okay with it and I was too.

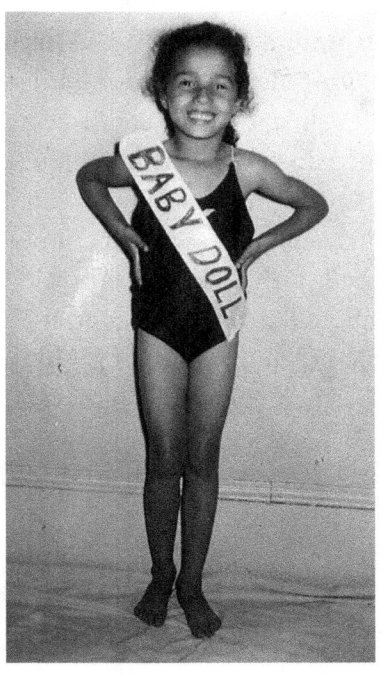

Where Justin was concerned, I was most cautious and apprehensive because he had been so extremely close to his Papa. He was the first grandchild, the eldest, and because I knew his heart it was a time to walk softly. For Justin there will never be another Papa. No way could he shift. Justin is fiercely loyal to those he

Norma-Jean,
Baby Doll,
kindergarten

loves and would need time to form his own relationship if there was to be one. This much I understood. I never interfered. I never told Dale he needed to give Justin space and I never talked to Justin about my desire for him to get to know Dale. If it was going to happen it would happen organically.

The first time Dale invited me to his house was on a Saturday afternoon. I drove for what seemed forever. He owned a home in a small town on the west side of the valley. I had lived in Arizona for years and never heard of El Mirage. When I arrived he was working in his garage covered in sawdust. He was working on a bedroom set he was building for a client. He told me he built furniture, but his primary job was with the airline. I was floored at his talent! He took me in the house to show me some of his work. He built his kitchen table and chairs and also his bedroom set. I fell in love with his bed. "Oh Dale, I love this bed. I would love to have one exactly like it." "We'll see." I was confused at his response back then, but now that bed does sit in our house. He introduced me to his nineteen-year-old nephew Todd who lived with him. I respected him for taking care of his nephew. I saw the pictures of his kids hanging on the family room wall, Dale, Randal, and Michelle, a nice looking family. We talked about family as we sat on the tailgate of his pickup truck eating pizza he ordered. I stayed for only about two hours but it was a nice visit. I went home feeling like I had a better picture of just who Dale was.

CHAPTER 39

Sweet Mama

O n the afternoon of December 22nd the director of Mi Casa popped in Mama's room to ask if I would come for a meeting with her and my daddy at eight in the morning. She wanted to discuss a care plan for my mama going forward. "Yes, of course," I told her I would be there. Mama had been keeping herself busy but had been experiencing a bit more fatigue than usual. The cardiologist saw her on a regular basis to monitor her heart condition but the real reason she was in Mi Casa was her legs. Those legs that had once carried her across many a midnight dance floor with Daddy had sidelined her life. However, she was still trying to press forward and find joy within the walls of her new home at Mi Casa.

I had decorated Mama's room for the holidays just like we did for every holiday. Christmas was going to be fun. I would go to visit and have dinner with her before going to church on Christmas Eve. We would be picking her up to join the family celebration Christmas Day. I told Mama I thought I would wait until a day or two after Christmas to bring Dale out to meet her. "I'll pick up some lunch for the three of us and we can sit on the patio and eat." She was looking forward to it all and so was I.

When I left on the evening of the 22nd I kissed Mama and told her I would see her in the morning. I told her I loved her. I don't think I ever left one of my parents without saying "I love you." I'm so grateful for a lifetime of I love you's.

> *I don't think I ever left one of my parents without saying "I love you." I'm so grateful for a lifetime of I love you's.*

I arrived at Mi Casa at around seven thirty the next morning to find Mama wide awake and sitting in her wheel chair. "Good morning, Sweetie." She patted my hand as I leaned in, resting on the armrest as I kissed her cheek. "Good morning Mama. How are you doing?" "Fine, just a little tired. Would you get me some coffee?" By the time I returned Daddy had arrived. We sat and talked with her for a few minutes, then he and I headed to the office. The meeting was jarring. The director explained that Mama was in rapid decline. "What do you mean? She's sitting up and talking to us." "Alice is having significant heart failure." By the time we finished our meeting, which was more or less to brace us for what was to come, the nursing staff had helped Mama back to bed. In the entire time of living in Mi Casa Mama had never gone back to bed, she had always stayed up until bedtime. I could see that she was fatigued. We sat in her room with her, chatting together and smiling at her familiar phrases, "oh for goodness sakes" delivered with her thick accent. Daddy and I looked at one another grinning. I wasn't sure what she was "goodness saking" about, but that was my mama! She nodded off now and then but just for a couple of minutes. I pulled the chair close to the bedside to hold Mama's soft hand. Daddy seemed very tired and looked like he hadn't slept at all. I told him to go home and get some rest but that I was going to stay and would see him later. I had no idea that things were as dire as they were.

There were no monitors hooked to Mama like there would have been in a hospital. No beeping machines to listen to, no gauges to watch. It was just me and Mama and the dull soft voices on the television in the background. She would look at the television and comment every now and then, barely audible. I stroked her head or patted her hand, chiming in or assuring her no worries about that. Every now and then she opened her eyes and looked right at me, saying nothing. Her green eyes seemed too sad and I knew she understood how sick she was. She wasn't fighting anymore. We were all alone and she didn't have the words to say to her baby girl, "Norma-Jean, this is as far as you can come with me. Our journey together is coming to an end. I am going to have to leave you; I know you know how much I love you. I have given my all to you. I want you to be okay in the world without me. I give you my heart and all my love to have forever." She couldn't say those things to me but I saw them in her eyes. I felt it in my soul connection to my mother, my sweet mama. I sat there with her. We were mother and daughter with an unbreakable bond. Every now and then she softly said, "Sveetie." "Yes Mama, I am here. I am not leaving, Mama. I am here beside you."

> *We were mother and daughter with an unbreakable bond. Every now and then she softly said, "Sveetie."*

Occasionally I would stand and smooth the covers over her bosom, brush her hair from her face, kiss her forehead and cheeks, and kiss my mama's beautiful, full lips. In my family we didn't have the rule of no kissing on the lips. Lips are made for kissing. I had kissed her a million times in my life and yet if I could kiss her a million times more it just wouldn't be enough. I felt overwhelmed with anxiety. Her room was filled with reminders of the season Her sudden illness took me back to the days before Charles passed away. I told myself Mama was surely sick but would definitely be able to hold on for a while. I mean, she didn't even need to go to the hospital. I held onto that small ray of hope.

Chrissy came to see Mama and I was glad to have her there with me. She pulled up a chair on one side of the bed and I stayed on the other. I held one hand and Chrissy held her other. We spoke to her and she was aware of us being there. Mama was not in pain, she was comfortable, but her breathing was slowly becoming shallow. Mama squeezed my hand ever so gently, barely discernable, and then one solitary perfect tear rolled gently down her cheek. She knew this was her goodbye. She took one deep breath and she was gone. Chrissy and I stared at each other for one long second in time. Our eyes met as our hearts broke for what we had just experienced together. It couldn't be! This wasn't supposed to happen!

In the years since Mama passed I have tried to mentally go back to that room, to that moment, to that day and piece it all together. I honestly have no recollection of the hours or days after Mama died. I was in shock. I don't remember planning her service, but I did. I don't remember informing my brother, but I did. I don't even remember telling my daddy, but I did.

I learned that the reason she wasn't transferred to a hospital was because Mama had a DNR or do not resuscitate order. If she had gone to the hospital they would not have taken any measures to save her as her heart stopped. I respect that. It was her decision. It is just hard to let go and say, "until we meet again." Never say goodbye.

When I told Dale about Mama he was very sympathetic. He expressed his own sadness at having never met her. He had his mother call me and pray for me. In what was probably the boldest step away from my life as it had been, I asked Dale to join our family and friends at Mama's memorial service at Arizona Community Church.

Once again my church family was so good to me and my family, holding me up through a dark and difficult time. Mama was cremated so there was no coffin at the church. I sat looking at the enlarged photograph of her and the lovely flowers scenting the air. Dale and his nephew Todd came and Dale sat right beside me. I know that in etiquette this is a place generally designated for the spouse or significant other of the surviving family members but I actually didn't care. He was of great comfort to me and I was glad to have him there by my side holding my hand. I knew how I felt about him even though I hadn't told him. We hadn't talked about our feelings yet but him being there with me was rather solidifying. It was his first introduction to many of my family members. It was the day he met my brother Andy. After the service was over and after we had mingled and talked a bit and ate a bit of food, Dale and Todd were heading home. He had a long night shift ahead. I walked him to the parking lot and thanked him from the bottom of my heart for coming. Todd took our picture. It's the first picture we took together and I'm glad to have it.

Norma-Jean and Dale at her mother's memorial service.

CHAPTER 40

Gerri was Right

Dale and I were spending a lot of time together. We often met at the mall because it was close to his job at the airport and not too far for me to travel. We would just walk and talk and sometimes have dinner.

Although our friend Gerri had M.S., it was under control and she was active. Not long after Dale and I began dating she had a massive heart attack and was flown to Arizona Heart Hospital where she was intubated and put on life support. This was an awful shock to everyone! We were so scared for her, her children, and granddaughter. Her parents flew to Arizona to be by her side. Things didn't look good. Looking at Gerri laying there so unaware of the world around her I thought about Charles and Mama. I was despondent. I wanted Gerri to know that Dale had been everything she said he was. I hadn't exactly said those words to her but I'm sure she knew I didn't want to be the first to tell Dale how I felt about him. I was holding back, trying to hold on to old fashioned norms. "Be a lady!"

As has happened with a few things in our relationship, Dale was giving me space and time to make a move. I was rather a coward about it. Speaking to him on the phone as I was walking around the less than romantic parking lot of Auto Mart I confessed how I felt. The words I used escape me. I'm sure they weren't eloquent, but they tumbled out and were met with, "Aah-haa, finally you say something!"

Gerri did pull through but had some lasting repercussions. She spent time in a rehabilitation facility regaining her strength before she could go back home to live with her boyfriend Charles. Dale and I never liked him at all, he wasn't good to Gerri, especially with her being sick now. She was going to need support and he wasn't capable of giving it from what she had confided in me.

For Valentine's Day Dale invited me to his house. First of all, let me say he greeted me at the door *every time* he would see me like he hadn't seen me for a year! He kissed me, hugged me, and expressed how good it was to see me. Nobody has ever been that happy to see me! It was wonderful and mind-blowing at the same time. He surprised me. "Why don't you go in the bathroom and wash up before we eat." On the bathroom counter lay a bouquet of two dozen gorgeous pink roses. *How thoughtful and sweet.* For dinner he cooked pork chops, dressing, and green beans with key lime pie for dessert. He played a variety of music from his expansive vinyl collection, took me by the hand, and we danced in the living room. It was our first holiday together and couldn't have been any better. It was a perfect first Valentine's Day together.

Our relationship blossomed quickly. In March we flew to Monterey to meet my bestie. It was March 13th, Alisa's birthday and I commented to Dale that he had to be pretty special to be able to whisk me away on my daughter's birthday. It was a bright

Norma-Jean and Dale,
Monterey, CA

sunny morning when I met him at the airport. As we waited for the shuttle from the parking lot he opened my hand and placed a single key in it and curled my fingers closed around it. "What's this for?' "It's to my house so you can get in anytime you like, whether I am home or not." "Oh wow! Thank you." I kissed him as the people around us stared. Oh well. I didn't care and neither did he.

As our flight departed Phoenix we held hands, looking down over the vast landscape trying to point out landmarks. Once we were leveled out Dale fell asleep, he had worked all night. I gazed at him instead of out the window. I had a lot on my mind. I knew it was going to be different to be in Pat's presence with Dale. For decades she had always seen me with Charles. She was the one person in my life who knew about all my melt downs since his death. I could confide in her to say, "I'm not okay, I still hear his voice" or "I don't think I'm getting through this." She was one person I had confided in about Dale, "I think I'm falling in love again, and I'm scared."

> *She was one person I had confided in about Dale, "I think I'm falling in love again, and I'm scared."*

So now here we were. Pat gave him the biggest hug and he of course being the hugger that he is gave her a great big hug back. She joked and said, "Oh my, let me feel those muscles" feeling his biceps. Then she teased about his six packs. Yes, he was in good shape. Having dedicated many years to the fitness industry herself Pat is always aware of others who are physically fit! We showed him around the Peninsula, where I had lived and raised my kids, places where Pat and I used to go frequently. We went to Cannery Row and ate at Bubba Gump's. My godson Charlie pointed out all the sights and gave Dale tips about the best things on the menu. Charlie and Dale hit it off right away. We walked down Fisherman's Wharf and visited Santa Cruz Beach and Boardwalk. We stayed with Pat for a couple of days, our trip packed with sightseeing and good company and much laughter. Pat told me she totally gave me her blessing and approval of my relationship with

Dale. She said she thought he was a genuinely nice man, a man of God, and he would always treat me well, which was what she wants for me. She makes me cry whenever she tells me things like that.

When we got home from the trip I smiled every time I thought about it. Maxine hadn't met him yet so I decided to make it happen. She and I drove out for a visit with a large pan of freshly baked lasagna. I love to cook, so I brought food. We sat at his kitchen table eating, laughing, and talking. Maxine was a decided yes! She liked him a lot.

✧✦✧ Connecticut ✧✦✧

In May Dale took me home to meet his family. We surprised his mom and dad late on Friday night when we arrived at the Bradley Airport in Hartford, Connecticut. I was excited, nervous, thrilled, all of it. The trip had been a good one. There was no strife when Dale and I were with one another. We clicked like the parts of a watch, just movement, keeping time together. I had huge butterflies in my stomach and was anxious to meet his parents in person. The first floor of their Cape Cod style house was lit up. It was late but it looked like everyone was still up. Dale pulled the rental car to the end of the side driveway. We walked to the backdoor and he knocked loudly and stepped off the porch leaving me standing alone under the light. The door opened and with a delighted squeal in her voice his mother looked hard at me and said, "Nooorrrma?" I said "Yes, it's me." Before I knew what was happening she scooped me in her arms and embraced me with the biggest hug. She started crying and I cried too. It was the sweetest moment. I felt like we were kindred souls. She called to his dad, "E.C. come look at who's here!"

They both were smiling at me. His mother said, "YOU are who we have been praying for!" I said, "Thank you. Thank you for the prayers."

Dale's dad was a big man with broad shoulders and strong arms. He gripped me very tightly in a warm embrace.... They both were smiling at me. His mother said, "YOU are who we have been praying for!" I said, "Thank you. Thank you for the prayers." They laughed.

Dale came in the house to join us, hugs and kisses going around between him and his parents. Their faces were full of joy looking at him. Clearly they loved their son! His mom had food cooking on the stove and she checked on it while we all congregated in the kitchen. Of course Dale was going to eat whatever his Mama was cooking! His parents clarified for me what they meant when they said they had been praying for me. Apparently, some time before he met me Dale had been sick with the flu. His mom felt badly because he was alone with no one to care for him. He had been single for a while, by choice but they had prayed for God to send him a good woman to be his wife. They thought I was that answered prayer. To be the answer to anyone's prayer is so humbling, but especially if they see you as whom God sent for their son!

That night I could see firsthand how much like his father Dale is. I could also see how much he was still in love with his bride after all the years of marriage. What a beautiful and wondrous thing it was to see. It is rare. His father is a big man yet strong, gentle, and caring, and very, very funny! He made me laugh a lot. I hope Dale will be like him as he grows older. I hope he follows his example.

Saturday was busy in the Coachman house. His brothers and sisters got news that we were in town and each one came by to visit. Mom cooked a huge, delicious dinner but due to work schedules his siblings each dropped by at different times. It was incredible to meet his family. Similarities do exist between the Sims and the Coachmans and that's kind of an odd thing.

The Sims family has seven kids, four boys and three girls; the Coachman family also has seven kids, four boys and three girls. When the family is together it is loud and fun and good food is always to be found. In both cases the kids had all grown up together in small houses filled with love.

We went to church on Sunday morning, Dale's father was preaching. Lord could his daddy preach! If you didn't feel anything, well, let's just say, you couldn't feel anything! Something in you is void. After church, more family time, more food, and a bit of sightseeing. "So this is where you grew up?" I liked Connecticut but Dale made it clear he would never want to live there again except maybe for a month or two at one of the beach communities in the summer once he retires. It was fun to see his hometown and meet his family. Everyone made me feel special, lucky, blessed, and welcome.

Just as I wanted my family to meet Dale and approve of him, he wanted his family to meet me. This trip was primarily to meet his parents and his siblings. I didn't meet his friends or his kids. Before I knew it the day was over and it was time to pack and prepare for our early morning flight.

While we were at his parents' home Dale and I were sleeping across the hall from each other. This may seem an old fashioned norm, but it is one of respect. We weren't married and under their roof unmarried you don't share a bed. He was in his old childhood room and I was in the girls' room. The house was quiet. His mom and dad were in bed watching television. I went to take a shower. When I came back upstairs Dale called to me. When I walked into his room he told me I looked beautiful. "Yeah right! I'm a hot mess." My hair was just washed, wet and curly all over my head. I was in my pajamas and bare feet, basically ready to go to bed, not ready to see the world. "Don't you want something to drink?" "Oh, no thank you. I'm good." He insisted I should have some juice and that he would go get it for me. I walked across to my room and sat on the bed. When he returned with the glass of juice he placed it on the night table. He

He stood in front of me for a moment and then he brought my attention to something shiny, "What's that?"

335

stood in front of me for a moment and then he brought my attention to something shiny, "What's that?" I looked down to see a shiny penny on the floor. I said, "It's a good luck penny," not realizing that he had dropped it down there on purpose. He knelt down as if to pick it up and I realized he was on one knee in front of me. He took my hand, looked in my eyes, and started talking to me saying the usual sweet things he says but this time he was a bit more serious. I could see it in his eyes and hear it in his voice. I was thinking, *Oh Dale, you are so sweet!* Then he went on to say he had something he wanted to ask me but I'd probably be mad or upset with him. I was puzzled. *Wow, it must be something serious. But, what?* He seemed concerned. I told him he could ask me anything or tell me anything and I wouldn't be upset. Why would he think I would be? I had never been angry with Dale. Then he said, "I should have asked you sooner," and pulled a white box out of his pocket and opened it. It held a splendid princess cut solitaire ring. I don't remember much else. I was overcome with joy and buried my face in his chest. He held me a long time. Finally, he put the ring on my finger and we kissed sweet, soft, tender kisses and I cried happy, happy tears. Then we went to share the news. By the time I got to the edge of his mom and dad's bed and held out my hand to show off the ring I was like a little kid, I just jumped right in the bed between the two of them! Honestly, I don't know what I was thinking; I was delighted and full of exuberant fun!

His parents were thrilled for us. They hugged and kissed and congratulated us both. His dad said, "It's about time!" Back upstairs I could barely get to sleep, adrenaline pulsed through my body and happy thoughts raced through my mind.

On our flight home we sat in first class and had congratulations all around from the crew. It was wonderful.

ᕙᕦ Both Feet In ᕤᕚ

Once Dale and I were engaged I joined his church. It was a big change for me after being a charter member at Arizona Community Church. I was going from a predominantly white yet very diverse congregation back to a predominantly black church. Comfortable in both, it didn't matter to me about the racial makeup but I had become used to the size of the church in numbers as well as the campus and all it had to offer. I had just never wanted to be anywhere that people were excluded because of who they were. That wasn't the case as the congregation was very welcoming. I jumped right in and wanted to be involved and make new friends. I quickly learned that Dale was the *catch of church* but hadn't dated or shown any interest in the single women. He was recognized as a gentleman, kind and stable. He was respected by the men as well. Any woman who dated him would be fortunate; I was considered very lucky to be marrying him. The women were genuinely sweet to me and immediately offered their assistance in planning and decorating for our day. Truthfully, I felt a bit overwhelmed and would have preferred to sit down with Dale and make a simple plan but I didn't articulate it. Why? I don't know. Perhaps it was still my old self very present indeed.

We set the date for July 31, 2004. There was no point in putting things off for a long time. We weren't having a big elaborate wedding. We knew that we wanted to be together. Thus we went forth with the plans.

Charles and Chrissy were moving to a new home at the end of June so I moved in with Dale just a month before we married. I was concerned about the day in the future when Shanay would tell me she wanted to live with her boyfriend. *Shack up* with him I guess I would say. Knowing it was years away, I was still concerned. I sat her down and told her, "The only reason I am moving in with Dale is I have an engagement ring on my finger and the invitations have been sent out!

Do you understand?" She did. Not that it would make any substantive difference, but it mattered to me.

Dale's best friend Ralph called most evenings to talk to me in the month before we married. He had lots of questions and wanted to make sure I was going to be good for Dale. He's a great guy, I like him a lot.

Ferol was the most encouraging person when it came to keeping me from almost changing my mind about a wedding. Dale had been teasing me about showing up one day with a wedding gown and us just running off to get married. I would laugh and say there was no way I could do that because my family would have a fit. But the reserved way my family acted toward me concerning the wedding made me rethink it. Ferol helped me with the wedding invitations and told me not to be discouraged. She said Dale was a really good man and I should not let him get away. "You hear me Mama-Jean? Don't let him get away!" She laughed out loud, her hazel eyes sparkling. With Ferol all her emotions were always reflected through her eyes. I had no plans to let him get away, just maybe plans for no wedding. In all fairness, I have to admit I didn't ask for much help. I just thought it would be offered. I only asked for help with finding a gown and picking invitations.

> *She said Dale was a really good man and I should not let him get away. "You hear me Mama-Jean? Don't let him get away!"*

I had hoped Alisa would go with me but I could see it was something she didn't feel comfortable doing, therefore I didn't push for it. That doesn't mean I wasn't sad. I had girlfriends I could have asked or I could have brought Chrissy, instead I went alone. I chose a gown that I thought was perfect. Fortunately I didn't need to have any alterations done to it. When my friend Anette saw it she said, "Girl, could you have picked anything other than this 'this is so Norma' dress? Step outside the box. Try something different than you usually wear. That's just like a dress you have already but a bit fancier. I will go with you!" And she did. We traded my matronly gown for a strapless fitted organza gown with a train. It was falling off me by our wedding day, but I was in love with it! Anette bought my necklace and earring set to wear. "Thank you Anette." She made all the difference.

Alisa, Chrissy, Cindy, and Ferol had a bridal shower for me. It was so much fun! I have given many, many showers over the years but I had never had one. I was very excited. LoVera even came from California. Pat couldn't come but she sent me a dozen roses and a gift. I had the most marvelous time. I laughed and felt like a kid. It was wonderful to have my family and friends there to bless me and wish me well.

Dale and I really didn't do anything much to plan the wedding. We ordered a simple, beautiful cake with fresh flowers and pearl beads. I made my bouquet of fresh flowers. My friend Rhonda sent tulips to include in my bouquet since that's my favorite flower. It was a lovely gift and it made me feel like she was part of my day.

We spoke with the pastor about the ceremony. We wanted traditional vows and prayers and there would be a few songs. Dale's father would pray over us and offer a special blessing. That was going to be the extent of our wedding. We didn't plan on a traditional reception, we were just going to serve some finger foods in the church hall with punch and cake.

On July 28 Dale's parents flew out to Arizona from Connecticut for the wedding. I was more than a little nervous as it was going to be the first time I would meet his son and daughter Randal and Michelle.

What I hoped for was to gently find my place in their life where they would become comfortable with me loving them.

I hoped they would like me. The first night when we were ready to eat and we were all sitting at the table Dale's father asked me what I thought of my new son and daughter. I was so happy he put it that way because it's exactly how I was feeling. I would never want to replace their mother in any way. I am big on that. I never wanted anyone to come in and be a part of my kids' lives and try to push me aside in some way. What I hoped for was to gently find my place in their life where they would become comfortable with me loving them. I was hopeful that they would grow to love me too. This was my opportunity to express that to them and I think I made it pretty clear. There was no pressure from me.

Michelle and I bonded fairly easily. She was a sweet, bright pre-teen. She could get a little rowdy which was fine by me since she always settled down when told to. She had a great sense of humor. We spent the first few days laughing a lot and talking and I learned that she did indeed like to shop. In preparation for the wedding she and I went to have manicures and pedicures. It was the first time for her and I was glad to have shared that with her.

Randal was in his late teens and such a gentleman. He washed my car and mopped the kitchen all without me asking! *Okay,* I thought to myself, *I have a son who is considerate and kind and does things like this without asking! Now I have another young man who is also kind and does things without having to be asked. Hallelujah!*

On Friday I left Dale and his family and went back to stay with my son and the gang. Charles' brother Emanuel had come down with a lady friend from Sacramento for the wedding and I wanted to spend some time visiting him. He was always there to support us. We were glad to see this but sad as we remembered back to that August day in 2003 when his wife LaVerne had passed away. The day I heard she had died my heart broke for him, but then went directly to their children Adrian and Sheri. Adrian had always been the epitome of Mama's boy and it was just so sad. Once again our large family came together to show support and love for Emanuel and his kids. We had all loved LaVerne and her gigantic bright smile. During Emanuel's visit with us for the wedding he and his friend went out dancing with Charles and Chrissy. I tossed and turned and could barely sleep. I have to admit I wondered about Charles Sr. I wondered what he would say. I hoped he'd want my happiness, want me to be loved.

⟡ Wedding Day ⟡

Charles walked me down the aisle. I was very disappointed that the minister had Dale standing with his back to me. Oh my goodness, this struck his father the wrong way. He actually wanted to perform our wedding over again because he felt

How could it be possible that just this one incredibly special, spectacular, splendid person is going to be mine for the rest of my life?

it hadn't been done right! I told him, "We're married now; it doesn't matter if we face north or south, east or west, and it's done." That

moment was not to be done over. For me, when Dale saw me standing beside him and he looked at me and smiled, that was everything. This is it! This is our moment to say there's no turning back, there's no choosing another, there's no time for thought, there's no second guessing. We know that we know, what we know, without any doubt. We found each other in this world with billions of people. *How could it be possible that just this one incredibly special, spectacular, splendid person is going to be mine for the rest of my life? How lucky could I be?* No, not lucky. I know I am blessed beyond measure.

Looking back, I know if I could do our wedding over I would have chosen to keep it very intimate

Top—Dale and Norma-Jean, Bottom—Rev. Coachman prays over Norma-Jean and Dale

and elegant. I would have married Dale in the little white chapel out at Luke Air force Base in a late afternoon ceremony. I would have filled the chapel with sweet flowers and candles and we would have all celebrated with dinner and dancing at the officers club. Maybe I would just go for a barefoot walk on the beach with our families there to celebrate. Our wedding day is still a sweet memory. We have pretty pictures and it was beautiful. Some of the pictures definitely reveal the room we had our reception in with vending machines in the background and children's toys piled high. We were just happy to be getting married. Although Pastor Thomas failed to murmur one personal word about our relationship, Dale's father certainly did make up for it with his heartfelt prayer over us. He stood facing us, large hands upon our heads, speaking words of love, asking God's blessing upon our marriage. We could feel his sincerity and passion as he raised his voice, he pressed gently on our heads. It was so sweet. My eyes filled with tears, I was overjoyed. He ended with a robust "Amen!" And we echoed "Amen." A picture of this moment hangs framed on our bedroom wall.

Remarkable family resemblance between Norma-Jean and her mother.

Norma-Jean and Dale with all the kids.

We took lots of beautiful pictures. We ate cake and punch before leaving for the Marriott at Desert Ridge. We had a suite for the night, a gift from Charles. We ate dinner in the steak house and a little girl thought I was a princess since I was still in my gown, tiara, and all, with Dale still in his tuxedo. Her mother asked if it was okay if she talked to me. "Of course it is okay." She was so cute. "You're so pretty. I love you." "Thank you, and I love you too! How old are you?" "Four years old." I reached for her small hand and said, "It's very nice to meet you." She made us smile.

What a delicious, unforgettable dinner we had. We wished we could have stayed to relax and enjoy our suite but since church service started at eleven and Dale's father was invited to deliver the sermon we had to get home. We ordered room service and had breakfast on the balcony so we could enjoy the beautiful view but then we had to get ourselves in gear. I don't know how, but we were actually on time. Later in the day Alisa and her family came over and we all went to Furr's Cafeteria. Charles and his family came too. We followed by opening wedding gifts in our home. Everyone oohed and awed at each gift, but Dale was most excited about the Home Depot gift card! To that he could relate and we all had a good laugh. He said most gifts are purchased by

*Norma-Jean and Dale with Gerri,
who got to say, "I told you so!"*

women, for women, in the case of wedding gifts. Not so true, but I knew what he meant.

Dale's parents left to go home but Michelle decided she wanted to stay longer. I would fly home with her since she was afraid to travel alone. This became a pattern. I'd fly to Connecticut, pick her up, and we'd fly home. At the beginning of our relationship it gave me and Michelle important time to bond.

With everything back to normal Dale and I were going to leave for the Bahamas to honeymoon but Hurricane Charley blew in and we had to cancel. We stayed home, slept in together, watched movies, ate out, and shopped. We actually had a marvelous time with nothing but our whole life ahead of us.

☙❦❧

We had settled into a very good beginning. Todd continued to live with us. He and I got along really well and he was welcoming to me as was the rest of the Coachman family. I was affectionately called Aunt Norma. Dale's father was proud to become a second great grandpa to the kids of my family. He was especially fond of the triplets and couldn't wait to get them back to Connecticut. He formed a special bond with Christopher, calling him on the phone and keeping up with him. Christopher was crazy about him too.

Dale and I were doing fine. We were happy and in love. Seeing me with someone else after a lifetime with Charles was a difficult adjust-ment for some of my family. They all really liked Dale and of course everyone wanted me to be happy, but from time to time things would be said that would deeply hurt me. I would have to be patient and let them come to accept that I wasn't the same person any longer, I wasn't dismissing my past, but embracing a future with Dale. My family would never lose importance to me but my family would now include Dale. If I was focusing on him, it didn't mean I had less love, less con-cern or caring for anyone. My heart has lots of room to love many people. The love that is shared between husband and wife is, of course, different, and now Dale would be my first priority. That was difficult for some to accept.

> *...I wasn't the same person any longer, I wasn't dismissing my past, but embracing a future with Dale.*

As soon as Dale and I married we should have insisted the kids drop the Mr. Dale and either begin to call him Grandpa or allow them to address him as Dale. As they have grown up and matured he is now addressed as Grandpa, Grandpa Dale, or just Dale by the oldest of my grandkids. I never thought about it until one day Dale said to me, "The people at work call me Mr. Dale. There's nothing endearing about that." I realized he didn't feel fully loved or accepted by my family.

We had our first holidays in the house on Dahlia. I was happy and content being married to Dale but the closer it got to Christmas my anxiety and depression set in. Everywhere I looked I saw Christmas decorations and lights and heard the music. I thought about Charles and how he died, replaying everything in my head until my grief was new again. Around the seventeenth of December I calculated the years we would have been married. I knew it was a day that everyone knew and they were used to saying, "Happy Anniversary" even after Charles passed. I decided I needed to consult someone to help me navigate my emotions before I was spinning out of control. It helped. I am still learning to compartmentalize my feelings. *Joy* for this, sadness for that, fear of this....

Daddy bought us an artificial Christmas tree as a gift and I dove in and decorated the house. We would have a good Christmas and start making memories of our own. Dale was working a lot of hours but we planned to go to Glendale Glitters, a nighttime light display with vendors and activities in the historic old town district. He was tired when we headed out the door and we were going later than we'd planned but I was just happy we didn't have to cancel. When we got there all the festivities had ended and the majority of the lights were off. Some of the trees were still lit with cascading strings of lights. It was beautiful, nonetheless. While we sat in the car Dale said, "I have something for you that glitters." He reached in his pocket and handed me a black velvet box. I opened it to see a sparkling pair of princess cut diamond earrings to match my ring. How sweet and romantic he is to me. It was an evening to remember. Our first Christmas was extraordinary.

CHAPTER 41

The Saddest Call

U nfortunately, it wasn't long before Dale's father became critically ill. He was hospitalized and we went to Connecticut
to visit him. Dale stayed as long as he could but after a few
days had to return to work. I stayed to help in any way I could. Mom
Coachman was dealing with an injury to her arm and couldn't drive
and was under a lot of stress. I drove her to and from the hospital each
day and tried to keep food prepared so she could eat without worrying about it. When she was doing better and it seemed Dale's dad was
stable, I flew home. I missed Dale.

Late one evening while Dale was in the shower, I answered the
phone. It was his sister Denise. His father had just passed. *Oh my God!* I
waited until he was out of the shower and with a broken heart I delivered
the news. His whole world just changed and all I could offer was arms
to hold him, my shoulder to cry on, and a heart breaking with his. We
would hold each other up and get through, although it was hard.

When we went home to Connecticut for the funeral the house was
full of people coming to pay their respects and drop off food. We were
sorrowful to see Mom Coachman in so much pain. Her face was void

of any expression but grief. She tried to smile and make small talk with friends, congregation members, fellow pastors from the community and family. She was still in shock to some degree. She would later tell me how thankful she was to have retired early to spend time with her beloved. They had done a lot, but had plans to do so much more. Now he was gone and she would have to carry on. I felt for her. I understood.

Germaine Coachman

The funeral was something fit for a celebrity or royalty. People overflowed the church into the halls and down into the basement as well as in the vestibule. The service could be viewed in different areas on closed circuit. Dozens of community faith leaders were in attendance as well as many pastors who spoke words of condolence and consolation to the family.

Alisa flew to be there in support of Dale. She just wanted to show her care for his loss, she loved his mom. It did give her a chance to see where he came from and the family he had been telling her about. All the family was there. She quickly bonded with Porchia, Dale's niece. I quickly bonded with his sister, Germaine, a police officer at the time. She opened her arms to me and embraced both Alisa and me into the family. Even though she was grieving she made us feel loved and welcome. We still talk regularly, laughing together and sharing secrets. We "get" each other on every level. Friends and relatives of EC Coachman paid him the loveliest tributes and said, "You look just *like* your Dad!" Indeed he did and he does.

With his dad laid to rest we returned home and settled back into our routine. It was all so hard. Hard to believe this awesome man had been in my life for such a short time. He made a big impact on me and I am indebted to him for raising the man I love. I was hopeful that in the future I could have a good relationship with all of his siblings. Most importantly, I wanted them to know that I love Dale and I will love them too.

CHAPTER 42

Searching

We began to look for a new home, searching for a place where our families could gather. Family is important to us both. We originally looked at homes in the east valley closer to where my family all lived. As we began to expand and explore we realized that we would get more home for our money in the west valley, but nothing was decided. We were just window shopping and then one day out of the blue Dale came home and said, "We're going to put the house up for sale." I was surprised because I thought with our window shopping a move would be in the distant future. We listed the house with a realtor and within a matter of days had staged our home and held an open house. The house sold immediately! We got full asking price with no debate or adjustments. The house passed inspection and within thirty days we moved. Adios to our home on Dahlia. It had been a superb first home together.

Since we knew our goal was a new home, we decided to rent a small place that was clean and inexpensive but nothing fancy. It was a small two bedroom patio home in an area of mostly senior citizens in Youngtown. We settled in and began to diligently search for our next place to live. The most important thing was it would be our own and reflect us both.

Once again we looked at tract homes as well as custom homes. We crisscrossed the valley, every bit of spare time became afternoons in the car driving and looking, stopping for McDonalds french fries and a drink, or an ice cream cone. We'd often arrive home tired, but we'd still sit down with flyers and brochures and discuss all we had seen. Finally we decided the best thing would be to purchase land and build our own home.

We first visited the lot in Buckeye and fell in love with the serenity there. It was one acre with views of mountains from every direction. We went early in the morning and noticed the beautiful sunrises. We returned in the evening and noticed the beautiful sunsets. The quiet neighborhood was surrounded by picturesque cotton and alfalfa fields. We continued searching but each and every time we came back to the lot on Desert Lane. Finally, we purchased it and began the process of finding a builder.

During that year in Youngstown while our new home was under construction we did so much! We certainly had some ups and down regarding my health. I would require another major surgery after the reoccurrence of my breast cancer. Dr. Holcomb was wonderful and assured us that everything was removed; however, I came home looking quite different. I opted not to follow up with any reconstructive procedures. I was released from the hospital with tubes and drains still in my chest. During this time I was grateful for the presence of Mom Coachman who came to stay for two weeks. I was at first embarrassed and humiliated to have her or Dale see me looking much like a patched together rag doll. I had no energy and couldn't be the hostess to my mother-in-law in the way I would have liked. I am happy to say that I got through it all and was given a cancer free, clean bill of health minus the existing lupus flare ups and daily fibromyalgia pain.

We had so much to be grateful for. Dale and I had found each other and our love just continued to grow as we learned more and more about being together and building a life. Dale was a very kind and caring husband from the start. I had given him my heart and I trusted him not to break it. I told him, "I will put my hand in yours and let you lead, as long as you are following Christ, the minute you stop. I stop." He was fully in agreement. He gave his solemn word and he meant it. He would love me and cherish me. Our vows were not just a formality but a soulful promise.

> *I had given him my heart and I trusted him not to break it. I told him, "I will put my hand in yours and let you lead, as long as you are following Christ..."*

Dale is a good provider and a hard worker. He would do many, many small things each day to show his love, but every now and then, he would wow me, knock me off my feet with a remarkable gift that made me feel extremely special, loved, and yes spoiled! He was always giving me sweet, tender, and loving compliments. Those words are little cherished gifts to my heart. I loved the days he would take me to Dillard's or Macys and he'd search the racks for things he wanted to have me try on. He'd find a seat and wait for me to come out of the dressing room to model for him. The first time he did that was my *Pretty Woman* moment. One day when Dillard's was having a sale we walked out with four suits and several dresses. We had bags of garments, shoes, and perfume. It was fun and amazing and felt good! I loved it.

❧ The Biggest Gift ☙

I can't tell the story of the beginning of our marriage and things that Dale did to make every day special without telling you about the biggest surprise of all. Alisa and I went to Texas on a weekend trip. We were flying standby and for some reason it was one of those weekends where everyone and their brother was flying. We kept getting bumped from one flight to the next for our trip home. I wasn't well and when they finally said that one seat was available, Alisa told me to take it and get home. She would come on the next flight which wouldn't be until morning.

When I finally made it home, I felt sick and exhausted. I waited at the curbside pickup bench for Dale, watching for our white Camry. Car after car pulled up to the curb dropping off or picking up passengers. I couldn't help but notice the beautiful black Chrysler 300 coming in my direction. *Oh, look at that car* I thought. For some reason I was in love with the 300, I think it's a beautiful vehicle, especially in black. I have never been a car person, but that model caught my eye the first time I saw it and every time we saw one I reminded Dale that I loved it. The black 300 slowed as it pulled closer to me and I couldn't take my gaze off it. It came to a stop and Dale stepped out to welcome me home. I hugged and kissed him and then I peppered him with questions, "What are you doing in this car?" "Did you rent it?" "Shhhh…wait a minute. How are you? Are you happy to see me? Are you happy to be home? Are you doing okay?" The suspense was killing me. He gave me a kiss; put the car in drive and off we drove toward home. He had not answered a thing I asked him. As we were driving he said, "Do you like this car?" "Like it, I love it! You know that I do." "Good Baby Doll because it's yours!" "What? What did you say?" "Open the glove box and pull out the contract." It was too good to be true. There it was, he had indeed bought the car, paid cash for it and it was *mine!* The tears flowed and flowed. My heart was filled with more gratitude than I could express. I was so overcome with *joy* at this absolutely, incredibly splendid gift from my husband. He called me his Baby Doll, his queen, and so many other endearing sweet names but he did go far beyond to make me know he meant every word.

I can honestly say that was the biggest and most surprising gift that I have ever received as an adult.

I can honestly say that was the biggest and most surprising gift

353

that I have ever received as an adult. Dale would mirror many of the things my daddy did for me in my youth. Daddy had indeed bought me a car, but I never drove it. This was so different. In my worst times of struggle I had cars financed in my son's name, but I paid for them. It was different. Ferol had given me a car so we'd have wheels, but that was different. Everything about this incredibly sweet, thoughtful, and generous gift set me on my heels. For weeks each time I got behind the steering wheel I was moved to tears. The reality of me being this special to any one person in the world was overwhelming. He was putting *me* first. Dale would continue to drive his truck and I had the keys to a beautiful, spanking brand new car. What a brat I felt like. I was a spoiled brat with a heart of gratitude.

The first years of being married to Dale gave me new freedom and I wasn't used to it. I often had to pinch myself. I was going places and doing things I could only dream of before. I flew to see my grandma in New Jersey. I went to New York City with my cousins and my sisters-in-law from the Sims side of my family. I couldn't imagine flying places and doing things on my own would be so liberating. I was enjoying it immensely. Sometimes I was walking on the edge with the rest of my family. I understood that they did of course want me to be happy but if I spoke too positively about my current joy, I had to be cautious to not say too much. There was always Charles, he was forever a part of me and I thought everyone understood just how much. But sometimes I was accused of things that were never true. I would always love him. I never fell out of love with him and divorced him, he died. We had been through a world of struggles and trauma as well as decades of drama, but we had love and joy too. I want to focus on the good of my life with Charles. I want to remember our family togetherness, caring, and laughter. There was always lots of laughing out loud. Truth is when you've been

...you have to work very hard to rise above the negative experiences and not have them affect you. Those experiences can determine...

through some things, you have to work very hard to rise above the negative experiences and not have them affect you. Those experiences can determine how you think about yourself. In my case I lost a big piece of myself through it all. I had grown to believe that maybe things weren't supposed to be carefree and happy. I was accustomed to stress and worry and complicated relationships. If I mentioned the lack of those elements in my day to day life, those around me deemed it as throwing Charles under the bus and elevating Dale to King of the World status. I am doing neither.

My present life is with Dale and so is my future. There's a reason God brought us together and we intend to honor that. Our happiness will not be at expense of others. We want them to respect our right to be happy and we want the same for them. Period. That's it in a nutshell.

⌦ Mexico ⌫

In September 2005 we flew to Paradise. We went to Puerto Vallarta, Mexico to finally have our honeymoon and celebrate Dale's 50th birthday. I actually fell in love with the city. The people, the culture, the food, it was all amazing, a little piece of heaven. Every day there was something new to explore. We went to the open air Mercado, the tequila factory, we did a city tour by bus and they showed us spectacular vistas blooming with bright bougainvillea and hibiscus. We saw the jungle and beautiful beaches. We stayed at the Crown Resort and experienced the five star treatment. They only allowed adults at this resort although there were children at their neighboring resort. We lay on the pristinely clean beach, which was raked every day multiple times a day. The sand resembled a carpet that had been carefully vacuumed in one direction. Birds chirped in the trees and the waves lapped upon the shore. In the restaurant every evening after dinner we were delighted by waiters making *sexy coffee*. It's quite an artful production, involving liquor and fire. We went into town with a group from the resort to experience the nightclub life. We danced and drank margaritas, slept late, and ate breakfast in the sunshine watching bees eat sticky jam from plates set out just for them. It was a great distraction to keep them from swarming around the patrons. It was a marvelous and glorious time to celebrate.

For Dale's 50th birthday I bought him a Movado watch. It was the most expensive piece of jewelry I have ever personally purchased but I wanted him to have an extraordinary gift to mark the occasion. I also gave him 50 birthday cards which took him quite a while to open and read.

The trip was one we would remember forever. We even talked about the possibility of moving to Mexico when Dale retired. We had immeasurable fun. When we got home I put together a scrapbook and vowed to keep up with photos of our life and adventures. I planned to scrapbook regularly but I have not kept my promise.

Puerto Vallarta, Mexico was the trip of a lifetime!

CHAPTER 43

Embracing Life

We were ecstatic when our builder broke ground for our new home. It would be Dale's and mine together and we reveled in the planning and progress. It was our project! We photographed every phase of the house being built. We picked out each and every light fixture, appliance, the bath tubs, the sinks, and paint colors. We decided where to place the walls or the windows and enjoyed working with our builder, Chuck Neidhart; he was great.

While we waited for our new home to be built from the foundation up, we rented a cute place in Buckeye, AZ about two miles from the new house. When it was finally completed and nearly ready for us to move in, I was admitted to the hospital with a medical emergency again. I felt drowned in disappointment laying there in that bed with bottles of medication and bags of IV fluid hanging on the pole over my head. The nearly silent noises of the machine monitoring my heart and controlling the drip speed seemed like sirens in my head. All I wanted was to be with Dale, especially now. We had waited so long for the day we could put our key in the door and walk right into *our* new home. Warm tears soaked the pillow under my head. I knew no matter how much I wished for this to be different; it was reality until I was better.

It wasn't until late in the day the doctor released me it was evening before I was actually discharged. I was surprised by my feelings of renewed joy and enthusiasm upon being released but embraced them gratefully. Dale was coming to get me and I was beaming. When we got to the house it was lit up bright and to my surprise the windows all had blinds! Dale had bought and installed them all. I'll never forget seeing the beautiful hardwood floors gleaming in the warm light.

> *I'll never forget seeing the beautiful hardwood floors gleaming in the warm light... This was HOME.*

We walked through the house from front to back over and over again taking it all in. This was HOME and it was ours. We did it. We had a dream and we made it come true!

Our home was a typical southwestern style territorial house with beautiful vigas, traditional log poles, in the ceiling and a big double wide front door. We had designed lots of big windows to bring in light in addition to the skylights. Dale could build furniture or work on his beloved classic cars in the roomy three car garage. Our home had all the small touches that were important to us both. But more importantly, we brought our family values, our love, and our dream of a place to live together and be happy for life. We were going to be in this home for a very long time, if not forever!

The day we actually moved in we were ecstatic, this was the beginning of the rest of our future. I put my hand in Dale's and we walked through the door of our new home on Desert Lane knowing that we were on solid ground. With determination and pride and our hearts bursting with love we made it. We were finally home! It would be a place to gather and celebrate with family and friends. Our home would be our sanctuary from the world, a place for us to live together and grow. There were no doubts and I finally had a sense of security. I had found a love to call my own and a place to call my own.

New house in Buckeye, AZ

I was filled with hope for the future. I will always embrace and remember my past. I will remember every wonderful and happy day. I will always remember my failures, my disappointments, and the crazy ups and downs as well because they have made me who I am. I am grateful for the love I shared with Charles and the children that we raised. I am a grandma filled with awe and humbleness. I'm incredibly thankful for the parents I was blessed with. So there it all is; my past colliding with my present and my future. All of it has come together to make me whole and I have clarity about my purpose; I am a daughter, sister, auntie, friend, grandma, and a wife.

I opened my heart in these pages and poured it all out. I have been transparent and told things about myself that only a few people in my life know.

I've been privileged to be Godmother to several and Auntie to many whom I love. Some I've never met! I've felt embarrassed that I couldn't send birthday and Christmas gifts like other Godparents and aunts do. I've regretted not being able to be there for many other special occasions. It's not how I ever wanted it to be, I was in survival mode and did the best I could. I hope that all will know I love them dearly in spite of this.

My purpose is to love and support and yes, guide if I can by speaking truth. I have opened my heart in these pages and poured it all out. I have been transparent and told things about myself that only a few people in my life know. I've shared details of things that I am ashamed to admit to but I can't keep in a closet because they need to be spoken about. I included the ugly and profane language because I didn't want to sugarcoat my experiences. I wanted to tell my story because I hope it has value to at least those who know me best and love me more because of who I have become, not less. I have spoken forthrightly because I pray that by showing the pitfalls of my life, some of the people I care most about will avoid repeating the same painful mistakes. I pray it helps someone, anyone who thinks they have given up on having the desires of their heart. Anything is possible for anyone. I hope after reading this you will reach high. Stretch your arms wide. Embrace what life has to offer. Renew your spirit. Believe in something bigger than yourself. Be the best version of yourself. Do not settle. Push for having an intentional life. Know that you are worthy and wonderful. You can do good things with the life you have been given. Don't be mediocre.

Know that God is real. Do not be deceived. To believe in God and put your faith in the goodness of His mighty love is not something that takes place in a church. It's something that takes place in your heart!

Love with all candor. Don't turn your back on the people who love you. This means never holding grudges, always forgiving, but being true to yourself. Live a life which reflects integrity. The definition of integrity is doing what is right when no one is looking. You will know in your heart when you are not. Try to never be cruel. Never forget where you came from as you chart your course in life. People are not dispensable. Live by the golden rule, always treating others as you want to be treated. Embrace those whom you love with no conditions on your love. If the people you love are toxic, it's okay to set boundaries. You are not obliged to participate in toxic relationships, but don't quit loving. Try to always leave the door open for things to improve. Conduct yourself with dignity. Don't air your dirty laundry at inappropriate times and in an inappropriate manner. Don't try to change others, it'll never work. Change yourself instead. You can do it. When you're setting out to change, ask yourself "Is this for the better or am I heading down the wrong path?" Examine yourself and ask if this is indeed who you desire to be. I know this and I believe this.

I had to face the fact that I could have torn it all down many, many years ago but I didn't know how then and looking back I think I didn't want to. I clearly didn't want to! I gave my children the flawed gift of a terribly dysfunctional home to grow up in but I cannot change that. My desire as a mother was to give them the best of all life had to offer. I realize how miserably I failed them by trying to follow my own desires and my own instincts. It wasn't entirely haphazardly that I failed. I was determined to give them a family and I was young, uneducated, unprepared, and unequally yoked with their father. Those are the facts. Had any of them been different my life and the lives of my children might have turned out entirely different.

There are many, many lessons to be gained within the pages of this book. I hope that someone will learn and take heed and change what they can, where they can and not wait until decades have passed to reflect on what could have, what would have, what should have been. You can breathe on your own! You may need to change your location to do it. Sometimes you don't get a cell phone signal where you stand and you must move, it's the same. Just move and perhaps the life flow will change. Don't be held back by your own insecurities. You do not need to be hooked to an oxygen tank, nor have others walk alongside you to feed you air. Just breathe! No foot is upon your neck and if you feel it is, resist with all your might! When you feel you can breathe again do not look back with a morsel of bitterness upon the circumstance you left. You experienced it for a reason. Everything I have, everything I feel, everything I have done, everything I have given or taken, everything I am thus far results from the wonder of having come to this day. I can look back and see it has all been for good. I do not want anyone to read this and think that it is a book of regret for the life I lived. It's exactly the opposite. I have learned so much. I have hope. I have hope and gratitude and I want my family to understand that when life seems difficult, remember that in everything we can learn and in everything we can give as well as take. Every person has crossed your path for a reason. Maybe it wasn't for you to gain anything, maybe they were there to gain and learn from you.

⌒◎⌒ A Lovely New Chapter ⌒◎⌒

"At last, I found a love to call my own," that line is from a beautiful love song that has become our song. We found a love. This is where a new chapter of our life begins. This is where the next chapter of *my life* starts!

When I look back over my life the one saving grace that God has given me is that I have never closed my heart completely. I held it close at times because it was surely breaking but in the end there was always a chance for love to redeem me. I thought I knew what I wanted but if I had followed my own path, I might have never met Dale. I'm so glad my friend Gerri was there holding up a detour sign pointing me to Dale. I'm so thankful for her

> *When I look back over my life the one saving grace that God has given me is that I have never closed my heart completely.*

persistence that I meet him. I'm even more grateful that I opened my heart to the possibility. He has been a blessing in my life; I am so very glad I didn't miss him!

I have sat at my computer staring at the keyboard so many mornings armed with my Coffee+Jesus mug pondering over the exact words to choose to say that would give my husband, my love, my encourager, my strength when I am weak, my voice when I am unable to speak for myself, my fierce protector at all times, proper credit.

This is my story and this is my life. It's about the extraordinary journey my life has taken me on. I have met so many wonderful people along the way and my heart has been touched. Although it's been broken, it has also been filled with love and joy. My heart has been renewed.

Dale Ray Coachman found a place in my heart I didn't know existed. We have a soul connection that is indeed special and infinite. I don't have enough words in my vocabulary to say thank you for listening to me, understanding, and inspiring me to write.

Most of all, Dale you are such a strong and principled man. You are a rare gem with a heart of gold. You have stood tall and firm and loving by my side but you told me you would always have my back. You lift me up and make me feel heard and important to you. You told me its important to you for me to be relaxed and stress free and cared for.

You told me I am the love of your life. This kind of love only comes around once in a lifetime. Thank you.

Dale, you make life fun. You can make me laugh when I want to cry. You make me laugh until I cry.

For the mysterious way my anxiety disappears when I am with you, I am more than grateful.

You walked into my life and everything changed profoundly. I've been wonderstruck, hypnotized, beguiled, I don't know what all to call it ….. Love struck!

You get so many things right and I often wonder.............then I remember my prayer,

"God, if there's going to be another man in my life let him be a man who puts God first and everything else will fall into place." God sent me you, Dale. I see it now. Just like your parents said I was the answer to their prayers, you are most certainly, without a doubt the answer to mine!

I think I will stick to what I know for sure. I am happy. I have Dale in my life and he is everything I could ask for. I will drink my morning coffee and reflect on my blessed life.

We will embrace family, friends, our children, grandchildren, and great grandchildren. We will honor our parents and we will always thank God for bringing us together. In our home and our life we choose to serve and follow Him. We will never force others to live as we do. Each person must decide his or her own journey.

My life is good. I am happy. My heart is full. My cup runneth over. I cannot shout enough Hallelujahs to the heavens. I marvel at the rainbows and the sunshine that come after the storms. I have sunshine on my shoulders after all.

There's a new purpose for my life. I know that life is worth living especially when I live intentionally. I will give of myself wholly and enthusiastically. I will embrace being an optimist, the world is too full of pessimists. Yes, it rains. Sometimes it pours but there is a rainbow after the rain. Thunder rolls and it can be scary but after the storm the birds serenade and the sun does shine. This I learned and I know that impossible dreams are just as likely to come true as any other dream. I hope to never give up and be an optimist with guts enough to reach high, love completely, work hard, and believe in myself. Be true to myself.

I am just an ordinary girl who has lived a quite extraordinary life. I am still a work in progress. I'm grateful to God for the challenges I have had because I am stronger. I'm grateful for the lessons I learned because if you don't learn, you can't teach. I'm the accidental matriarch now so I must take seriously my role to teach, guide, and offer advice when asked. I say *accidental matriarch* because I never gave a single thought to one day becoming the family matriarch, but here I am. I take it seriously. I have an obligation to my family to pass along some knowledge that will be helpful in the future when I am gone.

I have poured it all out; I have told you things about my family, my friends, and my experiences. Most of all I hope you'll see that although my life hasn't been perfect it has been full of goodness. The good has always outweighed any negative. I have no regrets, just lessons learned. I hope my family, my friends, and anyone who reads my story will realize, I'm not finished yet. I am still on my journey. I am yet a work in progress.

> *I am still a work in progress. I'm grateful to God for the challenges I have had because I am stronger.*

In the Bible James 1:2-6 reads:

> *Consider it pure joy, my brothers and sisters, whenever you face trials of many kinds, because you know that the testing of your faith produces perseverance. Let perseverance finish its work so that you may be mature and complete, not lacking anything. If any of you lacks wisdom, you should ask God, who gives generously to all without finding fault, and it will be given to you. But, when you ask, you must believe and not doubt, because the one who doubts is like a wave of the sea, blown and tossed by the wind.* (NIV)

I hope that you will glean something from my story that will inspire you to live your life intentionally. Give your best to each day, always believe in something greater than yourself. I know and clearly understand that my beliefs may not be what you believe. I didn't write my story to push my beliefs or religion on anyone. I didn't censor myself or the language. I am a Bible believing Christian, yet I respect others and their faith. I know it's important to have faith and believe in the greatness of someone, or something other than self. None of us got here alone. Trust others and always seek the better side of those you love. Try to be forgiving. We all fall short but we all have goodness in us. So when you face the trials of life, and they certainly will come, look for the silver lining.

Weeping may endure for a night, but joy comes in the morning. Psalms 30:5 (NIV)

Persevere and seek wisdom and when you walk through the storms of life and become more mature, more complete, look for that silver lining. I've found that silver lining was always there.

God is always there. I look at my life, where I started and where I have come and I am so elated to be in this moment. God has set my feet on solid ground. I endured much, learned much, and because of my faith I was expectant of the coming blessings. I have been truly blessed in many ways. Oh Lord, you have poured out on me Love, Mercy, and Goodness.

You have turned my wailing into dancing; you removed my sackcloth and clothed me with joy, that my heart may sing to you and not be silent. O Lord my God. I will give you thanks forever. Psalms 31:11-12 (NIV)

My heart will sing, and I will not be silent, I will dance and I will count it all joy!

Wishing you Joie de Vivre!

ACKNOWLEDGEMENTS

*T*hank you, first of all to my children for living life with me and being there through everything. You have been my joy and I love you more than can ever be expressed. My great love and appreciation to my husband, Dale for listening, encouraging, reading my story, understanding, and loving me more.

My grateful appreciation to Karen Ray, such a gifted editor. You have become a friend—you understood my words and you have been such a joy to work with.

ABOUT THE AUTHOR

Norma-Jean Sims-Coachman is a wife, mother of two adult children and two adult step-children, as well as a grand-mother and great grandmother.

This book is the first in a series. When she dropped out of a col-lege English class at Monterey Peninsula College, her professor, Dr. Bertha Hutchins, asked her to promise she would keep writing. This fulfills that promise but keeping it and telling her story took decades.

Norma-Jean traces her journey as a biracial child growing up in the fifties, traveling the world with her mother and military father. The story recounts her meeting her first husband as a teenager and building a family together until his untimely death and her struggle with grief. She realized life still held hope and began a vibrant chapter, coming alive with the new love of her life.

She writes of the stresses, hardships, family secrets, and tragedy of life while describing the ultimate, absolute joy she holds in her heart. Her love of God, family, and friends are the anchors in her life. Her motto is to live every day with intention.

Consider it pure joy, my brothers, whenever you face trials of many kinds, because you know that the testing of your faith develops persever-ance. James1:2 (NIV)